MW01615288

THE MINISTRY OF THE

EVANGELIST

BY

JOHN R. VAN GELDEREN

REVIVALFOCUS

All rights reserved. No part of this book may be reproduced in any manner whatsoever without prior written permission except in the case of brief quotations embodied in critical articles or brief reviews.

Originally published as THE EVANGELIST, THE EVANGEL, AND EVANGELISM
Copyright 2008 John R. Van Gelderen

Republished as THE MINISTRY OF THE EVANGELIST:
A Study of the Evangelist, the Evangel, and Evangelism
Reprinted 2021

Revival Focus
Ann Arbor, MI
revivalfocus.org

Book design by Mark Gillmore, cover by Harvest Media

Scripture quotations are from the King James Version of the Bible.

Acknowledgments

Truly I am thankful to the Lord for what He has taught me through this study. A special word of thanks to Dr. Steven Hankins for his encouragement to do this project, to Dr. Ward Andersen for his insight, precision, and encouragement in regard to the manuscript, and to Dr. Randy Leedy for his careful reading, meticulous comments, and fine-tuned help in articulating my burden.

On the practical side, I am grateful to my proofreader and editor, Carolyn Cooper, for her detailed and careful work, to Mark Gillmore for the excellent layout and design, and to Mike Moreau for the beautiful cover design. I am also especially thankful to my wife, Mary Lynn, for her encouragement, support, patience, and love through this project, plus hours of labor typing my handwritten work. Ultimately, I praise the Lord for the Spirit's enablement in this task.

Table of Contents

Tables and Diagrams

TABLES

DIAGRAMS

Introduction

In the providence of God, I was named after Evangelist John R. Rice. His emphasis through the periodical *The Sword of the Lord* was on revival and soulwinning. The heritage of being named after an evangelist has been a definite influence in my life toward the work of the evangelist. As a preacher's kid, I have been around evangelists from my earliest recollections and have nearly always been deeply stirred through their ministry. In fact, I have always loved the preaching of evangelists. It is no surprise that at the age of fifteen I surrendered to the call to preach after hearing Evangelist Monroe Parker. Initially and ever since, my heartbeat has been to be an evangelist. I studied for the ministry at Bob Jones University, which was founded by an evangelist.

Evangelists have been used of God since New Testament times to build and bless the church of the Lord Jesus Christ. In the last three centuries of church history, evangelists have played a leading role in revival and evangelism. Their names are familiar to many of God's people even today. Names such as George Whitefield, John Wesley, Asahel Nettleton, Charles Finney, D. L. Moody, R. A. Torrey, and Billy Sunday, to name a few.

But what is an evangelist? A study of the evangelist in Scripture helped confirm my calling in life and launch me into full-time evangelism in 1992. However, this study has continued over the years. Truly the Bible sheds much light on the person and work of the evangelist—much more light than many may realize.

The Need

In the latter half of the twentieth century, the concept of the evangelist deteriorated. The modern caricature is often someone with excessive illustrations and little substance. Certain ministries no longer use the ministry of the evangelist. In fact, in the theological realm of thought, the evangelist has been belittled and debunked by many, along with revival—one of the evangelist's burdens. Without seeking to be negative toward a particular organization, the criticism of the evangelist and revival is largely found in the theological journals of certain institutions of higher learning, as well as on blog sites. As a result, many young fundamentalists have a distorted view of the evangelist at the present time.

Part of the problem stems from a lack of biblical knowledge regarding the person and work of the evangelist, as well as an ignorance of the historical conception of the evangelist, which is much different from the modern perspective. Therefore, there is a need to thoroughly explore the biblical picture of the evangelist by investigating all of the related words and building a theological philosophy. Furthermore, there is a need to examine the understanding of and practice of the evangelist in church history. The scriptural foundation and historical perspective provide needed correction to the modern viewpoint of the evangelist.

The Terms

The three key biblical words regarding the evangelist all have the same stem *euangel*: *euangelion* (evangel), *euangelizo* (evangelize), and *euangelistes* (evangelist). The Greek words are as follows: ευαγγελιον, ευαγγελιζω, ευαγγελιστης.

First, the *evangel*, or gospel, is the good news of the saving death of Christ to sinners and the saving life of Christ to saints. Generally speaking, in recent decades there has been a lack of emphasis on the Spirit-filled life, which is the "present" aspect of the gospel. Christ is a present deliverer. Perhaps the neglect is due to an overreaction to the Charismatic excesses of the 1960s.

Second, *evangelize* means to preach the gospel (evangel).

Third, an *evangelist* is a God-enabled man specializing in preaching the gospel—both the gospel to sinners that proclaims freedom from the penalty of sin and the gospel to saints that proclaims freedom from the power of sin.

The Purpose

The purpose of this book is to inform the reader of the biblical information regarding the person and work of the evangelist. Therefore, there will be a thorough treatment of the three passages regarding the person of the evangelist that revolve around the word *euangelistes* and a thorough interacting with the biblical data regarding the work of the evangelist as demonstrated by the seventy-seven occurrences of the noun *euangelion* and the fifty-five occurrences of the verb *euangelizo*. Together the information provides a proper understanding of the person and the work of the evangelist. The conclusions will be supported throughout by historical examples, especially from the early centuries close to New Testament times and from the eighteenth and nineteenth centuries. Developing a thorough biblical understanding of the evangelist should aid both evangelists and pastors and churches to properly apply the ministry of the evangelist.

Yet in focusing on the ministry of the evangelist, there must of necessity be a focus on the evangel—the message of the gospel. Therefore anyone interested in being better equipped to declare the gospel may benefit from this study, especially the chapters addressing the evangel itself. The more accurate the understanding of the person and work of the evangelist, the better the application of the ministry of the evangelist by the grace of God. Also, the more accurate the understanding of the evangel, the greater the potential for all believers in both applying the full message of the good news individually and declaring the good news to others.

May the Spirit of God breathe life on the truth of God that the Son of God may be exalted as the personified Good News!

Part One

PANORAMA

OF THE BIBLICAL DATA

REGARDING

THE EVANGELIST,

THE EVANGEL,

AND EVANGELISM

Chapter One

THE PERSON AND WORK OF THE EVANGELIST

Little children sometimes have unique misunderstandings. An evangelist once had the opportunity to preach in a primary chapel at a Christian school. The elementary superintendent introduced him as the evangelist and then asked, "What is an evangelist?" Several children raised their hands. He called on a boy who was in the first grade. The boy replied, "A disease!"

Some today seem to agree with this boy, either by denying the existence of the evangelist beyond apostolic times or by downplaying the role of the evangelist. The latter is done by defining the evangelist in a limiting way, such as "a missionary church-planter."[1] Certainly an evangelist could apply his gift by planting churches on a mission field. In fact, this is a wonderful application of the gift in the divine leading of God. However, to limit the role of the evangelist by using one application as the entire definition is confusing "sense" and "reference." It would be like referring to a *chair* as the only sense of the term *furniture*. While the application is legitimate, the limitation is not. The same is true in limiting the role of the evangelist to one application. Furthermore, as will be seen, the Scripture provides broader applications.

---

1. William W. Combs, "The Biblical Role of the Evangelist," *Detroit Baptist Seminary Journal*, no. 7, (Fall 2002): 48.

Is there a solid biblical foundation for the existence of the evangelist? If so, is there a solid biblical foundation for defining what an evangelist is and what he does? Some argue that since the word translated *evangelist* occurs only three times in the New Testament, there is very little foundation for the evangelist in Scripture.[2] However, the biblical portrait of the evangelist is much larger than some have painted it. In fact, the New Testament provides a solid biblical foundation for the present-day person and work of the evangelist.

An Overview of the Biblical Data

A general survey of the words relating specifically to the person and work of the evangelist, noting their occurrences in Scripture, reveals objective data with which to formulate sound conclusions regarding the evangelist.

Key Words

The Greek word *euangelistes* reflects the person of the evangelist. In addition, the New Testament uses two other closely related words that have the same stem *euangel*: *euangelion* and *euangelizo*. These two words reflect the work of the evangelist.

The meanings of these three words, their number of occurrences throughout the New Testament, and their contextual usages greatly enlarge one's understanding of the evangelist. By noting the data regarding these three key words, one can form an objective foundation that undergirds the validity of the evangelist as a part of God's plan for the building of the church of

---

2. Ibid., 23-24. Combs comments, "When one turns to the pages of Scripture, it turns out that the amount of material dealing with the evangelist is rather sparse. The word *evangelist* . . . is used only three times in the NT." Later he says "the limited scriptural data."

Jesus Christ. As will be seen, the biblical information regarding the evangelist is not nearly as limited as some have suggested.

Lexical Definitions

Euangelistes (pronounced "you-an-gel-is-**tace**") is lexically defined as "preacher of the gospel, evangelist,"[3] "a bringer of good tidings, an evangelist,"[4] and "teller of good news, evangelist."[5]

Euangelion (prounounced "you-an-**gel**-i-on" with a hard "g") is defined as "God's good news to men, the gospel,"[6] "good tidings,"[7] and "good news, gospel."[8]

Euangelizo (prounounced "you-an-gel-**idz**-o" with a long "o") is defined as "bring or announce good news,"[9] "to bring good news, to announce glad tidings,"[10] and "to proclaim good news, preach the gospel, evangelize."[11]

Although the definitions of these three words can and will be expanded later in this chapter, simply put, *euangelistes* is the word for an "evangelist," *euangelion* is the word for the "evangel" or "gospel," and *euangelizo* is the word meaning to "evangelize," or "preach the gospel."

Total New Testament Occurrences

Euangelistes occurs three times in the New Testament, all referring to the person of the evangelist. *Euangelion* occurs 77 times, all referring to the gospel. *Euangelizo* occurs 55 times, of

---

3. William F. Arndt and F. Wilbur Gingrich, *A Greek-English Lexicon of the New Testament and Other Early Christian Literature*, 2nd ed. revised F. Wilbur Gingrich and Fredrick W. Danker (Chicago: University of Chicago Press, 1979), 318.

4. Joseph H. Thayer, *Thayer's Greek-English Lexicon of the New Testament* (Grand Rapids: Baker Book House, 1977), 257.

5. George V. Wigram and Jay P. Green, *The New Englishman's Greek Concordance and Lexicon* (Peabody, MA: Hendrickson Publishers, Inc., 1982), 355.

6. Arndt and Gingrich, 317.

7. Thayer.

8. Wigram and Green.

9. Arndt and Gingrich.

10. Thayer, 256.

11. Wigram and Green, 354.

which 53 refer specifically to salvific good news. Three of these occurrences involve angels.[12] Therefore, 50 occurrences refer to men preaching the gospel. The total comes to 135 occurrences of the same stem, of which 130 are pertinent to the person and work of the evangelist. Therefore, the subject of the evangelist is much broader than many realize. In fact, the evidence reveals that the whole realm of the evangelist is a solid emphasis in the New Testament and not just something that is barely mentioned. The larger perspective of the person and work of the evangelist is an important viewpoint. The messenger cannot be fully understood without understanding his message and "messaging" or preaching of the message. Just as songs and singing are vital to truly understand a singer, so *euangelion* and *euangelizo* are vital to truly understand a *euangelistes*. In both cases, the person and work form a complete whole. This enlarged picture reveals that the scriptural data is not nearly as limited as some have maintained.

By way of analogy, the word *kerux* [a preacher, herald] occurs only three times in the New Testament. The preachment or message represented by the word *kerugma* [preaching, proclamation] occurs eight times. The verb form *kerusso* [to preach, proclaim, herald] occurs 61 times. No one would suggest that since *kerux* occurs only three times, that therefore a "preacher" does not exist or does not have an important role. Obviously, the closely related words greatly expand the picture. Such is the case with the word *euangelistes*. In fact, there is more scriptural evidence for the concept of the person and work of the evangelist with 130 occurrences of the related words than there is for the concept of the person and work of the preacher with only 72 occurrences of the related words. The modern trend of downplaying the existence or role of the evangelist is not exegetically or theologically accurate.

---

12. The two non-salvific passages are 1 Thessalonians 3:6 and Revelation 10:7. The three salvific passages that involve angels are Luke 1:19; 2:10 and Revelation 14:6.

Book Occurrences

Euangelistes ("evangelist") occurs in Acts, Ephesians, and 2 Timothy. The occurrence in Acts is significant because it deals with the history of the early church. The occurrence in the fourth chapter of Ephesians is significant because that chapter is a foundational passage for church philosophy. The occurrence in 2 Timothy is also significant since the book gives ministerial instructions. Table 1.1 pinpoints the book occurrences of *euangelistes* in the New Testament.

Table 1.1. Book Occurrences of *Euangelistes*

Book	Occurrences	References
Acts	1	21:8
Ephesians	1	4:11
2 Timothy	1	4:5

Euangelion ("gospel") occurs in 17 of the 27 New Testament books. Romans contains the most usages, with a total of 10 occurrences. This is significant in light of the thorough gospel emphasis of Romans. Philippians contains nine occurrences, followed by Mark, 1 Corinthians, and 2 Corinthians with eight occurrences each, and Galatians with seven. Galatians emphasizes the full ramifications of the gospel. Surprisingly, neither Luke nor John as "Gospels" use the word *euangelion*. However, Luke uses the verb form *euangelizo* 10 times, and John describes the gospel by providing a detailed articulation of the full ramifications of the gospel for the stated purpose of bringing people to faith in Christ (John 20:31). Table 1.2 pinpoints the book occurrences of *euangelion* in the New Testament.

Table 1.2. Book Occurrences of *Euangelion*

Book	Occurrences	References
Matthew	4	4:23; 9:35; 24:14; 26:13
Mark	8	1:1, 14, 15; 8:35; 10:29; 13:10; 14:9; 16:15
Acts	2	15:7; 20:24
Romans	10	1:1, 9, 16; 2:16; 10:16; 11:28; 15:16, 19, 29; 16:25
I Corinthians	8	4:15; 9:12, 14 (2x), 18 (2x), 23; 15:1
2 Corinthians	8	2:12; 4:3, 4; 8:18; 9:13; 10:14; 11:4, 7
Galatians	7	1:6, 7, 11; 2:2, 5, 7, 14
Ephesians	4	1:13; 3:6; 6:15, 19
Philippians	9	1:5, 7, 12, 17, 27 (2x); 2:22; 4:3, 15
Colossians	2	1:5, 23
I Thessalonians	6	1:5; 2:2, 4, 8, 9; 3:2
2 Thessalonians	2	1:8; 2:14
I Timothy	1	1:11
2 Timothy	3	1:8, 10; 2:8
Philemon	1	13
I Peter	1	4:17
Revelation	1	14:6

Euangelizo ("evangelize") occurs in 12 of the 27 New Testament books. It is found 15 times in the book of Acts and

10 times in the book of Luke. These two books comprise 25 of the 55 New Testament occurrences penned under inspiration by Luke. Since Acts is the history of the early church, it is significant that this book contains the most occurrences. Therefore, the concept of the verb *euangelizo*, which emphasizes the work of the evangelist, is a prominent feature in the early church, not just a mere mention. Galatians ranks third in number of occurrences with seven (which is the same number of occurrences of *euaggelion* in Galatians). Table 1.3 pinpoints the book occurrences of *euangelizo* in the New Testament.

Table 1.3. Book Occurrences of *Euangelizo*

Book	Occurrences	References
Matthew	1	11:5
Luke	10	1:19; 2:10; 3:18; 4:18, 43; 7:22; 8:1; 9:6; 16:16; 20:1
Acts	15	5:42; 8:4, 12, 25, 35, 40; 10:36; 11:20; 13:32; 14:7, 15, 21; 15:35; 16:10; 17:18
Romans	4	1:15; 10:15 (2x); 15:20
1 Corinthians	6	1:17; 9:16 (2x), 18; 15:1, 2
2 Corinthians	2	10:16; 11:7
Galatians	7	1:8 (2x), 9, 11, 16, 23; 4:13
Ephesians	2	2:17; 3:8
1 Thessalonians	1	3:6
Hebrews	2	4:2, 6
1 Peter	3	1:12, 25; 4:6
Revelation	2	10:7; 14:6

General Conclusions

The macroscopic view of the key words and their placement throughout the New Testament provides a basis to draw some general conclusions.

Key Books

Acts is one of only two New Testament books that use all three words. Also, Acts contains the highest number of word usages, totaling 18. Acts uses *euangelizo* the most of the three words (15 of the 18) and contains the most occurrences of *euangelizo* in any New Testament book. *Euangelizo* ("preaching the gospel," "evangelizing") pertains to what an evangelist does. Therefore, Acts is the key book in highlighting the *work* of the evangelist (as Chapter 9: "Evangelism Applied" will show).

Romans, I Corinthians, and Galatians all contain 14 combined usages of *euangelion* and *euangelizo*. Romans uses the noun 10 times and the verb four times, I Corinthians uses the noun eight times and the verb six times, and Galatians uses each word seven times. These three books are doctrinal epistles, making Romans, I Corinthians, and Galatians key books in explaining the *message* of the evangelist. This conclusion is especially evident in Romans and Galatians and in chapter fifteen of I Corinthians.

Ephesians is the only book other than Acts that incorporates all three words, containing a total of seven occurrences. Ephesians is the foundational New Testament book for church philosophy. Therefore, Ephesians is the key book in addressing the *role* of the evangelist.

Key Chapters

Galatians I contains the most usages of *euangelizo* in one chapter (six occurrences) as well as the most combined usages of both *euangelion* and *euangelizo* in one chapter (a total of nine occurrences). Galatians 1 gives the strongest warning in the Epistles against perverting the gospel. Therefore, Galatians 1 is the key chapter emphasizing the *purity* of the gospel.

Acts 8 ranks second in number of usages of the verb *euangelizo* with five occurrences. The context of Acts 8 focuses primarily on the ministry of Philip, who in Acts 21:8 is specifically called an "evangelist" (*euangelistes*). Therefore, Acts 8, with its emphasis on evangelizing through the use of the verb, is the key chapter illustrating the *work* of the evangelist.

Philippians 1 uses the noun *euangelion* five times. Four of these five occurrences use the *gospel* as the genitive, making it grammatically dependent on another noun. Therefore, Philippians 1 is the key chapter highlighting the *facets* of the gospel.

1 Corinthians 15:1 uses both *euangelion* and *euangelizo*, with verse two using *euangelizo* one more time. Although this chapter does not use these words often, 1 Corinthians 15:1 states explicitly that the passage is a declaration of the gospel. Verses 1–11 provide the key details. Therefore, 1 Corinthians 15 is the key chapter in explaining the *message* of the evangelist (as Chapter 5: "The Gospel to Sinners" will show).

These conclusions regarding the key books and the key chapters are based on the objective data of the number of occurrences of the key words involved and their placement in Scripture by the Holy Spirit. At this point these are general conclusions. However, a closer investigation of the three key words themselves supports these conclusions.

An Analysis of the Key Words

The panoramic view of the person and work of the evangelist necessitates a brief focus on each of the key words.

Analyzing *Euangelizo*

A careful investigation of the usage of *euangelizo* reveals insight into both the number of evangelists in Scripture as well as the practical nature of their work.

Implied Evangelists

Although Philip is the only one explicitly labeled an evangelist (*euangelistes*) in the New Testament (Acts 21:8), many others are implicitly designated as evangelists through the verb *euangelizo*. Just as the label *baptistes* is derived from the verb *baptizo*, as expressed in John the Baptist or literally "the baptizer," so *euangelistes* is derived from the verb *euangelizo*.[13] Just as the verb *episkopeo*, meaning "to oversee," implies that the one overseeing is an *episkopos*, an "overseer" (as is seen by comparing the verb in I Peter 5:2, "taking the oversight," with the noun in I Timothy 3:2, "a bishop"), so the verb *euangelizo*, meaning "to evangelize," implies that the one evangelizing is a *euangelistes*, an "evangelist." Inspiration verifies this connection by using the verb *euangelizo* three times in the story of Philip in Acts 8:12, 35, and 40, who, in Acts 21:8, is labeled with the noun *euangelistes*. Therefore, through the use of *euangelizo* the New Testament implies that there may be many more evangelists than at first seems evident, although, as will be seen, some like the apostles were more than just evangelists.

---

13. See A. T. Robertson, *Word Pictures in the New Testament*, vol. 3 (Nashville: Broadman Press, 1930), 362. As it is fair to generally conclude that one who baptizes is a baptizer, so it is legitimate to generally conclude that one who evangelizes is an evangelist. However, does this apply to personal witnessing, and is it safe to assume that *only* those who are evangelists evangelize? The key is recognizing that while every believer is responsible to fulfill the Great Commission as a witness for Jesus Christ, the word *euangelizo* is predominantly used in Scripture to refer to a public ministry, not personal witnessing. This distinctive observation will be expanded in the next point, "Public Ministry." Unfortunately, the word *evangelism* in the present day is often used to simply mean personal evangelism. This confuses the scriptural usage of the word referring to the gift of the evangelist with the concept of personal witnessing.

As noted earlier, *euangelizo* occurs 55 times in the New Testament. Fifty-three of those occurrences focus on the good news of salvation in Jesus Christ. Three times the verb is used with an angel (Luke 1:19; 2:10; Rev. 14:6).[14] Therefore, 50 of the 55 occurrences refer to men preaching the gospel. Who are these evangelists implied in the verb *euangelizo*?

Jesus Christ is the prototype for all biblical ministry, and He is certainly the prototype for the evangelist. The verb *euangelizo* is connected to Christ frequently (Matt. 11:5; Luke 4:18, 43; 7:22; 8:1; 16:16; 20:1; Acts 10:36; Eph. 2:17; and possibly 1 Pet. 4:6, cf. 3:18-19).[15] The verb is used once with John the Baptist (Luke 3:18), who, although he was more than an evangelist in his ministry as a prophet, yet his ministry is called in Mark 1:1ff., "the beginning of the gospel." As a group of individuals, the twelve disciples or apostles are connected with the verb (Luke 9:6; 16:16; Acts 5:42). The apostles were endowed with a multi-faceted gifting, which, by observation, seems to include the gift of the prophet, the evangelist, and the pastor-teacher. Furthermore, beyond mere observation, based on the connection to *euangelizo*, every apostle

---

14. The first angelic occurrence is Gabriel in Luke 1:19, who announced to Zacharias the birth of John the Baptist, who would be used of God "to make ready a people prepared for the Lord" (1:17). The use of *euangelizo* may seem to focus more on the good news of the birth of John the Baptist, yet the ministry of John the Baptist in preparing the way for the Lord Jesus Christ is explicitly called "the beginning of the gospel" in Mark 1:1ff. TDNT states, "He is the one who brings glad tidings and therefore the longed-for eschatological salvation. His message, then, is good news. Even as a precursor of the Messiah, he is an evangelist. His story is the beginning of the Gospel (Mark 1:1; Acts 10:36f.)" (Gerhard Freidrich, "*Euaggelizomai*," in *Theological Dictionary of the New Testament* Vol. II, ed. Gerhard Kittel [Grand Rapids: Wm. B. Eerdmans Publishing Co., 1964, 1993], 719). Also, in referring to the angelic announcement of the birth of both John the Baptist and the birth of Jesus, TDNT explains, "In both cases the message is an evangel because the desired last time, the coming of Messianic salvation, is proclaimed" (Ibid., 721). The second angelic occurrence is in Luke 2:10ff., where the angel announced to the shepherds the birth of the "Savior, which is Christ the Lord" (2:11). The third angelic occurrence is in Revelation 14:6-7, where an angel, during the tribulation, preaches "the everlasting gospel."

15. In an article regarding *euangelizomai* in TDNT enumerating the evangelists intimated by the verb, the first evangelist listed is Jesus. "Jesus is the One who brings the good news of the expected last time" (Ibid., 718).

was an evangelist; however, not every evangelist was an apostle. Other specific names used with the verb are Peter and John (Acts 8:25), Philip (Acts 8:12, 35, 40), Paul and Barnabas (Acts 13:32; 14:7, 15, 21; 15:35), Paul and Silas (Acts 16:10), and Paul by himself (Acts 17:18; Rom. 1:15; 15:20; 1 Cor. 1:17; 9:16, 18; 15:1, 2; 2 Cor. 10:16; 11:7; Gal. 1:8, 11, 16, 23; 4:13, Eph. 3:8).[16] Other unspecified evangelists used with the verb are at least some among the scattered persecuted (Acts 8:4; 11:20, cf. 19), and several others who are unnamed (Acts 15:35; Rom. 10:15; Heb. 4:2, 6; 1 Pet. 1:12, 25).

It should be noted that Philip, Barnabas, and Silas were not among the twelve apostles, and their names are directly connected to *euangelizo*.[17] Others unnamed and unnumbered are connected to this verb. Also, although serving in other capacities, Jesus Christ, John the Baptist, and the apostles, including the Apostle Paul, are connected to this verb. Therefore, the evangelists of Scripture are much more numerous than many realize.[18] This fact alone greatly enlarges one's understanding of the evangelist in the New Testament.

Public Ministry

Of the 50 occurrences of *euangelizo* (out of a total of 55 usages) referring to men preaching the gospel, 49 seem to indicate a public ministry. The public nature of preaching the gospel (the work of the evangelist) is either directly stated or implied in the specific contexts of the verb. The majority of the contexts are very clear, a few are vague, but only one of the 50 is clearly

---

16. TDNT states in the article on *euangelizomai*, "Paul becomes the evangelist to the Gentiles" (Ibid., 719). A. T. Robertson states, "Men have different gifts and Philip had this of evangelizing as Paul was doing who is the chief evangelist" (Robertson, 362).

17. Barnabas is labeled an apostle in Acts 14:14. He may have been a prophet as well, according to Acts 13:1, but the same verse indicates he may have simply been a teacher.

18. TDNT notes in an article dealing specifically with *euangelistes*: "The number of evangelists must have been greater than one might suppose from the number of occurrences in the NT (Phil. 4:3; 2 Cor. 8:18; Col. 1:7, 4:12)" (Ibid., 737). For example, Colossians 1:7 and 4:12-13 intimate Epaphras may have been an evangelist.

to an individual and not to a group (Acts 8:35).[19] In some cases the audience may have been a small group, but nonetheless, a group of people as opposed to just one individual. The fact that all the contexts of *euangelizo* referring to men preaching the gospel, except for one, appear to be public in nature indicates that the ministry of the evangelist is primarily a public ministry. Clearly the emphasis of *euangelizo* as a word reaches beyond personal witnessing, which is a responsibility for all believers, to the public ministry of evangelists. Therefore, it is not accurate to say that *euangelizo* refers merely to "personal evangelism." In fact, the terminology "personal evangelism" would be more accurately stated as "personal witnessing" or "personal soulwinning" since the scriptural usage of *euangelizo* is predominantly public. Technically, the usage of *euangelizo* reveals that the work of the evangelist is primarily public in nature. Obviously, this gifting for public ministry enables the evangelist in personal witnessing as well. But the gift of the evangelist is primarily a gift for public ministry of which enablement in personal witnessing is a logical overflow.

Itinerant Ministry

Of the 50 occurrences of *euangelizo* referring to men preaching the gospel (out of a total of 55 usages), 25 indicate itinerant ministry. Of these 25 occurrences, 21 are found in the books of Luke and Acts, which are chronological narratives or histories. One more is found in the narrative of Matthew. This emphasis of itinerancy in the narratives is significant since the instructional nature of the Epistles, where there are other occurrences of *euangelizo*, would not be as likely to provide this insight.

The 25 occurrences of *euangelizo*, which contextually indicate the itinerancy of the evangelists connected to the verb, are

---

19. Acts 8:35 records Philip evangelizing the Ethiopian eunuch. Philip is called an evangelist in Acts 21:8. Although the work of the evangelist is primarily public in nature, obviously the gift can and should operate on an individual level as well. But the emphasis of *euangelizo* is public, not individual. This public emphasis of the verb is seen even with Philip in Acts 8:12 and Acts 8:40.

as follows: John the Baptist is connected to the verb in Luke 3:18, where the context says "he came into all the country about Jordan" (cf. 3:3ff.). Jesus is connected to the verb in Luke 4:18 at "Nazareth" (cf. 4:16), in Luke 4:43 referring to "other cities also," in Matthew 11:5 and Luke 7:22 in or around "Nain" (cf. Luke 7:11ff.) and/or possibly in "their [the disciples'] cities" (cf. Matt. 11:1-5), in Luke 8:1 "throughout every city and village," and in Luke 20:1 "in the temple" at Jerusalem. Philip is connected to the verb in Acts 8:12 at "Samaria" (cf. 8:5ff.), in Acts 8:35 at "Gaza, which is desert" (cf. 8:26ff.), and in Acts 8:40 "at Azotus" and "all the cities . . . to Caesarea." Peter and John are connected to the verb in Acts 8:25 "in many villages of the Samaritans." Paul and Barnabas are connected to the verb in Acts 13:32 at "Antioch in Pisidia" (cf. 13:14ff.), in Acts 14:7 at "Lystra and Derbe . . . and unto the region that lieth about" (cf. 14:6), in Acts 14:15 at "Lystra" (cf. 14:8ff.), in Acts 14:21 at "Derbe" (cf. 14:20), and in Acts 15:35 at "Antioch." Paul and Silas are connected to the verb in Acts 16:10 regarding "Macedonia," especially "Philippi" (cf. 16:12). Paul by himself is connected to the verb in Acts 17:18 at "Athens" (cf. 17:16ff.), in Romans 1:15 regarding "Rome," in Romans 15:20 "not where Christ was named," and 2 Corinthians 10:16 "in the regions beyond." The apostles are connected to the verb in Luke 9:6 "through the towns," and in Acts 5:42 "in the temple, and in every house." Unnamed evangelists among the scattered persecuted are connected to the verb in Acts 8:4 "everywhere," and in Acts 11:20 traveling as far as "Antioch" (cf. 11:19).

The narrative contexts of *euangelizo* clearly indicate that the work of the evangelist is generally an itinerant ministry.[20]

---

20. Speaking of one of Paul's journeys, Acts 18:23 states that Paul "went over all the country of Galatia and Phrygia in order." The terminology *in order* indicates that the itinerant travels incorporated common sense in their geographical order.

Analyzing *Euangelion*

A careful investigation of the usage of *euangelion* reveals insight into the message of the gospel.

The Body of the Gospel

Euangelion is used as an absolute (*to euangelion* "the gospel") at least 18 times (Mark 1:15; 8:35; 10:29; Rom. 1:16; 10:16; 11:28; 1 Cor. 4:15; 9:18, 23, 2 Cor. 8:18; Gal. 2:2; Eph. 3:6; Phil 1:5; 2:22; 4:3; 1 Thess. 2:4; 2 Tim. 1:8, 10). In this sense, *euangelion* is used as a body of truth.

The Facets of the Gospel

Euangelion is used as the genitive ("Y" in "X of Y" constructions) 15 times, revealing the many facets of the gospel. An example is "the mystery of the gospel" (Eph. 6:19). Other facets include "the beginning of the gospel" (Mark 1:1; Phil. 4:15), "the word of the gospel" (Acts 15:7), "the blessing of the gospel" (Rom. 15:29), "the truth of the gospel" (Gal. 2:5, 14; Col. 1:5), "the preparation of the gospel" (Eph. 6:15), "the confirmation of the gospel" (Phil. 1:7), "the furtherance of the gospel" (Phil. 1:12), "the defence of the gospel" (Phil. 1:17), "the faith of the gospel" (Phil. 1:27), "the hope of the gospel" (Col. 1:23), and "the bonds of the gospel" (Philem. 13). Each of these facets expands one's understanding of gospel ministry.

The Focus of the Gospel

Euangelion is also used as the pre-genitive ("X" in "X of Y" constructions). The predominant objective genitive usage reveals the focus of the gospel. An example is "the gospel of Jesus Christ" (Mark 1:1). With occasional variations of wording, *euangelion* is connected to Christ (Mark 1:1; Rom. 1:9, 16; 15:19, 29; 1 Cor. 9:12, 18; 2 Cor. 2:12; 4:4; 9:13; 10:14; Gal. 1:7; Phil. 1:27;

I Thess. 3:2; 2 Thess. 1:8), and the kingdom (Matt. 4:23; 9:35; 24:14; Mark 1:14).[21] The objective genitive focuses on the King and His kingdom and primarily on Christ, the King. Christ is, therefore, the object of the good news.

The Givers of the Gospel

The subjective genitive usage involves two basic ideas. First is the phrase "the gospel of God," which occurs seven times (Rom. 1:1; 15:16; 2 Cor. 11:7; I Thess. 2:2, 8, 9; I Pet. 4:17). The gospel is "God's gospel." It is God's good news to mankind. In this sense, God is the Giver of the gospel. Second is either the phrase "my gospel," which occurs three times (Rom. 2:16; 16:25; 2 Tim. 2:8), or "our gospel," which also occurs three times (2 Cor. 4:3; I Thess. 1:5; 2 Thess. 2:14). When the one preaching the gospel is in union with the indwelling Christ by faith, he can rightfully say "my/our gospel." This claim is legitimate, based on the example of Paul who wrote in I Corinthians 15 (which was noted earlier as a "key chapter") the testimony "I labored . . . yet not I, but the grace of God which was with me" (I Cor. 15:10) and the truth of "I live; yet not I, but Christ . . . by . . . faith" (Gal. 2:20).

The Extent of the Gospel

For many people the word *gospel* simply refers to the good news to the unsaved. This understanding is gloriously true as far as it goes, but the gospel goes further.[22] Previous generations called it "full salvation." Not only does the Scripture teach justification by faith based on the finished work of Christ, it also teaches sanctification by faith through the same finished work. The good news of the gospel reaches beyond positional change

21. The genitives *God* (I Tim. 1:11), *grace* (Acts 20:24), *salvation* (Eph. 1:13), and *peace* (Eph. 6:15) could be interpreted as uses other than objective.

22. TDNT states, "The evangelists continue the work of the apostles. They are not just missionaries, for, as [*euangelion*] is congregational as well as missionary preaching . . . ." (Ibid.). Also in speaking of Paul as "the evangelist to the Gentiles," TDNT says, "But the message is also addressed to Christians" (Ibid., 719-20).

to real practical change as well. The former is the gospel to the unsaved; the latter is the gospel to the saved. The gospel to sinners proclaims freedom from the penalty of sin; the gospel to saints proclaims freedom from the power of sin. The gospel to sinners is that "Christ died for our sins," emphasizing substitution; the gospel to saints is that "we died with Christ," emphasizing identification. The gospel to sinners focuses on the saving death of Christ; the gospel to saints focuses on the saving life of Christ. The gospel to sinners demands a response of faith for a new standing; the gospel to saints demands responses of faith for a new walking. The former speaks of receiving new life—the Eternal Life of Christ; the latter speaks of living in or being restored to that life—the Abundant Life of Christ. Restoration to Christ as one's life is the essence of revival. Revival is life again! Therefore, the extent of the message of the evangelist moves beyond the good news of receiving Christ's life when one is saved to the good news of living in or being restored to Christ's life after one is saved.

That the gospel to saints is to be considered "news" (good news) is observable for several reasons. First, when declared to new believers, it is obviously "news." Second, when declared to saints who have been saved for a while but never taught, it is good news. Third, when declared to saints who have been saved for a while and have heard the gospel to saints but never grasped it, when the truth is grasped, it is good news.

This double emphasis of good news to both sinners and to saints explains why some evangelists are known by that name and others are known by the label "revivalist." The revivalist is simply an evangelist who is preaching the gospel to saints in order that the saints might access the abundant life in Christ by faith. The revivalist is preaching not only for salvation but also for revival. Understanding the full extent of the gospel underscores the legitimacy of evangelists preaching for more than just the salvation of sinners and undergirds their ministry to the saints as well.

The extent of the gospel is implicit in the first five books of the New Testament. Since the history recorded in the four Gospels and in the book of Acts narrates how the gospel spread in virgin territory, it should not be surprising that many of the contexts would indicate the gospel to the unsaved. Yet there are overtones of extent in the words of Christ in Luke 4:18: "The Spirit of the Lord is upon me, because he hath anointed me to preach the gospel [*euangelizo*] to the poor; he hath sent me to heal the brokenhearted, to preach deliverance to the captives, and recovering of sight to the blind, to set at liberty them that are bruised." Consider Christ's words of purpose in John 10:10: "I am come that they might have life, and that they might have it more abundantly." Is not Christ's *deliverance* then beyond positional salvation (justification by faith) to practical salvation (sanctification by faith)? The abundant Christian life is a part of preaching Christ. It is a part of the good news.

Since Paul's first missionary journey was in altogether unevangelized territory, the emphasis most certainly was the gospel to the unsaved. However, in Acts 15:35 when "Paul also and Barnabas continued in Antioch, teaching and preaching [*euangelizo*] the word," the implication is more than just the gospel to the unsaved since the church in Antioch had already been established before Acts 15. Then on Paul's second missionary journey, "he went through Syria and Cilicia, confirming [strengthening] the churches" (Acts 15:41). Therefore, part of this journey involved more than just establishing churches. This second journey clearly involved edifying the already existing churches. Paul's third missionary journey also involved ministry to the saints as "he departed, and went over all the country of Galatia and Phrygia in order, strengthening all the disciples" (Acts 18:23). Therefore, Paul both established churches and strengthened existing churches. Today the former would be known as evangelistic ministry and the latter as revivalistic ministry.

In Acts 20:17-38, Paul addresses the elders at Ephesus. In verse 24 he states that his ministry was "to testify the gospel [*euangelion*] of the grace of God." In verse 27 he says, "For I have not shunned to declare unto you all the counsel [will, purpose] of God." Obviously this included more than justification. In fact, in verse 32 Paul states, "And now, brethren, I commend you to God, and to the word of his grace [cf. v. 24 "the gospel of . . . grace"], which is able to build you up, and to give you an inheritance among all them which are sanctified." Again his burden is beyond justification to sanctification as he states "the word of his grace which is able to build you up."

Beyond the implications in the narrative books, the extent of the gospel is explicit in the Epistles. The Pauline Epistles, which were written to some of the churches referred to in Acts, explain how Paul strengthened the churches. This included the good news to the saints.

As was noted earlier, based on the usage of *euangelion* and *euangelizo*, Romans and Galatians are "key books" explaining the message of the gospel. Romans specifically unfolds the gospel (Rom. 1:16). Romans 1-5 details justification by faith, emphasizing the saving death of Christ as the gospel to sinners. Romans 6-8 details sanctification by faith, emphasizing the saving life of Christ as the gospel to saints. Romans 6 revels in the implications of the finished work of Christ. Faith to access the victory of union with Christ is described with words such as "yield yourselves unto God, as those that are alive from the dead, and your members as instruments of righteousness unto God" (Rom. 6:13). The next verse explains that then "sin shall not have dominion over you" (Rom. 6:14). Faith for victory is also described in words such as "if ye through the Spirit do mortify the deeds of the body, ye shall live" (Rom. 8:13). Both emphases of the gospel to sinners and the gospel to saints relate to the provision of Christ's death and resurrection life. The gospel is that Jesus saves both positionally and practically. In fact, in Romans 15:15-16 Paul refers to what he has "written" in the entire book of Romans as "the gospel."

Galatians classically deals with a particular but common error. The error involved returning to "the weak and beggarly elements" of flesh-dependence (Gal. 4:9). The error was flesh-dependence to live the Christian life or sanctification by works. Galatians 3:2-3 confronts this error powerfully by asking the questions, "Received ye the Spirit by the works of the law, or by the hearing of faith? Are ye so foolish? having begun in the Spirit, are ye now made perfect by the flesh?" This emphasizes that as one is saved by faith, one also matures by faith. Any theology that minimizes a responsible faith is here labeled by Paul as "foolish."

As was noted earlier, Ephesians is another key book incorporating all three terms. Ephesians is the foundational book explaining church philosophy and is the key book dealing with the role of the evangelist. The Spirit-filled life or gospel to the saints emphasis permeates the book. Chapters 1-3 glory in the believer's inheritance in Christ. Chapters 5-6 command and provide practical application of the Spirit-filled life. Between both emphases is Chapter 4, stating in verses 11-12 that the evangelist is given to equip the saints ("evangelists . . . For the perfecting of the saints, for the work of the ministry"). To say that the evangelist is to have a ministry *only* to the unsaved is to ignore this explicit statement, which actually uses the term *euangelistes*, and to do injustice to the inspired wording. Verse 17 then says, "This I say therefore . . ." and continues to emphasize the believer's walk based on his wealth. It is no accident that verses 22-24 articulate the believer's co-death and co-resurrection with Christ as the foundation for Spirit-filled living. This is the good news to the saint. Colossians 3 is a beautiful parallel passage providing even greater detail.[23]

---

23. When the full extent of the gospel is analyzed and when Paul's itinerant ministry is studied (Chapter 9: "Evangelism Applied" expands on Paul's ministry), one simply

Much more could be cited demonstrating the extent of the gospel, but the examples given support the concept. The message of the evangelist is the evangel: the good news of eternal life to the unsaved and the good news of the abundant life or revival to the saved. The extent of the gospel is truly full salvation.

Analyzing *Euangelistes*

A careful examination of *euangelistes* in the light of *euangelizo* and *euangelion* reveals further insight into the person and work of the evangelist. As noted earlier, *euangelistes* occurs three times in the New Testament. Acts 21:8 designates "Philip the evangelist." Ephesians 4:11 explains that Christ gave gifts to the church, including "some, evangelists" to equip the saints to do the work of the ministry (Eph. 4:12). Second Timothy 4:5 commands "do the work of an evangelist," indicating that the evangelist has a specific work.

---

cannot validate the claim that the evangelist is *only* a missionary church planter. William Combs argues that "the NT evangelist was primarily a church planter" and further states "any ministry of itinerant evangelism that does not lead to new converts being formed into local churches is foreign to the NT. Thus, the evangelist would probably not have had his primary ministry in previously established churches" (Combs, 28). These claims do not stand when the gospel is understood in its full extent (Chapter 6: "The Gospel to Saints" expands on this) and when one observes that of Paul's three major missionary journeys, two involved much ministry to existing churches. In fact, the third journey was predominantly so. To be fair, Combs does admit "Paul, of course, did return to churches he had previously established, but this was probably more in his role as an apostle, rather than an evangelist" (Ibid., 40). However, this claim cannot be substantiated, and the word *probably*, used twice in the above quotations, reveals the lack of solid foundation for the claims. Combs' final conclusion states, "Although it is not possible to be overly dogmatic about the role of the NT evangelist in light of the limited biblical data, the evidence seems to strongly suggest that he functioned not as an itinerant revivalist preacher but as a missionary church planter"(Ibid., 48). While Combs' emphasis on evangelists planting churches ought to be well taken, and not just in foreign "missionary" settings but domestic settings as well, to limit the role of the evangelist to this one application overlooks the explicit statement of purpose in Ephesians 4:11-12, the full message of the gospel, the pattern of Paul in strengthening existing churches, and furthermore the possibility of mass evangelism through existing churches. (Chapter 9: "Evangelism Applied" expands on the example demonstrated in the book of Acts.)

As *euangelion* ("evangel") refers to the message of the gospel and *euangelizo* ("evangelize") refers to the preaching of that message, so *euangelistes* ("evangelist") refers to the man who does the preaching. Together these three words encompass the person and work of the evangelist.

The evangelist specializes in preaching the gospel: the good news of the saving death of Christ to sinners and the good news of the saving life of Christ to saints. Therefore, the evangelist is for the cause of evangelism and revival.[24] As evangelism focuses on the gospel to the lost, so revival focuses on the gospel to the saints. Both emphases form one gospel message of full salvation. The burden of evangelism is that sinners receive the eternal life of Christ, and the burden of revival is that saints be restored to the abundant life of Christ. In both emphases, the evangelist preaches Christ.

That the *euangelistes* exists today is biblically founded for several reasons. First, the very word is used in Ephesians 4:11-12 in the listing of the four leadership gifts Christ gave to the church—apostles, prophets, evangelists, and pastor-teachers—all for the building up of the body of Christ. This particular usage of the word is significant because Ephesians 2:19-20 speaks of the "saints" as "the household of God; And are built upon the foundation of the apostles and prophets, Jesus Christ himself being the chief corner stone." Since the "apostles" and "prophets" are explicitly said to be "the foundation" (indicated as well by the order of Ephesians 4:11), therefore the evangelists and pastor-teachers must be the ones to continue the work. To say that the evangelist does not exist today is to ignore or deny the inspired precision of Ephesians.

---

24. To keep in line with the evangel being for both sinners and saints, another word seems more suitable than *evangelism* here. Yet this word has come to be applied to preaching for the salvation of the lost. The words *witnessing* and *soulwinning* are good words, but apply more to personal ministry rather than public ministry. Therefore, due to a lack of a more specific word, *evangelism* will be occasionally used in the sense of preaching the gospel to the lost.

Second, the sheer weight of the 130 occurrences (out of 135) of the stem *euangel* ("evangel") that relates to the person and work of the evangelist, occurring in 70 percent of the New Testament books including 14 Epistles, indicate that the evangelist is a part of the continuing New Testament church. Furthermore, there is no biblical statement which indicates the ministry of the evangelist has ceased. In fact, the meaning of the three key words proves otherwise. The word *euangelion* means "the good news of the saving death of Christ to sinners and the saving life of Christ to saints." The word *euangelizo* means "preaching the gospel." The word *euangelistes* means "a God-enabled man specializing in preaching the gospel." The three words make a whole. Therefore, the person and work of the evangelist are part of God's plan for this age.

Part Two

FOCUS ON THE EVANGELIST

Chapter Two

A LEADERSHIP GIFT

"And he gave some, apostles; and some, prophets;
and some, evangelists; and some, pastors and teachers;
For the perfecting of the saints, for the work of the ministry,
for the edifying of the body of Christ."
Ephesians 4:11-12

The ministry of the gospel is so important, the crowning victory of Christ's finished work on the cross is so important, the winning back for God of His place in the hearts of fallen men that He might live His life through them is so important, that Christ gave the church an entire leadership gift—the evangelist—to be used of God to keep that focus in place. Of the three occurrences of *euangelistes*, the first of the didactic contexts is Ephesians 4:11-12. Christ, the head of the church, gave and still gives leadership gifts to the church. While Romans 12 and 1 Corinthians 12 primarily delineate service gifts *to believers*, Ephesians 4 delineates gifted men *to the church*. Among the list of these gifts to the church are apostles, prophets, evangelists, and pastor-teachers.[1]

---

1. Theologians differ as to whether the phrase "pastors and teachers" refers to one gifting with two emphases or to two separate giftings. Since the article translated *some* in verse 11 is used four times and not five, it seems that "pastors and teachers," both of which are following the last occurrence of *some*, refer to the one leadership gift of pastor-teacher.

It may be wondered why evangelists are absent from the passages in Romans 12 and 1 Corinthians 12 that also list various gifts. But Romans 12:3-8 emphasizes the interrelation of gifts as "members" in "one body." Therefore, the context is local, and only the gifts that constitute a local body are mentioned. First Corinthians 12 begins early in the chapter speaking of service gifts since the word *diakonia* is used to describe the type of gifts being addressed (12:5). Later in the chapter the leadership gifts are also mentioned: "And God hath set some in the church, first apostles, secondarily prophets, thirdly teachers . . ." (12:28). However, the context is referring to the local church in Corinth since the word "church" in verse 28 is singular, and Paul is addressing wrong thinking within that local body of believers. In contrast, Ephesians 4 addresses the gifts given to "the whole body" (4:16). Therefore, evangelists are listed only in Ephesians because they are a gift to the church as a whole, not just to one local body.

All the gifts of Ephesians 4:11 are given, according to verse 12, to equip the saints to do the work of the ministry for the building up of the body of Christ.[2] This stated purpose clearly implies leadership. The following verses in the context teach that the gifts of verse 11 are to be used of God to mature the body both spiritually and numerically (v. 13), to guard from false doctrine (v. 14), and to speak the truth in love (v. 15), all for the purpose of edification (v. 16). The grammatical flow of thought from verse 11 to verse 16 delineates the responsibility of the leadership gifts.

Christ gives evangelists a leadership role in the building up of His church. What exactly is the evangelist's leadership role? How does it differ from the other gifts? Ephesians 4:11-12 provides four clarifications regarding the leadership role of the evangelist.

---

2. In verse 12, the first *for* (*pros*) is a different Greek word than the last two occurrences of *for* (*eis*).

The Significance of the Order

The first clarification concerns the significance of the order of the leadership gifts. By comparing Ephesians 2:20 with Ephesians 4:11, one can categorize the gifts of Ephesians 4:11 into two groups. First, there are foundational gifts that ceased when the foundation was completed. Second, there are building gifts that continue to build upon the foundation.

Foundational Gifts

Unquestionably, the apostles and prophets had a tremendously important God-given role in leading the early church. The New Testament canon was not yet complete. Ephesians 3:5 speaks of the mystery "which in other ages was not made known unto the sons of men, as it is now revealed unto His holy apostles and prophets by the Spirit." The completion of the canon of Scripture was critical to the founding of the early church. Ephesians 2:20, referring to the church, states, "And are built upon the foundation of the apostles and prophets, Jesus Christ Himself being the chief corner stone." Notice "the foundation of the apostles and prophets" was to be aligned with "Christ . . . the chief cornerstone," but they were *the foundation*.[3] Since the apostles and prophets were the foundation of the church, they are no longer

---

3. John F. Walvoord and Roy B. Zuck, eds., *The Bible Knowledge Commentary, New Testament Edition* (Wheaton: Victor Books, 1983), 627. *The Bible Knowledge Commentary* explains, "The words could be translated, 'the foundation which consists of the apostles and prophets.' This makes the best sense when one sees in 4:11 that the apostles and prophets were gifted men given to the church as its 'foundation.' Furthermore, this fits well in the present context, which states that Christ Jesus Himself is the Chief Cornerstone; that is, He is part of the foundation. In ancient building practices 'the chief cornerstone' was carefully placed. It was crucial because the entire building was lined up with it. The church's foundation, that is, the apostles and prophets, needed to be correctly aligned with Christ. All other believers are built on that foundation, measuring their lives with Christ." Although there may be broader usages of *apostles* and *prophets*, in the narrow sense these gifts were foundational gifts.

functioning because the foundation was completed through their specific ministry. The canon was completed, and the church of Jesus Christ begun. The fact that evangelists are not listed in this statement proves that they were not just for the foundational era of the church but for the entire church age. To deny this conclusion ignores the precision of Ephesians 2:20. Therefore, to deny the present-day validity of the evangelist is neither exegetically nor theologically accurate.

Because the book of Acts provides the history of this foundational era, it is not surprising that more information is given regarding the work of apostles and prophets than to evangelists and pastors. However, early church history immediately records the use of evangelists. For example, Eusebius, one of the historians of early church history, records that "Thomas, one of the twelve apostles, under divine impulse sent Thaddeus, who was numbered among the seventy disciples of Christ, to Edessa, as a preacher and evangelist of the teaching of Christ."[4]

Building Gifts

The foundation having been laid, evangelists and pastors began a greater usefulness in the building upon the apostolic foundation. This follows since the next gifts listed after the apostles and prophets are "evangelists" and "pastors and teachers" (pastor-teachers).

The placement of the gift of the evangelist by Christ indicates a leadership responsibility for the building of the church following the foundational era. Eusebius, in a chapter entitled "The Evangelists that Were Still Eminent at that Time," speaks of one Quadratus and "many others . . . who were known in those days, and who occupied the first place among the successors of the

---

4. Philip Schaff and Henry Wace, eds., "The Church History of Eusebius" *Nicene and Post-Nicene Fathers*, Second Series, 2nd ed., vol. I, bk. I (1952; reprint ed., Peabody, Mass.: Hendrickson, 2004), 100.

apostles. And they also, being illustrious disciples of such great men, built up the foundations of the churches which had been laid by the apostles in every place."[5] The time period is just following the apostolic era. Also, evangelists were viewed as "successors of the apostles." This does not imply that they had the authority of apostles, but rather were building on the foundation of the apostles. Clearly, Eusebius viewed the evangelists as operative following the apostolic era. In fact, later in the chapter he wrote, "It is impossible for us to enumerate the names of all that became shepherds and evangelists in the churches throughout the world in the age immediately succeeding the apostles."[6] Notice Eusebius refers to two operating gifts: "shepherds and evangelists."

In addition to noting the two valid building gifts, the scriptural placement of evangelists in the list of leadership gifts as the first to follow the apostles and prophets indicates a definitive leadership responsibility. The order of placement has significance. When seen in the light of other Scripture, the evangelist is likely listed before pastor-teachers because his ministry is broader, affecting many churches, not just one. In the least, evangelists are not beneath the rank of pastor-teachers. This placement, however, does not mean hierarchy over pastors and churches in an organizational sense. Nor does it give evangelists the authority to violate a church's autonomy. However, it does mean evangelists clearly have a vital leadership role in the building of Christ's church.

An Office of Declaration

A second clarification regarding the leadership role of the evangelist in Ephesians 4:11-12 concerns the nature of the leadership role that the evangelist has. Occasionally, reference is made to the "office of the evangelist." Since this phrase is never used

5. Ibid., bk. 3, 169.
6. Ibid.

in Scripture, is this a legitimate concept? The word *office* in the English language "applies usually to the function of or the work to be performed by a person as a result of his trade, profession, employment, or position with relation to others."[7] But what nuance does the scriptural usage of the word indicate? The KJV uses the word *office* eight times; however, only six Greek words are used. Two pairs of the six terms come from the same root. So in essence, four different root stems are involved. By investigating the eight contexts of the translation *office* with the four Greek root stems involved and then comparing them all to the leadership gifts of Ephesians 4:11-12, noting the difference between local church offices and offices to the church at large, there is reason to conclude that the evangelist is an office of declaration to the body of Christ.

The Concept of an Office

Of the eight occurrences of the translation *office* in the KJV, three refer to the priesthood of Old Testament Israel. These three references involve two Greek words that come from the same root. Since these three references refer to the Old Testament priesthood, they do not refer to the New Testament church leadership gifts.

Of the five remaining occurrences of *office*, four Greek words and three root stems are used. The first occurrence is in Romans 11:13: "For I speak to you Gentiles, inasmuch as I am the apostle of the Gentiles, I magnify mine office." The word the Apostle Paul uses here under inspiration is the noun *diakonia*, which means "service, office."[8] Interestingly, this word most often translates as *ministry*. Romans 11:13 is the only time this word is translated as

---

7. *Webster's New Dictionary of Synonyms* (Springfield, MA: Merriam-Webster, Inc., 1984), 366.

8. William F. Arndt and F. Wilbur Gingrich, *A Greek-English Lexicon of the New Testament and Other Early Christian Literature*, 2nd ed. revised F. Wilbur Gingrich and Fredrick W. Danker (Chicago: University of Chicago Press, 1979), 184.

office. The emphasis is on the apostle's service or function as an apostle. Is it fair then to even refer to the gift of the apostle as an office? Acts 1 clarifies the question. The context deals with choosing someone to take Judas's place as one of the twelve. Acts 1:17 says, "For he was numbered with us, and had obtained part of this ministry." The word *ministry* is the same word translated as *office* in Romans 11:13. Acts 1:17 uses it as referring to the twelve apostles. But Acts 1:20 refers to the replacement of Judas by quoting the Psalms as saying "and, his bisophrick let another take." The word *bishoprick* is the same word translated as "the office of a bishop" in 1 Timothy 3:1. Therefore, the gift of the apostle was definitely an office and even involved oversight.

Romans 12:4 provides the second occurrence: "For as we have many members in one body, and all members have not the same office." The context is addressing the service gifts. The word translated *office* is the noun *praxis*, which means "acting, activity, function."[9] It is translated most often as *deeds* or *works*. This is the only context where *praxis* is translated "office," and it does not impact the discussion at hand.

The third occurrence gives even more understanding of the subject. First Timothy 3:1 states, "This is a true saying, If a man desire the office of a bishop, he desireth a good work." The noun *episkope* is used here and means "position" or "office as an overseer."[10] The word emphasizes oversight. Obviously, it is related to the noun translated *bishop*, meaning "overseer." The sense of office as a position of organizational oversight is clear. The word *bishop* is one of the words referring to the New Testament leadership gift of the pastor-teacher and emphasizes the oversight emphasis of that office.

The final two occurrences of the word *office* both occur in 1 Timothy 3, along with the word just noted. However, these two references use another Greek term. Verse 10 says, "And let these

9. Ibid., 697.
10. Ibid., 299.

also first be proved; then let them use the office of a deacon, being found blameless." Finally, verse 13 says, "For they that have used the office of a deacon well purchase to themselves a good degree, and great boldness in the faith which is in Christ Jesus." Both verses dealing with deacons use the verb *diakoneo*, which means generally to "wait on someone" or "serve" and here "serve as deacon."[11] In the New Testament it is translated primarily as *minister* or *serve*. First Timothy 3:10 and 13 are the only two times it is translated as *office* in the KJV, while many other translations just say *serve*. This indicates that the emphasis is serving, and yet verse 13 indicates that the position should be respected.

If *office* means only a pastoral position of organizational oversight, then "the office of a bishop" (overseer) would be the only office in I Timothy 3. But if *office* also includes a respected position with a specific function, then it is fair to use the terminology "the office of a deacon." The first deacons of Acts 6 were to be "men of honest report, full of the Holy Ghost and wisdom" (v. 3). These qualifications meant that their new position demanded integrity and Spirit-enablement. The position was implemented to put down "murmuring" (v. 1). Although the deacons were under the apostles, they were "over this business" (v. 3) of the "daily ministration" (v. 1). Interestingly, *ministration* translates from *diakonia*, which is the word Paul used in Romans 11:13: "I magnify mine office [*diakonia*]."[12] Therefore, there is a "leadership function" sense in which *office* is applied to deacons and a "leadership oversight" sense in which the word is applied to overseers/bishops.

Evidently many Baptists have followed the sense opted for in the KJV since most Baptists believe in the two offices of pastor and deacon. If, then, it is legitimate to refer to the office

---

11. Ibid., 184.

12. That the men of Acts were deacons seems clear from the fact that all the words have the same root: "ministration" [*diakonia*] in Acts 6:1; "let them use the office of a deacon" [*diakoneo*] in I Timothy 3:10; and simply "the deacons" [*diakonos*] in I Timothy 3:8.

of a deacon, based on the concept of a position with a specific leadership function, then it is also legitimate to refer to the office of an evangelist. Yet choice of words is not really the issue. The issue is that the evangelist is a valid ministry today, and that ministry has a specific leadership function. However, if the word *office* is embraced, care must be taken to distinguish between local church offices and offices to the body of Christ.

Local Church Offices

First Timothy 3 gives the qualifications for pastors and deacons. The fact that this pastoral epistle addresses only these two categories indicates that there are only two offices when it comes to a specific local church. Philippians 1:1 supports the concept of only two local church offices by referring specifically to bishops (overseers) and deacons in the context of addressing the church at Philippi: "Paul and Timotheus, the servants of Jesus Christ, To all the saints in Christ Jesus which are at Philippi, with the bishops and deacons." The former is an office of oversight; the latter is an office of service. These two offices specifically relate to local churches.[13] The Scripture gives no indication that the office of the evangelist is a local church office.

Offices to the Body of Christ

Ephesians 4:11-12 delineates four gifts to the body of Christ. The emphasis of the office of pastor-teacher is to a specific local body of believers. However, the emphasis of apostles, prophets,

---

13. Since 1 Peter 5:1-2 speaks of "elders" synonymously with those who "feed the flock" [verb of noun "shepherd"/pastor] and "taking the oversight" [verb of noun "bishop"], it appears that this passage refers to one position with three major elements emphasized. Acts 20:17 and 28 use the words *elder, overseer,* and *shepherd* to refer to the same men. On this basis, most Baptists strongly hold to two offices: pastor and deacon. However, the point here is that the office of the evangelist is not among the local church offices.

and evangelists is not scripturally specified as relating primarily to only one local church. Therefore, these three gifts are offices to the body of Christ or church at large. Except for the apostles, these offices do not have a scriptural right to violate a church's autonomy through organizational hierarchy, even though their ministry is to many churches.

The apostles had the greatest responsibility as an office. Not only were they an office to the body of Christ, but they also had the authority as overseers of the early church to demand obedience. A classic example of this can be found in I Corinthians 5, dealing with church discipline. The founding of the early church needed more than local church overseers (the office of the pastor-teacher); it also needed authoritative oversight from the apostles.

Prophets and evangelists are never designated as "offices" of oversight such as those of apostles and pastors because their function is primarily truth declaration. However, they are listed between the office of the apostle and the office of the pastor-teacher, which may imply that they, too, are offices. This conclusion is similar to the conclusion of many Baptists that there are only two local church offices because the ministry of pastors and deacons are placed together in several passages. If *episkope* (bishoprick) is the only word truly relating to an "office," then the offices would be limited to apostles and pastors, not prophets and evangelists or, for that matter, deacons on the local church level. However, if the word *office* may be taken to mean more than the oversight concept of *episkope* and to emphasize a position with a specific leadership function, then prophets and evangelists may be legitimately labeled an "office" to the body of Christ (and deacons to local bodies). In other words, if a strict sense of the word *office* is meant as an organizational position with oversight authority, then evangelists should not be labeled an "office." But if a broader sense of the word *office* is meant as a position of declaring specific truth (the evangel), not just to one local church but to the body of Christ at large, then evangelists may be properly termed an "office." This is the sense used in this discussion of "the office of the evangelist."

The Office of the Evangelist

The bottom line is that the evangelist is an office of dec-laration. The leadership gifts to the church are offices with a definite primary function. Apostles were an office of over-sight and declaration to the church at large. Prophets were an office of declaration to the church at large. Evangelists are an office of declaration to the church at large. And pastor-teachers are an office of oversight and declaration primarily to one church. It should be noted that when the gift of the pas-tor is specifically called an "office," the word *bishop* is used (I Timothy 3:I). Not everyone with the gift of pastor-teacher serves in the office of a bishop, since some may be assistant pastors, and so on. It is possible, therefore, although certainly not the norm, for an evangelist to serve in the office of a bishop for a time. Pothinus of the second century is referred to as an evangelist,[14] but he later became the bishop of Lyons.[15] Also, the Gospel writers are constantly referred to in early church history as "the Evangelists," yet Hippolytus refers to "Mark the evange-list, bishop of Alexandria."[16] This is the exception, not the rule, and would be only for providential purposes.

---

14. Alexander Roberts and James Donaldson, eds., "Introductory Note to Irenae-us Against Heresies," *Ante-Nicene Fathers*, vol. I (reprint ed., Peabody, MA: Hendrickson Publishers, 2004), 309.

15. Diana Severonce, "Blandina: A Faithful Witness Unto Death," *Glimpses*, ed. Ken Curtis, no. 51 (1993): 2.

16. Alexander Roberts and James Donaldson, eds., "The Same Hippolytus on the Seventy Apostles," *Ante-Nicene Fathers: Translations of the Writings of the Fathers Down to A.D. 325*, vol. 5 (reprint ed., Peabody, MA: Hendrickson Publishers, 2004), 255.

Evangelists do have their own scriptural New Testament office, whether or not it is called an "office." The question of terminology is somewhat beside the point. The issue is that there is a valid role the evangelist is to fulfill in the building up of Christ's church. However, historically in the broader usage of the word, *office* began to be applied to the role of the evangelist. Origen of the third century uses the phrase "the office of the evangelist."[17] Also, Eusebius, writing in the early fourth century, uses the phrase "the office of evangelists."[18]

The gift of the evangelist is a valid leadership role. Evangelists lead primarily through the means of declaring truth and not necessarily through oversight in a local church. The nature of the leadership of the evangelist is through a declarative voice. But what do evangelists declare?

A Leadership Focus on the Evangel

A third clarification of the leadership role of the evangelist seen in Ephesians 4:11-12 concerns the emphasis of the word *evangelist* itself. Since there are two leadership gifts functioning today for the purpose of equipping the saints to do the work of the ministry, what is the difference between the two gifts? The difference lies in the focus of the words involved. A pastor has a broad focus (shepherding), and an evangelist has a specialized focus (the evangel).

As a pastor may be likened to a general practitioner who must know a lot about a lot, so an evangelist may be likened to a specialist who must know a lot about a little. While it is true that a pastor also declares the gospel, an evangelist specializes in the

17. Alexander Roberts and James Donaldson, eds., "Origen's Commentary on the Gospel of John," *Ante-Nicene Fathers*, vol. 10 (reprint ed., Peabody, MA: Hendrickson Publishers, 2004), 299.

18. Schaff and Wace.

gospel in its full ramifications. As the general practitioner and the specialist work together as colleagues in a common cause, each with his own specific responsibility, so the pastor and the evangelist work together as colleagues in a common cause, each with his own specific responsibility. As general practitioners have the responsibility for the ongoing physical welfare of their patients and specialists have the responsibility to address specific physical needs more thoroughly, so pastors have the responsibility for the ongoing spiritual welfare of their churches and evangelists have the responsibility to address specific spiritual needs more thoroughly.

The general practitioner is the constant, overall caregiver physically; the specialist brought in by the general practitioner is a short-term, focused caregiver. One is not superseding the other. For example, the family doctor is glad for the heart surgeon to come in and do his specialized work. Also the heart surgeon is glad after his work is done to turn his patient back over to the family doctor. Likewise, as the pastor is the constant, overall caregiver spiritually, the evangelist invited by the pastor is a short-term, focused caregiver. Pastors and evangelists are colleagues that ought to respect and appreciate each other's giftings, and work together in the ministry. Both are a part of God's plan for the New Testament church.

The specialty of the evangelist is inherent in the word *evangelist*. The narrow focus of the evangelist is *the evangel*. In the previous chapter it was noted that the evangel is both the gospel to sinners as well as the gospel to saints. The evangel is the glorious good news of the saving death of Christ to sinners and the saving life of Christ to saints. This latter emphasis to the saints is simply revival, or life again, to the defeated Christian. The life of Christ in the believer may be accessed by faith as the animating power to one's personality. This is the "engine" that pulls the responsibilities and privileges of the Christian life. Evangelists focus on this engine—the evangel.

Regarding this twofold burden of revival and evangelism, some evangelists may be more involved in one aspect than the other. For example, George Whitefield's ministry largely focused on the lost. Yet John Wesley, though God used him to reach many unsaved, had a tremendous ministry of strengthening churches. All evangelists will be used to some degree in both aspects, and certainly all have a burden for both revival and evangelism.

Although pastors address these emphases as well, evangelists specialize in them. Part 3 will discuss the evangel in much greater detail. At this point, it must simply be understood that the evangelist has a leading role in the theology of the evangel. If the theology of the evangel becomes confused or incorrect, it is the responsibility of evangelists more than any others in the body of Christ to address the issues involved, for that is their specialized focus.

Therefore, in equipping the saints for the work of the ministry, the evangelist's equipping focuses specifically on the evangel. Evangelists must preach revival truth to the saints so that they are accessing the power of the Holy Spirit to do the work of the ministry. This is true "equipment." Also, they must equip the saints with a clear understanding of the gospel so that the saints in turn might clearly declare the gospel.

The wording of Ephesians 4:11-12 makes it clear that evangelists have a specific ministry to the saints, not just to the lost. John R. Rice emphasizes:

> But does the Bible teach that the evangelist is only, or principally, a missionary to the heathen and unevangelized? Not at all! This Scripture expressly states that he is given as a gift of the ascended Christ to men, "for the perfecting of the saints for the work of the ministry" . . . The evangelist is to perfect saints in soul winning and is to edify the body of Christ.[19]

---

19. John R. Rice, *The Evangelist* (Murfreesboro: Sword of the Lord Publishers, 1968), 24.

Evangelists and pastors are, by divine enablement, keenly aware of evangelism and shepherding respectively—not so they can be the only ones to evangelize and shepherd, but so they can equip the saints to evangelize and shepherd. The gifts provide divine understanding to the respective men in order to teach others.

The evangelist is different from the pastor. Obviously, they have some elements that overlap. However, the emphasis for each one is different. The word *pastor* means "shepherd." The shepherd is one who leads the sheep, feeds them, and cares for the members of the flock by encouraging them, comforting them, and helping them.[20] But the evangelist is not a pastor. Though there may be areas that overlap, the primary emphasis is different.

The primary emphasis of the evangelist is not to lead the sheep as a congregation in an ongoing situation, or else he would be a pastor. Beyond the legitimate application of establishing churches, some evangelists have pastored established churches. However, if an evangelist pastors too long, it may be to the detriment of the church unless there are true pastors working with the evangelist.

The primary emphasis of the evangelist is not to tend the flock. Although it is a blessing to fellowship with people, go out to eat with them, get to know them, and be there during times of crisis and times of joy, all of which produces a bond with people, is the evangelist supposed to be building bonds with the pastor's flock? Certainly there is a balance to all this, but tending the flock is pastoral and bond-building. This is not the evangelist's primary emphasis.

The primary emphasis of the evangelist, in keeping with the analogy of sheep, is to "shear" the sheep. But this does not mean

---

20. Charles Ryrie, *The Holy Spirit* (Chicago: Moody Press, 1997), 135. Ryrie says, "The word *pastor* means to shepherd; therefore, the gift of pastor involves leading, providing and caring for, and protecting the portion of the flock of God committed to one's care."

to skin them. If they were skinned, they would be dead. A pastor spoke of a time when an evangelist said to him during the song service, "I'm going to skin your people tonight!" The pastor wisely replied, "My people need their skin."

The word *shear*, in reference to sheep, simply means "to cut or clip the hair, wool, etc. from."[21] A sheep is sheared so that its wool can be used. In other words, the idea is to make the sheep useful.

A certain pastor who also has a farm mentioned that he is particular as to who he lets shear his sheep. If the sheepshearer is careless and nicks the sheep, causing needless bleeding, the pastor will not use that sheepshearer again. He wants one who will carefully shear the wool pelt from the sheep. The pelt is then sold and put into various avenues of usefulness.[22]

Bob Jones, Sr. pointed out the following:

> As an evangelist, I may have access to more sinners than some other Christian; but what I am doing in winning souls to Christ is what every other Christian is supposed to do. My responsibility as an evangelist is to stir up Christian people to win souls, to live separated Christian lives, to do the job that God expects of them, and to be the kind of people that God expects them to be. The evangelist is supposed to stimulate the sheep into real spiritual activity.[23]

Thus, God uses the evangelist to lead people in a specialized way to be useful in God's great cause. The pastor continually equips the people in many ways on a long-term basis. All of this is so that the saints will do the work of the ministry.

---

21. *Webster's New World Dictionary*, 2nd college ed. (U.S.A.: William Collins and World Publishing Co., Inc., 1978), 1310.

22. From a personal conversation with a pastor.

23. Bob Jones, Sr., *Evangelism Today* (Greenville, SC: Bob Jones University Press, 1955), 6.

Although the ministries of a pastor and evangelist are alike in some ways, each calling has a unique purpose. Furthermore, both are a part of God's plan for the church, and God's plan has not changed. Providentially, God works these emphases together to further the body of Christ. A church that refuses to use a pastor is not following God's plan for the New Testament church. It would follow that a church that refuses to use the evangelist is incomplete in following God's plan for the New Testament church as well. "The pastor and the evangelist are given by Christ Himself to the local church and should be utilized by the church in their distinct capabilities."[24]

How well are churches and evangelists applying the gift? Obedience is vital. The gift of the evangelist is a part of the plan of Christ in the New Testament church age. If a part of Christ's plan is ignored or rejected, the health of the body of Christ will be affected. However, when Christ's plan is implemented, the body of Christ is healthy, and God is truly glorified.

Evangelists are to lead in their specialized focus. True leadership, as Christ taught it, is serving others. True leadership is not being ministered unto, but ministering (Matt. 20:28). When an evangelist humbly, yet boldly, exercises his gift in God-dependence for Spirit-enablement, he is serving as well as leading. While it is true that an evangelist must have a servant's heart, it is also true that he has a God-given leadership responsibility.

The pastor is equipping in an ongoing setting. When the evangelist comes in, he must quickly diagnose what is hindering the body from healthy maturity and growth. Then he must administer what is needed to correct or enhance the body of Christ in that setting. Although at times this may involve the path of confrontation, this is part of the specialized work of the evangelist.

---

24. Phil Shuler, *The Shepherd and His Dog* (Poway, CA: Phil Shuler Crusades, Inc., n.d.), 6.

As general practitioners invite specialists, so pastors invite evangelists. Although there is a sense in which the specialist is "under" the general practitioner as an invited extension of his work, there is also a sense in which the general practitioner is "under" the specialist in regard to his specialized focus. Likewise, although there is a sense in which the evangelist is "under" the pastor as an invited extension of his work, there is also a sense in which the pastor is "under" the evangelist in regard to his specialized focus. The issue is not who is over whom, but colleagues working together in a common cause, each respecting the other's role. Obviously, it makes sense for the evangelist to lead in the work of an evangelist because he is an evangelist.

Where Spirit-filled men are involved, there is a high respect for the other's role. In fact, when an evangelist is operating in the Spirit, the congregation he is ministering to will have a greater love and respect for their pastor. Asahel Nettleton, used of God in the Second Great Awakening, was known for turning congregations' hearts toward their pastors.[25]

A Ministry of Itinerancy

A final clarification of the leadership role of the evangelist, implied in Ephesians 4:11 and supported through the analogy of faith, concerns the extent of the evangelist's leadership. The very word *pastor* (shepherd) indicates a local leadership over one's flock. The word *evangelist* does not provide this concept. First Peter 5:2 exhorts pastors to "feed the flock of God which is among you, taking the oversight thereof." The flock is God's, yet God

25. Bennet Tyler and Andrew Bonar, *Asahel Nettleton: Life and Labours* (Edinburgh: The Banner of Truth Trust, 1996), 58-59. Asahel Nettleton believed evangelists had a "duty not to weaken the hands of settled pastors, but to do all in their power to strengthen them." "He would treat ministers with such kindness, and speak of them with such respect, as to make the impression on the minds of their people, that they were worthy of their confidence."

gives pastors the responsibility of overseeing the flock. First Peter 5:3 says, "Neither as being lords over God's heritage, but being ensamples to the flock." The idea of "God's heritage" refers to those God allots to each pastor.[26] Hebrews 13:17 states that pastors "must give account" for those under their leadership. Unquestionably, pastors are responsible for the flock God puts under their care.

For whom, then, are evangelists responsible? What is the extent of responsibility given by God to evangelists? The extent of a pastor's responsibility is primarily to the flock over which God has given him the oversight. However, as noted earlier, the evangelist's responsibility is toward many flocks. The God-given gift of the evangelist is a leadership gift to churches or the church as a whole. Scripture indicates this, and history supports it.

Since the responsibility of the evangelist reaches toward many churches, he must usually be itinerant. For example, in Acts 21, Philip is called "the evangelist." In Acts 8:5, Philip "went down to the city of Samaria, and preached Christ unto them." Verses 4-13 speak of his ministry in Samaria. Then, according to Acts 8:26-39, Philip, under divine leading, went south to reach the Ethiopian eunuch. After being "caught away" in verse 39, "Philip was found at Azotus: and passing through he preached in all the cities, till he came to Caesarea" (v. 40). Obviously, Philip had an itinerant ministry. This example of an evangelist in Acts sets the precedent for itinerancy.

However, beyond the example of Philip, it was noted in the previous chapter that of the 50 contexts of the verb *euangelizo* referring to men preaching the gospel, 25 of them indicate an itinerant ministry. Twenty-two of these are found in narratives. Obviously, the contexts in didactic literature would not provide this insight.

---

26. Arndt and Gingrich, 435.

The Scripture does not indicate how short or long an evangelist's ministry is to be in a given church. Before modern transportation, the itinerancy may have been somewhat regional from a practical standpoint. It is interesting to note in Acts 21:8 that Philip, who is called an evangelist, did have a house from which he evidently based his ministry: "the house of Philip the evangelist."

The concept of itinerancy is generally true of the work of the evangelist. However, the real issue is ministry to many churches. Before modern transportation and large buildings, individual churches were generally small. But in the present time there is a sense in which several churches meet together under one roof in a large church building. In this larger setting, an evangelist may be "local" and yet ministering his gift to "several churches." Also, when an evangelist serves as a college president, a camp director, or the like, he is ministering his gift to people from multiple churches. However, the people are coming to his location, rather than his going to their location. But the general application of the work of the evangelist involves itinerancy.

Church history also indicates the extent of an evangelist's responsibility. Eusebius continues in the passage cited earlier that evangelists "preached the Gospel more and more widely and scattered the saving seeds of the kingdom of heaven far and near throughout the whole world."[27] This statement reveals a broad extent of responsibility and implies itinerancy. Eusebius later speaks of "Pantaenus, a man highly distinguished for his learning," who "had charge of the school of the faithful in Alexandria" and who "displayed such zeal for the divine Word that he was appointed as a herald of the Gospel of Christ to the nations of the East, and was sent as far as India. For indeed there were still many evangelists of the Word who sought earnestly to use their inspired zeal, after the examples of the apostles, for the increase and building

---

27. Schaff and Wace.

up of the Divine Word."[28] The statement that the evangelist was sent to "the nations of the East," implies an itinerant range.

The "Introductory Note to the First Apology of Justin Martyr" in *Ante-Nicene Fathers* states regarding Martyr: "From this time he acted as an evangelist, taking every opportunity to proclaim the gospel as the only safe and certain philosophy, the only way to salvation. It is probable that he travelled much."[29] Justin Martyr lived in the second century. The word *evangelist* is ascribed to him, and itinerancy is mentioned in that context.

Also Polycarp, the disciple of Apostle John, is referred to in *Ante-Nicene Fathers* in the "Introductory Note to Irenaeus Against Heresies": "Polycarp had sent Pothinus into Celtic Gaul at an early date as its evangelist."[30] Notice Pothinus was sent to the region of Celtic Gaul as "its evangelist." Gaul, at the time of the Roman Empire, included the region of modern France, Belgium, and the very northern part of Italy.[31] Therefore, this evangelist's responsibility was to this entire region, indicating an itinerant ministry.

In nineteenth-century American history, Peter Cartwright stands out as a colorful Methodist circuit rider. A brief study of his life reveals clearly that Peter Cartwright had the gift of the evangelist. The following account highlights his sense of responsibility:

> Two men on horseback said goodbyes. "I should not be surprised if I never see you again," said the first.
> "Well," answered the second, "if I fall and you never see me again, tell my friends that I fell at my post trying to do my duty."

28. Ibid., bk. 5, 224-25. Interestingly, Eusebius further records, "It is reported that among persons there [India] who knew of Christ, he found the gospel according to Matthew which had anticipated his own arrival. For Bartholomew, one of the apostles, had preached to them, and left with them the writing of Matthew in the Hebrew language, which they had preserved till that time."

29. Roberts and Donaldson, "Introductory Note to the First Apology of Justin Martyr," vol. I, 160.

30. Ibid., "Introductory Note to Irenaeus Against Heresies," 309.

31. *Webster's New World Dictionary*, 578.

Illinois was flooded. Not a path could be seen beneath the sheet of water. Treetops, which might guide a bold traveler, stood miles away but would be out of sight whenever he rode into a hollow. He could easily lose his way or flounder into a hole. Even if he reached the trees, a swollen creek beside them would compel him to swim twenty yards. He might have to spend the night on the sopping prairie. The rider paused. On one hand was his duty to the souls of his frontier parish; on the other, serious danger. At that moment he recalled his motto: "Never retreat till you know you can advance no further." He rode forward.[32]

"Souls of his frontier parish" articulates Cartwright's extent of responsibility as an evangelist. Peter Cartwright's burden to fulfill his specific responsibility even in the midst of difficulty challenges evangelists to take their leadership role seriously.

Conclusion

Ephesians 4:11-12 clarifies the leadership role of the evangelist. The significance of the order of the gifts reveals that the evangelist, along with the pastor-teacher, is a "building gift," given by Christ to build upon the foundation of the apostles and prophets. The nature of the leadership role is an office of declaration. The focus of the declaration is the evangel. And the extent of the declaration is to the body of Christ.

---

32. Ken Curtis, et al. eds., "Peter Cartwright: Perhaps America's Most Colorful Country Preacher," *Glimpses*, no. 85 (1997): 1.

Chapter Three

A PREACHING GIFT

*"Preach the word; be instant in season, out of season; reprove,
rebuke, exhort with all longsuffering and doctrine . . .
do the work of an evangelist."*
2 Timothy 4:2, 5
*"Therefore they that were scattered abroad went everywhere
preaching the word. Then Philip went down to the city of
Samaria, and preached Christ unto them."*
Acts 8:4-5

The first New Testament evangelist intimated by the verb
euangelizo was John the Baptist, who was also the greatest Old
Testament prophet. When asked "Who art thou?" John answered,
"I am the voice of one crying in the wilderness" (John 1:22-23).
This is an articulate description of the evangelist—a *voice*. In the
previous chapter it was noted that the gift of the evangelist is an
office of declaration—a voice. The nature of the gift of the evangelist is preaching.[1] The evangelist is a preacher of the evangel.

It is no accident that in the same context where the admoni-
tion to "do the work of an evangelist" is found, the ministerial
mandate to "preach the word" is also given. Second Timothy 4:5

---

1. Jimmy Cook, "And He Gave . . . Some Evangelists," *Preach the Word Newsletter*,
vol. 5, no. 4 (1996): 2. With this perspective, Evangelist Jimmy Cook defines the gift of
the evangelist as "a preaching gift to the church."

provides one of the three occurrences and the second didactic context of *euangelistes*. *Euangelistes* is the person who does the work represented elsewhere by the verb *euangelizo*.

In Acts 8:4, the present participle of the verb is translated *preaching*, and the context further states "preaching the word." Acts 8:4 connects *euangelizo* with the *logos*. However, 2 Timothy 4:2 uses *kerusso* with the *logos*. What is the difference? *Kerusso* by itself means "to proclaim (as a herald), from *kerux*, a herald; without reference to the *matter* proclaimed . . . ; and without including the idea of *teaching*."[2] *Euangelizo* means "to announce a joyful message; having regard to the matter announced (not the manner)."[3] Therefore, *kerusso* by itself emphasizes manner, while *euangelizo* emphasizes matter.

Both Acts 8:4 and 2 Timothy 4:2 refer to preaching "the word." Acts 8:5, speaking specifically of Philip, says that he "preached Christ unto them." Here the verb is *kerusso*. Acts 8:12 uses *euangelizo* of Philip's preaching in Samaria. Also, *euangelizo* is used in Acts 8:35 when the scene shifts to the Ethiopian eunuch as Philip "preached unto him Jesus." Since both *kerusso* and *euangelizo* are used of Philip, and since Philip is called an evangelist in Acts 21:8, clearly both terms pertain to the preaching of the evangelist, even though *kerusso* is not limited to the evangelist.

Second Timothy 4:2 stands as the classic passage on preaching. In the same context, we observe the imperative "do the work of an evangelist." However, the phrase does not include a definite article before the word *evangelist*. This indicates the person is not what is in mind but rather the operation.[4] Thus Timothy was not an evangelist but a pastor who was to have an evangelistic

---

2. E. W. Bullinger, *Appendixes to the Companion Bible* (Grand Rapids: Zondervan Bible Publishers, 1974), 160 [emphasis original].

3. Ibid.

4. D. Edmond Hiebert, *Second Timothy* (Chicago: Moody Press, 1958), 108. Hiebert here states, "The term, used without an article, does not here designate a distinct office but rather characterizes him as one whose chief activity is the bringing of the good news of the Gospel of Christ. His ministry must be evangelistic in nature."

dimension in his ministry. On the other hand, it is significant to note that one of the three occurrences of the word *evangelist* occurs right in the classic context on preaching.

The nature of the work of an evangelist is the preaching of an evangelist. But what is the preaching of an evangelist? What makes the preaching of the evangelist different from all other preaching? According to 2 Timothy 4:5, at times even pastors are to apply the preaching of an evangelist. In Chapter I it was noted that the emphasis of the verb *euangelizo* is a public ministry. Therefore, there is a work of the evangelist that is a specific type of public preaching. It is not merely a matter of personal witnessing, which is an obligation given to every believer in the Great Commission.

To discern the preaching of the evangelist, one must understand what makes preaching preaching, and then beyond that, understand what makes the preaching of the evangelist distinctive.

The Characteristics of All Biblical Preaching

According to 2 Timothy 4:2, the characteristics of all true biblical preaching involve issues of content, readiness, and empowerment.

Substantive Content

Second Timothy 4:2, among other truths, delineates three components that involve the *substance* of preaching. Without any one of these three components, the speaking is not true biblical preaching.

Based on the Authority of the Word

Biblical preaching is authoritative. The first component involving the substance of preaching is found in the phrase "preach the word." Here *kerusso* (emphasizing manner) is tied to the *matter* to be heralded. The authority is the *logos*, the Word of God. Outside of this authority, preaching has no authority. "The preacher is not to air his own opinions but to proclaim God's eternal, authoritative Word of truth."[5] Ultimate authority resides in the Word of the living God.

The use of *kerusso* emphasizes proclaiming as a herald.[6] A herald was "a *messenger* vested with public authority, who conveyed the official messages of kings, magistrates, princes, military commanders, or who gave a public summons or command."[7] Although the verb *kerusso* emphasizes manner and not matter, the *logos* emphasizes the content. Also, the definition of the noun *herald* emphasizes an outside authority. In preaching, the authority is the Word of God. Preachers are simply the spokesmen for the King's message. This concept focuses on the greatness of God, where the authority actually lies. Thus God is to receive the glory.

First Peter 4:11 states, "If any man speak, let him speak as the oracles of God . . . that God in all things may be glorified through Jesus Christ, to whom be praise and dominion for ever and ever. Amen." Notice that it does not say "speak the oracles of God." Preachers are not just to speak to people the words of God; they are to speak *as* the utterances of God. When a preacher preaches "as the oracles of God," the dynamic of the "manifold grace of God" mentioned in the previous verse enables the preaching through the power of the Spirit so that the audience senses that it is hearing from God Himself. The preacher is lost in the One he represents. This is truly authoritative preaching that honors the Lord. The focus is on the message, not the messenger.

---

5. Frank E. Gaebelein, ed., *The Expositor's Bible Commentary*, vol. 2 (Grand Rapids: Zondervan Bible Publishers, 1978), 411.

6. Fritz Rienecker and Cleon L. Rogers, *A Linguistic Key to the Greek New Testament* (Grand Rapids: Zondervan Bible Publishers, 1980), 647.

7. Joseph Henry Thayer, *A Greek-English Lexicon of the New Testament* (Grand Rapids: Baker Book House, 1984), 346 [emphasis original].

Intended to Persuade through the Word

Secondly, biblical preaching is persuasive. This second component involving the substance of preaching is found in the series of imperatives "reprove, rebuke, exhort." These words reveal a persuasive nature to true preaching and imply the applicatory nature of true preaching. "Reprove" comes from the Greek verb *elencho*, meaning "to convict or convince someone of something."[8] The idea conveys "convincement." It is "to prove with demonstrative evidence."[9] "It is so to rebuke another with such effectual wielding of the victorious arms of the truth as to bring him, if not always to a confession, yet at least to a conviction of his sin."[10] Jesus Christ uses this verb of the Holy Spirit's work in John 16:8: "He will reprove the world of sin, and of righteousness, and of judgment." Ultimately, the Spirit of God, through the truth of God heralded by the man of God, convicts and convinces people. Is this not persuasive in nature?

The next imperative of persuasion is "rebuke." This is a synonym of "reprove." From the verb *epitimao*, "'rebuke' is a stronger word, 'chide, censure, blame'"; therefore, the preacher "must reprimand the sinner and not tone down his sin."[11] "The word implies a *sharp, severe* rebuke."[12] By itself the word *rebuke* may be ineffective "to bring the offender to own it; and in this possibility of 'rebuking' of sin, without 'convincing' of sin, lies the distinction between these two words."[13] However, notice the imperative to "rebuke" follows the imperative to "reprove," which emphasizes the convincing nuance. Once a hearer is convinced, then the

---

8. William F. Arndt and F. Wilber Gingrich, *A Greek-English Lexicon of the New Testament and Other Early Christian Literature*, 2nd ed. revised F. Wilber Gingrich and Fredrick W. Danker (Chicago: University of Chicago Press, 1979), 249.

9. Rienecker and Rogers, 647.

10. Richard C. Trench, *Synonyms of the New Testament* (Grand Rapids: Wm. B. Eerdmans Publishing Company, 1983), 13.

11. Hiebert, 105.

12. Marvin R. Vincent, *Word Studies in the Greek New Testament* (Grand Rapids: Wm. B. Eerdmans Publishing Company, 1980), 319 [emphasis original].

13. Trench, 13.

rebuke has fertile soil to take root. The biblical order of these terms emphasizes persuasion.

The third imperative provides a positive turn to the persuasive component of preaching. "Exhort" comes from the biblical word *parakaleo*, meaning "to urge, to encourage."[14] After one is convinced of his error and rebuked for his error, he must be encouraged out of his error. The combination of these three commands makes up the persuasive component of preaching. This persuasive component relies on reasoning from the Scriptures, not on a worldly basis of reasoning. Scriptural reasoning stands in opposition to worldly reasoning. Thus the apostle clarifies to the Corinthians in I Corinthians 2:1, "I . . . came not with excellency of speech or of wisdom, declaring unto you the testimony of God." Notice human reasoning is differentiated from "the testimony of God." Verses 4-5 continue, "And my speech and my preaching was not with enticing words of man's wisdom, but in demonstration of the Spirit and of power: That your faith should not stand in the wisdom of men, but in the power of God." This is truly persuasive preaching.

Filled with Instruction from the Word

Thirdly, biblical preaching is instructive. This third and final component involving the substance of preaching is found in the last word of 2 Timothy 4:2, *doctrine*. This word comes from *didache*, meaning "*teaching* as an activity, *instruction*."[15] The preacher is not just stating facts; he is to help his hearers learn. Preaching involves the activity of instructing. Thus, instruction is a part of the substance of preaching.

This didactic component implies that preachers must be learned in the Scriptures. Men of God should be men of depth. Both the gift of the evangelist and the gift of the pastor-teacher are "for the perfecting of the saints, for the work of the ministry."

---

14. Rienecker and Rogers, 648.
15. Arndt and Gingrich, 192 [emphasis original].

The leadership gifts must equip the saints to do the work of the ministry. In order to equip, one must be equipped. In order to train, one must be trained. This training may come through formal education or informal education. The bottom line is that the leadership gifts must be learned in the Scriptures in order to teach as they preach the Word of God. Second Timothy 4:3 says, "For the time will come when they will not endure sound doctrine." This implies that the "doctrine" to be preached in verse 2 is "sound doctrine." Accuracy and depth are implied. This must be true for all preaching, even the preaching of evangelists.

Speaking of the "elementary nature" of the third- or fourth-century work entitled "The Teaching of the Twelve Apostles" in *Ante-Nicene Fathers*, it is suggested in the "Introductory Notice" that the document may have been affected by the "incompetency" of a "local church as yet unvisited by learned teachers and evangelists."[16] This comment implies that the evangelists were learned and doctrinally correct. Interestingly, this depth confronts the shallowness of the caricature of modern evangelists.

John Wesley, an evangelist by gift, "wanted his men to be well read and careful preachers. He personally urged each minister to spend five hours out of every day in reading. He once said, 'Read, or get out of the ministry!'"[17] Preaching implies learning first so that one can teach the Word of God.

Three components of the substance of preaching are seen in 2 Timothy 4:2. Biblical preaching is authoritative, persuasive, and instructive.[18] All three components constitute preaching and must

---

16. Alexander Roberts and James Donaldson, eds., "Introductory Notice to the Teaching of the Twelve Apostles," *Ante-Nicene Fathers*, vol. 7 (reprint ed., Peabody, MA: Hendrickson Publishers, 2004), 371.

17. John H. Armstrong, *Five Great Evangelists* (Great Britain: Christian Focus Publications, 1997), 109.

18. Bryan Chapell, *Christ-centered Preaching* (Grand Rapids: Baker Books, 2000), 81. Chapell delineates "word presentation," "word exhortation," and "word explanation" regarding the same three components in 2 Timothy 4:2. Also, Bill Rice III uses the acrostic APT to specify the same three elements of preaching as "authority," "persuasion," and "teaching." He defines preaching as "speaking and teaching with the intent

be applied in order to have true biblical preaching. For example, teaching without persuasion is only teaching, not preaching. Persuasion without teaching is shallow. Some may be great teachers of the Word without really affecting people's lives because the persuasive component is lacking. Others may be great pulpit-pounders with dramatic style without really affecting people's lives because rebuke without teaching is mere dramatics. One component may characterize a particular preacher more than the others, but true preaching demands that all three be present.

Fearless Readiness

The second characteristic of biblical preaching is a fearless readiness. One of the imperatives of 2 Timothy 4:2 addresses the duty of preaching instead of the substance of preaching. The command is "be instant in season, out of season." The verb translated "be instant" means to "be ready" or "be on hand."[19] The concept conveys faithfulness "at one's task."[20] "In season, out of season" indicates at an opportune time or an inopportune time; that is, whether the occasion seems favorable or not.[21] Preachers must preach the Word when the hearers welcome the message as well as when they do not. Preachers must be faithful to the leading of the Spirit, not the likings of the audience.

For itinerant evangelists, this need for consistency increases because their audience constantly changes. Evangelists must remain steadfast in their message even though at times they will face those in their audience who do not want to hear it. The key is God's truth empowered by God's Spirit. The philosophy of catering to the market cannot be espoused by evangelists who must preach the Word "in season, out of season."

---

to persuade from a point of authority." Bill Rice III, *Preach the Word Newsletter*, vol. 4, no. 2 (1995): 3.

19. Arndt and Gingrich, 330.
20. Rienecker and Rogers, 647.
21. Hiebert, 105.

This need to be steadfast in the substance of preaching is balanced by the phrase "with all longsuffering," which means with "patient endurance."[22] Arrogantly "brow-beating" people reveals a flesh-filled preacher. Strong confrontational preaching enabled by the Spirit will still be accompanied by a patient endurance that waits for God to do in hearers' hearts what man cannot do. This aspect focuses on God to meet men's needs through the truth and therefore helps the preacher to be broken over men's needs and not arrogantly telling them what they need to hear. Brokenness produces the right spirit in the preacher.

Spirit Empowerment

The final characteristic of biblical preaching is Spirit-filled preaching. Three aspects in 2 Timothy 4:2 reveal this necessary element. First of all, the content of preaching is the Word, which clearly demands the life of the Spirit to be effective. Second Corinthians 3:5-6 states, "Not that we are sufficient of ourselves to think any thing as of ourselves; but our sufficiency is of God; Who also hath made us able ministers of the new testament; not of the letter, but of the spirit: for the letter killeth, but the spirit giveth life." The issue here is "the Spirit," not *spirit* as an attitude. Fleshly preachers can use the Word with a seemingly good attitude, but it does not give life to the Word. The issue is the Spirit giving life, or the letter will kill. Preaching the Word intensifies the need for Spirit-filled preaching; otherwise the preaching deadens without the Spirit giving it life. It is no wonder the Apostle Paul clarifies under inspiration to the church at Thessalonica in I Thessalonians 1:5: "For our gospel came not unto you in word only, but also in power, and in the Holy Ghost."

Secondly, the concept of "convincing," seen in the word *reprove*, reveals the need for the Spirit's work in preaching. As previously noted, the verb translated *reprove* [*elencho*] is used

---

22. Rienecker and Rogers, 648.

of the Spirit in John 16:8: "He will reprove the world of sin, and of righteousness, and of judgment." To be truly convincing in regard to biblical truth, which runs contrary to the grain of man's flesh, a preacher needs the convincing work of the Spirit. It is not enough to reason with men about the truth if God's Spirit is not making the truth convincing. The Spirit of God is the great Lawyer who convinces people of the truth. The noun of "reprove" is used in Hebrews 11:1 as the "evidence" or convincement needed to exercise faith.

Thirdly, the need to "exhort" the audience to victory over sin implies the aid of the Spirit in the exhorting. The word *exhort* translates from *parakaleo*, which is the verb form of the name *Paraclete* [*parakletos*], one of the titles for the Holy Spirit (John 14:16, 26; 15:26; 16:7). As the preacher exhorts in cooperation with the Exhorter, the hearers are filled with light and hope.

God is honored through Spirit-filled preaching. The Spirit's enabling grace for God-honoring preaching is referred to in I Peter 4:10-11: "As every man hath received the gift, even so minister the same one to another, as good stewards of the manifold grace of God. If any man speak, let him speak as the oracles of God . . . that God in all things may be glorified through Jesus Christ, to whom be praise and dominion for ever and ever. Amen." Spirit-filled preaching glorifies the Lord Jesus Christ.

The characteristics of all true biblical preaching, whether by evangelists or pastors, includes first a substantive content based on the authority of the Word, intended to persuade, and filled with instruction; second, a fearless readiness to preach regardless of how the ecclesiastical or worldly winds are blowing; and finally, a Spirit-empowerment that gives life to the truth preached. But what makes the preaching of the evangelist definitive?

The Distinctive Characteristics
of the Preaching of the Evangelist

In addition to the characteristics of all true biblical preaching, there are several characteristics that distinguish the preaching of the evangelist. These distinctive characteristics revolve around the relationship of the evangel to the three components of the substantive content.

Concerning Authority: The Evangel Demands a Focus

The *Logos* is the authority for all true biblical preaching. This involves the whole counsel of God. However, the God-given terminology of the *evangelist* implies a necessary focus on the *evangel*. Part 3 will present this focus in greater detail. In summary, the evangel, or the gospel, is the good news of the saving death of Christ to sinners, and the good news of the saving life of Christ to saints. Romans 5:10 emphasizes this glorious good news with the words "For if, when we were enemies, we were reconciled to God by the death of his Son; much more, being reconciled, we shall be saved by his life." That an enemy of a holy God could be reconciled by the saving death of Christ is truly good news. But that the reconciled ones "much more" then "shall be saved by his life" and thus experience the saving life of Christ is even, if it were possible, a greater good news.[23]

---

23. W. Ian Thomas, *The Indwelling Life of Christ* (Sisters, OR: Multnomah Publishers, Inc., 2006), 60. The British preacher Major W. Ian Thomas beautifully emphasizes this with the comment, "If your Christian experience is limited only to being reconciled to God by the death of Christ, yet you are not *being* saved by the present reality of His life, then you are obviously missing the 'much more' of your salvation. In fact, you are missing the whole purpose for which Christ died. You are cheating Him of that for which His blood was shed." This truth is an awakening concept to a defeated Christian. After emphasizing the necessity of faith to enjoy Christ's life, Thomas says, "This is the gospel, the whole of it. Anything less than this falls short of the gospel as revealed in the Word of God."

In preaching the gospel to sinners, sin and judgment must be addressed to reveal one's need so that Christ may be lifted up as the Savior and answer to that need. Similarly, in preaching the gospel to saints, the sins of the converted life must be exposed so that the provision of the blood of Christ to cleanse and the Spirit of Christ to enable may be lifted up as the divine answer to the need. This provides the platform to further expand on the Spirit-filled life, which is the essence of revival on the personal level. Also this demonstrates that the focus of the evangel still addresses many issues. Yet there is a focus on the good news of Jesus Christ to meet man's problem of sin and sinfulness in every way. The preaching of the evangelist focuses on the evangel within the biblical authority.

Concerning Persuasion: The Evangel Demands a Verdict

Since the goal of the evangel is that sinners actually receive the eternal life of Christ and that saints actually live in or become restored to the abundant life of Christ, then it follows that the component of persuasion is heightened for the evangelist in his preaching. The evangelist by nature of his message is preaching for a verdict. This is revival preaching. Although both the authority of the Word and instruction in the Word are necessary for the component of persuasion to be truly persuasive, God gives evangelists the burden of preaching for a verdict. This burden involves a heartbeat of seeing people saved *now* and seeing Christians revived *now*. Therefore, persuasion is of particular importance.

This persuasive emphasis in the preaching of the evangelist focuses on the imperatives "reprove" (convince), "rebuke" (censure), and "exhort" (encourage). This combination of words speaks of preaching that aims at the conscience. The conscience is a moral monitor within man that encourages him to shun what he believes is wrong and to do what he believes is right.

It condemns him for violating its urgings and commends him for obeying. The conscience is an exhorter, based on one's knowledge, and a judge passing sentence, based on one's choices in light of that knowledge. Therefore, when preaching seeks to convince (reprove), the basis of the conscience (knowledge) is what is to be affected. When preaching censures (rebuke), the judicial aspect of the conscience (a judge passing sentence) is what is to be affected. When preaching encourages one to obedience (exhort), the urging of the conscience (an exhorter) is what is to be affected. The goal of all this is to ultimately affect the will so that right choices are made.

The preaching of the evangelist, by nature heavy on persuasion, goes directly for the conscience. God wonderfully used the ministry of an evangelist by the name of Duncan Matheson in the awakening in Scotland from 1857 to 1859, which occurred when many English-speaking countries were touched by God. Matheson was influenced by his grand-uncle, George Cowie, a godly Dissenter in Scotland, who also was an evangelist by gift. "Cowie's views regarding true preaching, learned well by Duncan Matheson, were summed up in this counsel: 'Go direct to the conscience, and in every sermon take your hearers to the judgment-seat.'"[24] Preaching to the conscience for a verdict involves all three commands: "reprove, rebuke, exhort." The nature of each command seen in this light affects the preaching of the evangelist.

Specific Preaching

The nature of *reprove*, or convince, demands specificity. The goal of specific preaching aimed at the conscience is to move the will. The Spirit uses specific truth to convince and thus bring conviction. The believer is given a sword in the list of armor in Ephesians 6: "the sword of the Spirit, which is the word of God."

---

24. Armstrong, 206.

The word *sword* refers to a short sword, not a long sword.[25] This "dagger" is then explained as "the word of God." The term *word* is *rhema*, which refers to a specific part of the *logos*.[26] Therefore both *sword* and *word* emphasize specific truth. The sword is given to the believer, but it is called "the sword of the Spirit." Therefore, believers must wield the Sword in dependence on the Spirit to pierce with it. But it is specific truth that the Spirit uses to bring conviction, which is part of persuasion. This applies directly to the preaching of the evangelist because he has, by gift, a persuasive heartbeat.

Specific preaching aimed at the conscience must be clear in its articulation. A lady commented, "Is this the great Mr. Wesley?" after hearing a sermon entitled "The One Needful Thing." She continued, "Why the poorest person in the chapel might understand him!"[27] Many are the comments made to evangelists regarding the clarity of the truth presented. This is a God-given enablement for the execution of the gift.

As noted earlier, the pastor could be likened to a general practitioner in the medical realm. The general practitioner must know about many different matters, medically speaking. Occasionally, he will bring in a specialist to shed more light on a given case. The specialist does not work against the general practitioner, but with him. Likewise, the pastor must preach "the whole counsel," but at times, under God's leading, will bring in the evangelist to add more light on a focused issue. Every evangelist should be a specialist on the gospel, both to sinners and to saints. Every evangelist must focus on the sins of the day that are harming the health of the church and therefore hindering revival. As a specialist, the evangelist must know his subject matter well. Since he does not have three or more new sermons to prepare each week, he must put in the extra time that is necessary to be a

25. Rienecker and Rogers, 542.

26. Stewart Custer, *A Treasury of New Testament Synonyms* (Greenville, SC: Bob Jones University Press, 1975), 82.

27. Armstrong, 123.

"specialist" on his subject. This does not mean that a pastor does not have areas of expertise or that he does not preach on salvation and revival. However, an evangelist must be a specialist on gospel-related issues. This precision in presenting truth is incisive when enabled by the Spirit. Often the evangelist preaches what the pastor has already preached. Yet God uses the gift of the evangelist to bring the truth home to the hearers.

The clarity of specific preaching involves not only the clear articulation of truth but also the clear application of truth. A pastor, noting the lasting nature of Asahel Nettleton's ministry in his church twenty-nine years earlier during the Second Great Awakening, questioned the congregation regarding Nettleton's preaching. He wrote, "I am told that his sermons were in a high degree practical. Doctrinal sermons were frequent, but these had a practical turn. They were eminently scriptural, and plain and made men feel that they were the men addressed, and not their neighbors."[28] Notice the doctrinal content along with the last statement dealing with specific application of truth to the hearers—*and made men feel that they were the men addressed, and not their neighbors.*

The specific application of truth to the hearers is vital to arousing the conscience. Evangelist Sam Jones, mightily used of God in the late 1800s, said:

> There is a difference between preaching the truth and applying it to the hearers . . . Abstract truth has influenced the mind to some extent, but it's the consecrated truth vigorously applied to the conscience that arouses the mind and produces the conviction which brings results . . . The more conscience that I awake, the more people will be converted; as you know, it is the shoemaker who gives the best fit that has the most customers.[29]

---

28. Ibid., 177.
29. Laura Jones, *The Life and Sayings of Sam P. Jones* (Atlanta: Franklin-Turner Company, 1907), 72.

What does "the shoemaker who gives the best fit" refer to? It refers to specific preaching that is fearless in its application. This is the reason that many describe the preaching of the evangelist as preaching that "goes for the jugular."

Some call into question this aspect of application being preached with conviction, thinking one can preach only principle with conviction. However, biblical example reveals that application of principle should also be preached with conviction. In Luke 11:43 Jesus decries, "Woe unto you, Pharisees! for ye love the uppermost seats in the synagogues, and greetings in the markets." Is this not specific application to the principle of the sin of pride? Also, Jesus named the very people He was targeting. Galatians 5:19-22 lists the "works of the flesh." At the end of the list of sins, verse 21 says "and such like." If application is not valid, this phrase would be out of order. Clearly God means for truth to be applied. While distinguishing between the explicit statements of the text and valid applications of the explicit statements, it is nonetheless needful to apply the truth to the hearers.

The preaching of the evangelist is specific preaching—preaching aimed at the conscience through clear articulation of truth as well as clear application of truth. The persuasive emphasis of this kind of preaching demands intensity. Intense preaching is not necessarily a particular style, although it may lend itself to certain styles of preaching. The issue, however, is not stylistic. The uneducated D. L. Moody's style differed greatly from the educated, dignified style of R. A. Torrey. However, both were evangelists who employed specific preaching effectively.

Confrontational Preaching

Not only is preaching for a verdict demonstrated through specific preaching, it is also manifested through confrontational preaching. The nature of "rebuke" especially demands confrontation. The evangelist is to be a voice that confronts. Confrontational preaching confronts worldliness; it confronts moral laxity that pollutes clean channels; it confronts compromise regarding media, modesty, music, and so forth; it confronts the attitude sins; and it confronts unbelief and ineffectiveness in reaching people for Christ.

Christ equips the church with gifted men to fight especially the battles in which the church's effectiveness is at stake. Evangelists must squarely face the issues. Evangelists must address even controversial issues that hinder the usefulness of God's people. A pastor once mentioned that an evangelist had stated, "I'm not here to stir up trouble or be controversial; I'm here to be an encouragement." The pastor continued by stating his disappointment because he needed the evangelist's support regarding certain controversial issues. Recognizably, an evangelist operating in the flesh can be obnoxious and unnecessarily stir up trouble. But for an evangelist to shy away from confronting needful issues is to abdicate his God-given responsibility. He must confront the issues, and he must be filled with the Spirit when he does. The hearers will then answer to God for their response.

Some believe that if an evangelist knows that his audience believes something different than he believes, then he should not preach on that subject. However, that may be the very reason that God brought the evangelist to that congregation. If an evangelist does not preach his convictions when God leads him to do so, he is selling his soul and becomes ineffective. The key is preaching God's message under the leading of the Spirit. The Spirit will give a freeness to say what needs to be said with a prudence that will help and not hinder. It will be "speech . . . with grace, seasoned with salt" (Col. 4:6). This is much different than fleshly boldness that could easily harm and not help. The dangers of flesh-dependent ministry will be addressed in the next chapter.

Justin Martyr, an evangelist as noted earlier, was one of the great Christian philosophers of the second century. He was an apologist, which means "a person who writes or speaks in defense or justification of a doctrine, faith, action, etc."[30] Note the following excerpt from the "Introductory Note to the First Apology of Justin Martyr":

> The writings of Justin Martyr are among the most important that have come down to us from the second century. He was not the first that wrote an Apology in behalf of the Christians, but his Apologies are the earliest extant. They are characterized by intense Christian fervor, and they give us an insight into the relations existing between heathens and Christians in those days. His other principal writing, the "Dialogue with Trypho," is the first elaborate exposition of the reasons for regarding Christ as the Messiah of the Old Testament, and the first systematic attempt to exhibit the false position of the Jews in regard to Christianity.[31]

Although apologetics is not the exclusive domain of evangelists, the nature of their responsibility clearly involves Christian apologetics. However, the defense is still declarative in nature. Also, the declaration must be made in dependence on the Spirit, not the apologetics. Notice the phrase "intense Christian fervor" in regard to Justin Martyr's apologies. The work of the evangelist also shines through in his "First Apology." Justin Martyr addressed it to the emperor of the Roman Empire, humanly speaking the most powerful man living at that time. He respectfully and ably defended the Christians' cause and, in the midst of a period of persecution, bravely stated, "You can kill, but not hurt

---

30. *Webster's New World Dictionary*, 2nd college ed. (U.S.A.: William Collins and World Publishing Co., Inc., 1978), 64.

31. Alexander Roberts and James Donaldson, eds., "Introductory Note to the First Apology of Justin Martyr," *Ante-Nicene Fathers*, vol. 1 (reprint ed., Peabody, MA: Hendrickson Publishers, 2004), 160.

us."[32] Later in the apology he warns the emperor of the judgment of God.[33]

Years later in A.D. 165, Justin Martyr courageously stood for Christ through a final examination and ultimately was beheaded.[34] This is a classic example from church history of the voice of the evangelist. The nature of the evangelist's responsibility means running to—not from—the battle being fought in God's cause. Though every believer ought to be a soldier of Jesus Christ, as a leadership gift, the evangelist has an even greater responsibility in the matter of militancy.[35]

For example, after giving the benefit of the doubt to Billy Graham in the mid-1950s and even defending him, both Evangelist Bob Jones, Sr. and Evangelist John R. Rice openly denounced the compromise of Graham when his philosophy and practice were clear.[36] They were not eagerly waiting to stand against Graham, but when the truth was at stake and the issues had crystallized, both of these evangelists alerted Fundamentalism to the dangers of such compromise. Later, Jones and Rice fulfilled the "voice of declaration" regarding the compromise at Fuller Seminary.[37]

Declaring truth is the duty of the evangelist. Just as a pastor would be considered negligent if he did not oversee his flock by leading and feeding them, so an evangelist who shuns

---

32. Ibid., "The First Apology of Justin," 163.

33. Ibid., 186.

34. Ibid., "The Martyrdom of the Holy Martyrs," 305-6.

35. Ernest Pickering, *Biblical Separation: The Struggle for a Pure Church* (Schaumburg, IL: Regular Baptist Press, 1979), 149. Ernest Pickering, writing to expose the unscriptural fallacies of ecumenical evangelism, emphasizes the need for evangelists to be a voice that confronts: "The evangelist is to 'perfect the saints' (that is, build them up, make them strong in the faith, Eph. 4:12). He cannot do that if he is silent about the terrible apostasy and the deceitful ministries of the Devil's preachers. An evangelist is to warn his converts about the false 'winds of doctrine' (Eph. 4:14)."

36. George Marsden, *Reforming Fundamentalism* (Grand Rapid: William B. Eerdmans Publishing Company, 1987), 159-66. It is interesting to note that Marsden usually mentions Jones and Rice in a negative light. However, he is still documenting their separatist stand.

37. Ibid., 190-92.

needful declaration and, therefore, confrontation is being negligent in fulfilling his office. Declaring truth is the primary function of the office of the evangelist. For example, evangelists must preach in such a way that worldliness, materialism, and lukewarmness are not valid options for believers.

This type of ministry emphasizes the acute need for the leadership and enablement of the Holy Spirit, who is the one that convinces the hearers of the truth declared. The Holy Spirit will lead to the appropriate disposition for the confrontation at hand. At times this may be a prudent chiding. On occasion this may be a Spirit-filled confrontation much like Christ cleansing the temple. Some may question the intense disposition of such confrontation. However, Christ's disposition had to be sinless, even though it was undoubtedly intense. The key to correct disposition is to have a disposition energized by the Spirit appropriate to the truth being declared. Therefore, the disposition will not always be quiet, but it will always be right because it is controlled by the Spirit.

Since the gospel to the saints declares the good news of freedom from the power of sin, it is unconscionable for evangelists to be weak on moral issues of holiness. Tolerating worldliness keeps people enslaved to sin. But evangelists must have discernment to know what is truly important, what is truly needed at a particular time, and what is the appropriate disposition for the communication to be the most effective at that time. This discernment of "style of confrontation" is also exemplified by Paul in his letters to the church at Corinth. At times he was quite bold. At other times he made prudent appeals. The Holy Spirit will guide those who truly look to Him for discernment.

The nature of the evangelist's responsibility also encourages a deep level of learning in the Scriptures, whether through formal education or by some other means. Since the nature of his work is declarative and confrontational, he must know how to accurately wield the Sword with the power of the Spirit. Since he must face the issues squarely, he must know how to put biblical authority in the forefront so that his hearers are faced with truth and know that it is the truth they are facing.[38] Otherwise the audience is left with what appears to be a man's own opinions rather than the authoritative Word of God.

If biblical Fundamentalism weakens, it is the responsibility of evangelists to lead in confronting the need. Since evangelists have a wider sphere of ministry, they should be more aware of the need and have more opportunity to address the need. If weakening continues because evangelists fail to speak out, then they will answer to God for it in a greater way than anyone else in the body of Christ.

Urgent Preaching

Although the nature of "exhort" connotes much more than urgency, when seen in light of "reprove" and "rebuke" in 2 Timothy 4:2 and in the context of the preaching of the evangelist, there is an urgent aspect to the exhorting. In fact, as noted earlier, *parakaleo* means "to urge."[39] This is the positive urging of the hearers to respond to truth and benefit thereby. The preaching of the evangelist demands a verdict. Hearers must recognize that a choice will indeed be made and then must be encouraged to make the right choice. This element of persuasion is especially undergirded by the last component of preaching.

Before examining the last component, however, it must be remembered that specific, confrontational, and urgent preaching in the power of the Spirit comes from a compassionate heart truly desirous of the best for the hearers.

---

38. An ill-quipped evangelist often relies on the authority of his dogmatic style (which is no authority at all by itself) rather than the clear authority of the Scripture empowered by the Spirit.

39. Rienecker and Rogers, 648.

Concerning Instruction: The Evangel
Demands an Explanation

The focused biblical authority on the evangel and the height-ened obligation for a verdict demand thorough teaching. This is especially evident in the full concept of "exhort with . . . doctrine." Specific, confrontational, and urgent preaching is necessary to awaken need. But then there must be an emphasis on *how* the need can be met. Truly there is instruction when convincing of and confronting sin through the authority of God's Word. But when presenting the solution of Christ to the problem of sin, there is a special need to teach the glorious truths of Christ cru-cified and risen. The glorious details of the good news of freedom from both the penalty and the power of sin must be delineated, and the access by faith must be clearly taught. Spiritual truth de-mands spiritual instruction, looking to the Holy Spirit to enlighten the eyes of the understanding.

Conclusion

The truth is sometimes unpopular, but the evangelist must still declare it. Some confrontation is not welcomed. It is vital that evangelists function in accordance with the Word and the Spirit so that if various forms of persecution come, they do so because of faithfulness to God and not a lack of prudence by man. Yet if an evangelist declares all that God leads him to declare, there may be a price to pay. Meetings may be canceled. Other doors may be closed. This unpopularity is similar to that experienced by some of God's faithful Old Testament prophets. Although the prophets proclaimed new revelation, they did have a declarative ministry as evangelists do with the revealed Word of God.

Micaiah was unpopular in Ahab's reign for his truthful declaration. Second Chronicles 18 unfolds the story. When called upon by Ahab at the urging of King Jehoshaphat, who respected true prophets of Jehovah (18:6), Micaiah was pressured by the messenger to compromise his message. Second Chronicles 18:12 records, "And the messenger that went to call Micaiah spake to him, saying, Behold, the words of the prophets declare good to the king with one assent; let thy word therefore, I pray thee, be like one of theirs, and speak thou good." As a faithful voice for God, Micaiah declared: "As the LORD liveth, even what my God saith, that will I speak" (18:13). Micaiah did declare the truth and was physically smitten by a false prophet (18:23), and King Ahab commanded that he be put in prison to be fed "with bread of affliction and with water of affliction" (18:26).[40]

Pressure to compromise will always be felt as long as Satan is at work. Pressure to preach abstractly instead of specifically is an old tactic that the Devil has used effectively. Pressure not to offend anyone is a common wind of compromise. Pressure to not face people with decision is a subtle softening. Insecure evangelists will follow right along, but God-secure evangelists will "speak [God's] word faithfully" (Jeremiah 23:28). Man-fearing evangelists will bow to pleasing men, but God-fearing evangelists will kneel at the throne of pleasing God. Flesh-dependent evangelists will buy into the sales pitch of carnal marketing, but God-dependent evangelists will use the marketing strategy of Micaiah: "As the LORD liveth, even what my God saith, that will I speak" (2 Chronicles 18:13).

---

40. Interestingly, Micaiah initially used the sarcasm of "Go ye up, and prosper." This was what King Ahab wanted to hear. Apparently, Micaiah used this tactic to alert King Ahab to the fact that it is God's truth that really matters, not man's desires.

Chapter Four

A SUPERNATURAL GIFT

"Full of the Holy Ghost and wisdom . . . Philip . . . every-
where preaching the word . . . preached Christ . . . and the
people with one accord gave heed unto those things which
Philip spake . . . and there was great joy in that city . . . when
they believed Philip preaching the things concerning the king-
dom of God, and the name of Jesus Christ, they were bap-
tized both men and women . . . Philip the evangelist."
Acts 6:3, 5; 8:4, 5, 6, 8, 12; 21:8

From the late 1920s through the early 1940s, God greatly empowered the ministry of an evangelist by the name of John Sung.
This evangelist ministered in China and Southeast Asia. From the
years 1933 to 1936, God poured out His Spirit on the Chinese
church, and 100,000 lost souls were brought to Christ through
the ministry of John Sung.[1] Early in his ministry, before he ever saw
this outpouring of the Spirit, John Sung learned the importance
of the enabling of the evangelist. Regarding theological degrees,
Sung wrote,

---

1. Timothy Tow, *The Asian Awakening* (Singapore: Christian Life Publishers, 1988),
144.

The best is that no certificate be awarded merely on academic qualifications (if so, what difference is there from the secular?). Certificates and degrees should be given to those who qualify academically, who also have the abundant life of Jesus Christ. For the 'recession' in the Chinese Church today is due not to a lack of theological graduates, but rather to a lack of Spirit-filled men with the new life to do a holy work. . . . Since my preaching has now extended to all parts of China, I am more than ever convinced from more things I have seen that preaching does not depend on man-made scholarship, intellectualism, or talents, but rather on whether one has the new life or not. The results of a preacher with the new life and of one without it are like the "gold, silver, and precious stones" versus the "wood, hay, and stubble" mentioned by the Apostle Paul.[2]

Although John Sung saw the outpouring of the Spirit in revival during part of his ministry, when he speaks of the abundant life of Jesus Christ and connects it to gold, silver, and precious stones, he is speaking of the filling of the Spirit. This is the enabling of the evangelist. What a difference it makes when an evangelist is enabled by God to do what the flesh cannot do!

The third and final occurrence of *euangelistes* to be investigated is found in Acts 21:8, simply describing "Philip the evangelist." In the last two chapters, the didactic occurrences in Ephesians and 2 Timothy were investigated, revealing that the evangelist is both a leadership gift and a preaching gift. The leadership is primarily through the venue of preaching. Although the occurrence in the narrative of Acts 21 does not reveal much regarding the gift of the evangelist, the broader context of the book of Acts does. Acts describes the coming of the promised Spirit, His empowering work

---

2. Timothy Tow, *John Sung, My Teacher* (Singapore: Christian Life Publishers, 1985), 94.

among the saints, and His convicting work among the lost. Even the brief biographical sketch of Philip in Acts 6 and 8 demonstrates the supernatural dimension of a life that is "full of the Holy Ghost." As a result, the people of Samaria "gave heed unto those things which Philip spake" and were filled with "great joy." After they "believed . . . they were baptized," forming a core of believers. The operation of the gift of the evangelist in the life of Philip the evangelist reveals a supernatural enablement. This enabling is also seen in the lives of others connected to the verb *euange-lizo* throughout the narrative of Acts.[3] This insight of supernatural enablement as the power for the work of the evangelist demonstrated in Acts is further supported in Ephesians 4, where the gift of the evangelist is by "grace" (vv. 7, 11).

Since a grace gift demands supernatural enablement to operate correctly, the gift of the evangelist demands supernatural enablement to operate to the glory of God. Why is the supernatural emphasis so necessary? And how does the evangelist operate by grace? These questions may be answered by scripturally contrasting the flesh versus the Spirit in ministry.

Flesh-dependent, Flesh-filled Ministry

Since evangelists are given to equip the saints to do the work of the ministry so that the body of Christ is edified, why do some pastors say that they have to "clean up" after certain evangelists? Is this an overstatement by pastors, or has this been a reality at times? Is it possible that the ministry of an evangelist could literally be harmful?

---

3. Chapter 1 noted that Peter, John, Paul, Silas, Barnabas, others among the apostles, and others unnamed are all designated as evangelists through their direct connection to *euangelizo*. Their ministries in Acts all demonstrated a supernatural dimension.

The Scriptures warn against two major avenues of the flesh. One avenue is the works of the flesh. Galatians 5:19-21 delineates the manifestations of "the works of the flesh" as "adultery, fornication, uncleanness, lasciviousness," and so on. Other passages such as Ephesians 5:3-6 and Colossians 3:5-6 have similar emphases. Obviously, the hypocrisy of acting like a man of God but living in wickedness brings great shame and dishonor to the ministry. However, the other avenue of the flesh is not as obvious. It can be described as the strength of the flesh. This is the arm of the flesh of which Jeremiah 17:5 warns. The issue here is not deeds but rather dependence. It is possible to attempt to do the work of the ministry in dependence on the strength of the flesh, but there are dangers to this kind of ministry.

The Dangers of Flesh-dependent, Flesh-filled Ministry

Notice four reasons that ministry done through the arm of the flesh is harmful, especially for evangelists.

Unprofitable

John 6:63 teaches, "It is the Spirit that quickeneth; the flesh profiteth nothing." This is a sobering truth to consider. Even the work of the ministry done in fleshly dependence profits "nothing." The word *opheleo* means "help, aid, benefit, be of use (to)."[4] The emphasis with the negative conveys uselessness or that which is of no value. The work of God done through the power of man is unprofitable in God's record book. Though man may be impressed and the work appear magnificent, flesh-dependent ministry will go up in smoke as wood, hay, and stubble at the Judgment Seat of Christ (I Cor. 3:11-15). The word *opheleo* with the negative occurs in the Septuagint in Jeremiah 2:11-13: "But my

---

4. William F. Arndt and F. Wilbur Gingrich, *A Greek-English Lexicon of the New Testament and Other Early Christian Literature*, 2nd ed. revised F. Wilbur Gingrich and Fredrick W. Danker (Chicago: University of Chicago Press, 1979), 900.

people have changed their glory for that which doth not profit. Be astonished, O ye heavens, at this, and be horribly afraid, be ye very desolate, saith the Lord. For my people have committed two evils; they have forsaken me the fountain of living waters, and hewed them out cisterns, broken cisterns, that can hold no water." Choosing the broken cistern of fleshly dependence does "not profit" and is, therefore, unavailing. Even though one may desire to do the work of God, if an evangelist depends on the energy of the flesh, he is in reality unprofitable in God's cause. Is this not a real danger for a church's time, effort, and support?

Counterproductive

Second Corinthians 3:5-6 states, "Not that we are sufficient of ourselves to think anything as of ourselves; but our sufficiency is of God; who also hath made us able ministers of the new testament; not of the letter, but of the spirit: for the letter killeth, but the spirit giveth life." The context of verse 3 (which mentions the ministry of "the Spirit of the living God") all the way to verse 18 indicates that the "spirit" mentioned in verse 6 is the Holy Spirit. The emphasis is not spirit as an attitude but the Spirit, who gives life.

The passage emphasizes that in and of "ourselves," man, even saved man, is not sufficient—not even the Apostle Paul. However, "our sufficiency is of God." Through God there is the enablement to be "ministers of the new testament." But this ministry is "not of the letter, but of the spirit." Ministry enabled by the Holy Spirit gives life; otherwise, the letter kills.

Without the Spirit giving life, even ministering the "new testament" can be deadening. Is this not counterproductive? This truth may come to some as an alarming discovery. No wonder the Apostle Paul writes under inspiration in I Thessalonians 1:5, "For our gospel came not unto you in word only, but also in power, and in the Holy Ghost." Word only preaching is incomplete, but the Word made convincing by the Holy Spirit is the power of heaven.

Orthodoxy without the life of the Spirit is dead orthodoxy. The life of the Spirit without orthodoxy is not the life of the Holy Spirit, it is unorthodoxy. However, orthodoxy with the life of the Spirit is living orthodoxy. In other words, the Word without the Spirit is deadness, leading to no fire. The Spirit without the Word is deception, leading to strange fire. But the Word and the Spirit is dynamic, leading to true fire.

Some may object on the basis of Isaiah 55:10-11: "For as the rain cometh down, and the snow from heaven, and returneth not thither, but watereth the earth, and maketh it bring forth and bud, that it may give seed to the sower, and bread to the eater: So shall my word be that goeth forth out of my mouth: it shall not return unto me void, but it shall accomplish that which I please, and it shall prosper in the thing whereto I sent it." However, notice that the Word accomplishes that which God pleases, not what flesh-dependent man may desire.[5] To preach the Word without the life of the Spirit does not guarantee God's blessing. God may bless the Word for the sake of a seeking hearer, but there is no guarantee to a flesh-filled preacher that He will. The only way an evangelist can be assured of God's life manifested through the preached Word is to be filled with the Spirit.

Many parents scratch their heads and wonder, "Why did my children turn away from God? We were all in church every time the doors were open. We sent them to a Christian school. We had high standards and good rules. Why did they rebel against God?"

---

5. E. J. Young, *The Book of Isaiah*, vol. 3 (Grand Rapids: Wm. B. Eerdmans Publishing Company, 1972), 384. Young comments, "The word does not return to God in vain, but rather accomplishes what He has desired and succeeds in that for which He has sent it. What is stressed is the utter efficaciousness of God's Word to accomplish the purpose for which He has sent it forth." J. A. Alexander, *Isaiah* (Grand Rapids: Kregel Publication, 1992), 332. Also, J. A. Alexander says, "The general design of these two verses is to generate and foster confidence in what Jehovah has engaged to do."

It may be that the good positions were upheld largely through the strength of the flesh, and, therefore, were counterproductive. In the same way, when an evangelist functions in the energy of the flesh, though he may preach truth, without the Spirit's quickening, it is lifeless—it kills. For one who ministers from church to church, many could be adversely affected. Is this not a grave danger?

Sinful

Isaiah 64:6 declares "all our righteousnesses are as filthy rags." Man's righteousness, whether it is unsaved man's righteousness or saved man's righteousness, if it is man's righteousness, it is "as filthy rags" in God's sight. Flesh-dependent actions of obedience are merely ritualistic religious exercises. In fact, Romans 14:23 states, "Whatsoever is not of faith is sin." Faith, simply put, is dependence on God, based on His Word. The opposite of God-dependence is flesh-dependence. Therefore, the essence of flesh-dependence is unbelief. Though an evangelist who is attempting to minister in the power of man may impress man, God is not impressed. To God it is actually the sin of unbelief. Would it not be fair to say that what God considers sinful ministry is a danger to churches?

Displeasing

Finally, flesh-dependent ministry is displeasing to God. Hebrews 11:6 clearly states, "But without faith it is impossible to please him." God is displeased not only with the works of the flesh but also with the strength of the flesh. How much ministry produces the form of godliness but denies the power, or life, thereof and, as such, is not pleasing to God? It is possible for an evangelist who operates largely out of flesh-dependence to be in a position where his ministry is actually displeasing to God.

Since flesh-filled ministry endangers others, it is important to be aware of the marks of fleshly ministry.

The Marks of Flesh-dependent, Flesh-filled Ministry

A man's heart, which is deceitful, is truly known only by God. Also, one may slip in and out of flesh-dependence in the day-to-day work of the ministry. No one has the right, according to Matthew 7:1, to judge another man's heart. "Judge not, that ye be not judged." On the other hand, there is a responsibility to judge words. First Corinthians 10:15 declares, "Judge ye what I say." Also, there is a responsibility to judge actions. The scriptural mandate for church discipline indicates this. Without looking into a man's heart, what would be some legitimate marks of flesh-dependence? This discussion will be limited to that which relates directly to the work of an evangelist.

Manipulation

Manipulation can be a temptation in invitations. For example, some invitations are couched in such a way that nearly everyone in the audience feels pressure to "go forward" or face the possibility of looking bad in front of others. The problem is that the conviction of the Spirit is not necessary for this type of invitation. Many may go forward. People may talk about the unusual "visible results." But in God's record book, if it was merely a flesh-dependent maneuver, it profited nothing, was spiritually deadening, and actually sinful and displeasing to God.

On one occasion, a preacher said something to the effect of, "If you desire to come forward but find that you cannot get all the way to the front of the auditorium, just go as far down the aisle as you can and kneel. In fact, if you make your way toward the aisle but find it is so crowded that you cannot get there, just go as far down your row as you can and kneel." Now what does all this imply? It suggests that everyone is going to come forward. Not surprisingly, a huge crowd came forward.[6] Is this depending on the flesh to manipulate a big invitation?

---

6. This account is from personal observation as a young preacher.

Evangelists must not bow to such tactics even though their ministry may look comparatively less effective. God's records, not man's, are the ones which count. It is a real matter of faith.

Arrogance

A second mark of flesh-dependence is arrogance. Cockiness is not Spirit-led. Egotism and self-glorification are not of God. Pride is of the flesh. Self-righteousness and condescension are the antithesis of humility that depends on the Lord. Even an infatuation with being the "farthest to the right" is also suspect. Obviously, all preachers ought to be for standing right—right on the Word of God. But some are not looking for the authority of the Word; they want only to be perceived as the furthest to the right, whether there is a scriptural basis or not. This is pride.

Intimidation

A third example is reliance on intimidation to "move" a crowd. Some exhibit a macho image—pounding the pulpit and yelling—in order to pressure an audience. Obviously pulpit-hitting and loudness are not intrinsically evil and, at times, are quite appropriate, but to depend on them to intimidate is to depend on the flesh.

Sometimes, rudeness goes along with intimidation. Though people may take offense at Spirit-filled preaching, the offense ought never to be the arrogance or rudeness of a flesh-filled evangelist.

Focus on Finances

A fourth mark of flesh-dependence is making an issue of money. This indicates a lack of dependence on God to meet one's financial needs. Many are the stories on this point.

Charlatans bring shame to the cause of Christ. Unfortunately, this is an age-old mark of flesh-dependence. "Misusing the gospel for financial gain is by no means the invention of twentieth-century religious hucksters. One of the earliest Christian documents after the New Testament, 'The Didache,' a kind of manual on church practice, warns about traveling preachers who come and ask for money."[7]

Interestingly, in the same passage which teaches churches to provide materially for those who minister spiritually, Paul, under inspiration, also speaks of his making the gospel "without charge" (I Cor. 9:18). Although those who "preach the gospel should live of the gospel" (I Cor. 9:14), Paul's example shows that he did not demand a "charge" for his ministry.

Evangelist Sam Jones, who ministered in many city-wide crusades, did not demand an amount for remuneration. He trusted God. Evangelist John R. Rice "made a solemn covenant with God that if He would look after his business, he would look after His . . . from that day on he never made any requirement . . . as to what remuneration he should receive. Almost fifty-five years of personal experience abundantly proved God's gracious faithfulness in fulfilling His part of the agreement."[8]

Insecurity

A fifth mark of flesh-dependence is insecurity. A defensive spirit when criticized by a well-meaning pastor or even a church member reveals insecurity. A God-secure evangelist recognizes that God may be teaching him through criticism. "Overconcern" as to whether or not man is pleased also exposes a "man-security." God-secure evangelists are primarily concerned that God be pleased. Jealousy over blessing on another evangelist's ministry again shows insecurity. Insecurity reveals flesh-dependence. God-security reveals God-dependence, which rejoices over any blessing in God's cause.

---

7. Ken Curtis, et al. eds., "Foundations of Our Faith: A Look at the Early Church," *Glimpses*, no. 7 (1990): 2.

8. Robert L. Sumner, *Man Sent from God: A Biography of John R. Rice* (Murfreesboro, TN: Sword of the Lord Publishers, 1959), 69-70.

Compromise

A sixth mark of flesh-dependence is compromise. Without God's power, the demands of the Christian life are frustrating. Sadly, many simply lower the high road of the Christian life down to a level attainable in the flesh. This may ease their conscience and bring a type of relief, but it is not the right relief. The real answer is to access God's enablement to live as God says to live. When an evangelist compromises in order to get or keep a crowd, the glory of God has departed.

Impulsiveness

A seventh mark of the flesh is impulsiveness. The Spirit works through the faculties of man, including his mind. Impulsiveness acts without weighing a matter as to whether or not God is in it. First John 4:1 admonishes "try the spirits whether they are of God."

Fear of Man

Finally, when an evangelist changes the message God led him to preach for fear of who is in the audience, is he depending on God? If God led him to preach a certain message, then if he will depend on God, blessing can come from it. However, if in an attempt to avoid man's reaction, he changes the message in the name of not being offensive, then he is not depending on God. Yet, as noted earlier, this flesh-dependence is actually what is harmful. Certainly an evangelist must be prudent to do only what the Holy Spirit leads. On the other hand, when God does lead, the message cannot be changed for fear of offending someone because Proverbs 29:25 states, "The fear of man bringeth a snare." Therefore, evangelists must walk with God. If an evangelist is deceived by Satan's counterfeits, the results may be harmful to many.

God-called evangelists must beware of the danger of functioning after the flesh, which is unprofitable, counterproductive, sinful, and displeasing to God. Their enablement must come from God for genuine usefulness in God's cause. When God enables the work of the evangelist, He is pleased with the work of the evangelist. But how does an evangelist know he is operating in the Spirit and not in the flesh?

God-dependent, Spirit-filled Ministry

The danger for the evangelist arises when he functions after the flesh. By contrast, when the evangelist ministers after the Spirit, God receives glory. Since natural ability without the Holy Spirit is spiritually negative, how does one receive supernatural ability? Ephesians reveals two watershed truths that teach that God-dependence accesses Spirit-enablement.

The Ability Is Grace

The first watershed truth is that the ability is grace. Ephesians 4:7, in the context of admonishing believers to "walk worthy" of their calling, focuses on "grace" as the key to fulfilling this instruction. This provides the context of the gift of the evangelist in Ephesians 4:11. Ephesians 3 precedes this by providing the foundation for understanding grace. What is grace?

Referring to the ministry of the "gospel," the Apostle Paul writes under divine inspiration in Ephesians 3:7-8: "Whereof I was made a minister, according to the gift of the grace of God given unto me by the effectual working of his power. Unto me, who am less than the least of all saints, is this grace given, that I should preach among the Gentiles the unsearchable riches of Christ." Five discernible aspects provide the foundation to define *grace*.

The Nature of Grace Is a Gift

First, the phrase "the gift of the grace of God" reveals that grace is clearly a gift. Therefore, grace is unmerited, undeserved, and truly free to the recipient. It is a true gift.

The Giver of Grace Is God

Second, the phrase "the gift of the grace of God" also indicates that God is the giver of true grace. Therefore, grace cannot be produced or manipulated by man. Rather, the giver of grace is God Himself. Grace is not something man does, it is something God gives and man receives.

The Essence of Grace Is Supernatural Enablement

Often grace is defined as "unmerited favor." Truly it is unmerited. Also, the fact that God gives that which is undeserved is also genuine *favor*. But what is the favor? Is there a more specific understanding of grace? Usage of words determines their definition. Therefore, noting how the Spirit of God uses the word *grace* helps one to fine-tune his understanding of grace. Ephesians 3:7 provides an enlightening phrase: "the grace of God given unto me by the effectual working of his power." The phrase "effectual working" comes from the Greek word *energeia*. Transliterations do not always mean what they sound like, but the basic meaning of *energeia* is "energy."[9] The word *power* comes from *dunamis*, which emphasizes strength in the sense of ability.[10] So the text connects the *energy* to God's *ability*. The energy of God's ability is surely supernatural enablement. Grace is explained here as God supernaturally energizing Paul. This is a transforming concept of ministry.

Galatians 2:8-9 provides another example to investigate. In verse 8, Paul writes under inspiration, "For he that wrought

9. Stewart Custer, *A Treasury of New Testament Synonyms* (Greenville, SC: Bob Jones University Press, 1975), 33.

10. Ibid.

effectually in Peter to the apostleship of the circumcision, the same was mighty in me toward the Gentiles." The verb phrases "wrought effectually" and "was mighty" are both from the Greek word *energeo*, which is the verb form of the noun just noted in Ephesians. So Paul states that He who energized Peter to minister to the Jews also energized him to minister to the Gentiles. Verse 9 labels what this "energizing" was: "And when James, Cephas, and John, who seemed to be pillars, perceived the grace that was given unto me." Again the word *grace* describes God supernaturally enabling His servants to minister.

Of many other examples that could be studied, in I Corinthians 15:10, Paul clarifies, "But by the grace of God I am what I am: and his grace which was bestowed upon me was not in vain; but I labored more abundantly than they all: yet not I, but the grace of God which was with me." The word *labored* is parallel to "the grace of God which was with me." Again, grace is God's supernatural enablement for ministry. Understanding grace as "supernatural enablement" directly confronts the problem of serving God through the natural energy of the flesh.

The Agent of Grace Is the Holy Spirit

Fourth, the Holy Spirit is the Enabler of enabling grace. Paul's Epistles all begin essentially saying, "Grace be unto you, and peace, from God our Father, and from the Lord Jesus Christ" (Rom. 1:7; I Cor. 1:3; 2 Cor. 1:2; Gal. 1:3; Eph. 1:2; Phil. 1:2; Col. 1:2; I Thess. 1:1; 2 Thess. 1:2; I Tim. 1:2; 2 Tim. 1:2; Titus 1:4; Philem. 3). Why is the Holy Spirit not mentioned? Perhaps it is because the Holy Spirit is the divine agent of grace. The Spirit is the person of the Godhead who enables or graces believers. He is the Spirit of Christ who lives in the believer to enable the believer. As I Corinthians 15:10 states, "I labored ... yet not I, but the grace of God which was with me," so Galatians 2:20 parallels, "I live; yet not I, but Christ liveth in me." This is the reality of the Spirit-filled life—the Spirit of Christ living through one's spirit, soul, and body. The enablement is not just a power; it is the Person of power. It is not just an influence; it is the Person of influence. The enablement is the Spirit of the glorified Christ living His divine life through the believer and, more specifically, the evangelist. Although other contexts apply this enablement to different aspects of the Christian life, such as holy living, the three examples cited in the previous point (Eph. 3:7-8; I Cor. 15:10; Gal. 2:8-9) apply specifically to enablement in the ministry of the gospel.

The Purpose of Grace Is to Do God's Will

Finally, grace is given for one to do God's will. Ephesians 3:8 explains, "Unto me . . . is this grace given, that I should preach among the Gentiles the unsearchable riches of Christ." In other words, grace was given so that Paul could do God's will. The passages noted in Galatians and I Corinthians specify the same truth.

By combining the five aspects of grace just noted, a scriptural definition of grace can be formulated. Grace is the God-given gift of the supernatural enablement through the Holy Spirit to do God's will. In short, grace is Spirit-enablement.

Grace for salvation includes the undeserved favor of the Spirit's convincing work in order to point one to faith in Christ, and then the Spirit's regenerating work (and so forth) when one has believed in Christ as Savior. Grace for the Christian life also involves the Spirit's convincing work in order to point Christians to choices of faith, and then the Spirit's energizing work providing the power to obey when one walks by faith. "For it is God which worketh in you both to will and to do of his good pleasure" (Phil. 2:13). Faith is not a work; therefore, although the Spirit enables man to make right choices and then to follow through on those choices, faith has nothing to do with human merit. Grace for justification is "positional enablement," and grace for sanctification is "practical enablement."

Grace, then, in the life of the believer is clearly another way of stating the Spirit-filled life. Grace, or the Spirit-filled life, is the Spirit filling one with the life of Christ. Interestingly, it is Ephesians that commands "be filled with the Spirit" (5:18). Much more could be investigated on the fullness of Christ through the Spirit. However, to apply this definition of grace to the enabling of the evangelist is simply that *the ability is grace.*

How, then, do evangelists become recipients of this divine enablement? The second watershed truth teaches that the enabling of the evangelist comes through faith in Christ.

The Access Is Faith

After explaining the empowering nature of grace in Ephesians 3:7-8, the passage continues to relate the Apostle Paul's burden for the Ephesians to also know this divine enablement. The phrase used to describe this in Ephesians 3:16 is "to be strengthened with might by his Spirit in the inner man." This is, in essence, the definition of grace. The next verse describes how to receive this power by saying, "That Christ may dwell in your hearts by faith." The access to Spirit-enablement is "by faith." Faith is not a work, but it accesses the Worker. The culmination of the chapter resounds with the doxology of verses 20-21. Ephesians 3:20 truly pictures grace with the praise "Now unto him that is able to do exceeding abundantly above all that we ask or think, according to the power that worketh in us." When this grace abounds, God is glorified because the work accomplished through the instruments of men could never have been done by the strength of the flesh. And so verse 21 proclaims, "Unto him be glory in the church by Jesus Christ throughout all ages, world without end. Amen."

The access to the ability of grace is through faith in the power of the resurrected Savior. Romans 5:2 emphasizes this truth by declaring, "By whom [Christ] also we have access by faith into this grace wherein we stand, and rejoice in hope of the glory of God." Faith accesses grace.

Since the access to grace is faith, what is faith? If faith is conceptually misunderstood, is it even possible to live by faith? Although much could be covered, it is important to note two key concepts regarding faith.

The Nature of Faith

Hebrews 11:1 states, "Now faith is the substance of things hoped for, the evidence of things not seen." The topic is found in the word *faith*, which means "trust."[11] The key idea is dependence. The discussion of the topic then involves the next two phrases. These two phrases describe biblical faith and, in that sense, aid in defining faith, though they themselves do not define faith. First, in the phrase "the substance of things hoped for," the word *substance* means "realization, reality."[12] The verb is a present, passive participle indicating linear action. Therefore, the first phrase simply means "the reality of things being hoped for."

The second phrase is "the evidence of things not seen." The word *evidence* means "proof, proving"[13] and is used only twice in the New Testament. The other occurrence is translated "reproof" in 2 Timothy 3:16, the great verse on inspiration. The connection between "evidence" and "reproof" may, at first, seem remote. However, the verb form used in the New Testament illuminates the meaning. For instance, as noted earlier in John 16:8, Christ says of the Holy Spirit, "He will reprove the world of sin, and of righteousness, and of judgment." The verb translated *reprove* means "convict or convince someone of something."[14] The noun idea, therefore, would be a conviction or "convincement." A conviction is a strong belief because of being convinced of something. It is

---

11. Arndt and Gingrich, 662.
12. Ibid., 847.
13. Ibid., 249.
14. Ibid.

proven. Thus, there is a clear link to the definition of the noun form *proof*. Simply put, "evidence" is the state of being convinced by the Holy Spirit.

But what is the convincement about? The last half of the phrase says "of things not seen," which again involves a present, passive participle. The next point will address what the *things* are.

Summarizing these thoughts provides part of a scriptural definition of faith. Faith is depending on the reality of things being hoped for, being convinced of those unseen things. Faith is God-dependence based on Spirit-convincement of unseen realities. Understanding the nature of faith, how can one be so convinced as to depend on the reality of the unseen?

The Basis of Faith

The basis of faith is stated succinctly in Romans 10:17: "So then faith cometh by hearing, and hearing by the word of God." The basis of faith is "the word of God." The New Testament uses two words referring to the Word of God. The word *logos* often refers to the entire revealed Word of God. This is not the word in Romans 10:17. Rather, the word *rhema* is used, which refers to a specific word, statement, or part of the *logos*.[15] The usage of *rhema* indicates that the foundation for faith is not general; rather, the basis is specific. Adding this to the nature of faith, faith is depending on the reality of things being hoped for, being convinced of those unseen things, based on specific truth. Faith is God-dependence based on Spirit-convincement of the reality of God's words. Therefore, faith is the simple choice to depend on the reality of the words of God. In short, faith is God-dependence. Since Jesus Christ is the living Word, as John 1 explains, then depending on the Word of God is depending on Christ.

For example, in Jeremiah 23:29 God thunders out, "Is not my word like as a fire? saith the Lord; and like a hammer that breaketh

---

15. Custer, 82.

the rock in pieces?" When is this the case, since the letter kills without the life of the Spirit? The answer is in the previous verse. Jeremiah 23:28 says in contrast to the flesh-dependent prophet telling his own dreams, "He that hath my word, let him speak my word faithfully." When an evangelist declares God's Word, under the leading of the Holy Spirit, depending on God to empower it, he is fulfilling the condition, "let him speak my word faithfully." Then the promise (*rhema*) of verse 29 can be expected, and God's Word will be "as a fire" and "like a hammer."

The enabling of the evangelist comes through faith in Christ. The ability is grace, and the access is faith. Every evangelist must apply God-dependence for Spirit-enablement to fulfill his calling to the glory of God. Evangelist James Stewart of Scotland states correctly that "true evangelism is the work of a man in cooperation with the Holy Spirit for the salvation of the lost. . . . Was there ever a day when we had so much evangelistic equipment and so little of the demonstration of the power of the Spirit?"[16] The way one can become a recipient of the enabling grace of God is to cast his dependence on the Lord Jesus Christ. Then the Spirit of Christ enables with divine life. The result is Spirit-empowered preaching. How many times are evangelists content with false fire manufactured by the flesh? How needful is the fire of God set ablaze by faith in the One whose eyes are as a flame of fire!

Conclusion

In writing of the preaching of George Whitefield, John Wesley, and Howell Harris (evangelists who were all used of God in the First Great Awakening, which affected the British world of that time), a biographer of Harris noted that all these men had

---

16. James A. Stewart, *Evangelism Without Apology* (Grand Rapids: Kregel Publication, 1960), 73-75.

variations, but "each felt deeply the absolute priority and unique authority of preaching in the power of the Holy Spirit."[17] These men understood the necessity of the supernatural dimension.

Another example of the enabling of the evangelist comes from the life of Duncan Matheson. God wonderfully used this Scottish evangelist during the mid-1800s. After being born again and ending a major struggle over trusting Christ alone and not himself for salvation, Matheson entered a new struggle. In his own words he describes this battle: "Gradually my joy began to abate. I had been soaring on the eagle wings of praise, but now my song failed. At any rate, I thought, I am free of sin; but, alas, I soon discovered that in my flesh dwelleth no good thing. I could see two distinct principles at work in me—the flesh and the Spirit."[18]

This struggle continued intensely for two years. "When the dawn broke again, he was never to be the same. His soul had learned the comforts of grace and his understanding of the fight of faith was profound."[19] Understanding "legalism" for what it really is (flesh-dependence) and "liberty" for what it truly is (the liberty to do right by the power of the Spirit), John Macpherson, a contemporary and biographer of Matheson writes of this time in Duncan Matheson's life:

> These two years were spent on the hardest bench in Christ's school. That lowly seat of spiritual discipline has been occupied in turns by the most distinguished servants of God. During the years preceding his conversion, he had been taught the mad and desperate opposition of the natural man to the grace of God. Now he learned how the flesh lusts against the Spirit; how legalism counterworks grace in the believer's heart; how

17. John H. Armstrong, *Five Great Evangelists* (Great Britain: Christian Focus Publications, 1997), 141-42.

18. Ibid., 216.

19. Ibid., 217.

it fetters liberty, mars the joy, hinders the progress, dis-figures the character, and lessens or even destroys the usefulness of the Christian.[20]

When Duncan Matheson learned to depend on God for di-vine enabling, God began to open doors of usefulness for his life. For the next twenty years of his life, he served as an evangelist with the obvious blessing of God, and God used this evangelist, as well, in the awakening in Scotland during the 1850s.

The gift of the evangelist demands supernatural enablement to operate to the glory of God. God-dependence accesses Spirit-en-ablement. The result is supernatural so that God receives the glory.

20. Ibid.

Part Three

FOCUS ON THE EVANGEL

Chapter Five

THE GOSPEL TO SINNERS

*"I declare unto you the gospel . . . For I delivered unto you
first of all that which I also received, how that Christ died
for our sins according to the Scriptures; And that he was
buried, and that he rose again the third day according
to the Scriptures: And that he was seen . . .
and so ye believed."*
I Corinthians 15:1, 3-5, 11

George Whitefield wrote in a letter: "O that I could do more
for Him! O that I was a flame of pure and holy fire, and had a thousand lives to spend in my dear Redeemer's service . . . the sight
of so many perishing souls affects me much, and makes me long
to go if possible from pole to pole to proclaim redeeming love."[1]
What is this message of *redeeming love?*

The Apostle Paul, under inspiration, wrote "I declare unto
you the gospel." Although there are many passages that articulate the gospel message, I Corinthians 15:1 explicitly claims that it
is a declaration of *the gospel.* In fact, it is the gospel Paul had "received" (I Cor. 15:3). In Galatians 1:11–12 Paul explains, "But I certify
you, brethren, that the gospel which was preached of me is not

---

1. John H. Armstrong, *Five Great Evangelists* (Great Britain: Christian Focus Publications, 1997), 56.

after man. For I neither received it of man, neither was I taught it, but by the revelation of Jesus Christ." The noun translated "gospel" in both contexts is *euangelion,* which means "good news."[2] But what is this *good news?* What exactly is the gospel of Jesus Christ as it relates to the unregenerate? More specifically, what must one understand in order to be saved? Since "the natural man receiveth not the things of the Spirit of God: neither can he know them, because they are spiritually discerned," what must be communicated to "natural" men to bring them to salvation?[3]

The Lord Jesus Himself answers this question in John 16:8 by delineating that of which the Holy Spirit will convict unsaved men: "He will reprove the world of sin, and of righteousness, and of judgment." The Holy Spirit will reprove ("convict or convince")[4] the world (unregenerated people) of sin, righteousness, and judgment. Therefore, these three emphases form the outline of gospel declaration.[5]

Jesus promised in John 16:7, "I will send him [the Holy Spirit] unto you." But the next phrase then says, "And when he is come,

---

2. William F. Arndt and F. Wilbur Gingrich, *A Greek-English Lexicon of the New Testament and Other Early Christian Literature,* 2nd ed., revised F. Wilbur Gingrich and Fredrick W. Danker (Chicago: University of Chicago Press, 1979), 317.

3. Some argue that one must start with explaining and defending Creation. But since the "natural" man cannot discern spiritual truth, it is better to assume the reality of biblical Creation as Paul did in Acts 17:24: "God that made the world and all things therein, seeing that he is Lord of heaven and earth." Paul simply declared Creation (not defended it) and then confronted his audience with the folly of worshiping idols (Acts 17:25–29). Then he drove home their responsibility by saying "God . . . now commandeth all men everywhere to repent" (Acts 17:30), based on the resurrection of Christ (Acts 17:31). Paul used Creation as a steppingstone to confront the idolatry of his audience and point them to Christ. This is the correct use of Creation in declaring the gospel. For example, in some primitive settings missionaries have started with Creation to explain the origin of sin and then God's redemptive plan.

4. Arndt and Gingrich, 249.

5. The key is to declare these three truths. The order may vary. For example, in Acts 24:25 Paul "reasoned" with Felix "of righteousness, temperance [sin], and judgment to come."

he will reprove the world." Jesus did not say, "I will send the Spirit to the world, and He will convict the world." He said, "I will send him unto you. And . . . he will reprove the world." The Holy Spirit convicts the world of sin, righteousness, and judgment as believers declare these truths of the gospel.

Therefore, it should be no surprise to see the corresponding emphasis of the truths of *sin, righteousness*, and *judgment* in I Corinthians 15:3 as Paul declares the gospel: "Christ [righteousness], died [judgment] for our sins [sin]."

The gospel to sinners is that Jesus Christ saves from sin and hell everyone who believes in Him. Simply put, there are three truths one must understand and agree with, and then one decision that must be made in accordance with these three truths.[6]

The Problem of Sin

In the phrase "Christ died for our sins," it is "our sins" that articulates the first truth of man's problem of sin. Because of Adam's sin in the Garden of Eden, all who are of Adam's race are born sinners (Rom. 5:12). Being born in a sinful condition manifests itself through sins or sinful acts. The following four concepts reveal man's problem of sin.

Universality of Sin

Sin is a universal problem. Ecclesiastes 7:20 states, "For there is not a just man upon earth, that doeth good, and sinneth not." Regardless of country, culture, or ethnicity, humanity is born depraved. Nobody is perfect. No one is without sin. But what is sin?

---

6. Van Gelderen, John R., ed. *Netcasters Evangelism Training* (Germantown, WI: Revival Focus Press, 1995; revised ed. 2008). This chapter reflects the gospel presentation as taught in the *Netcasters Evangelism Training* course.

Definition of Sin

The Bible defines *sin* in 1 John 3:4 as "the transgression of the law." Sin transgresses or breaks God's law. It is lawlessness. It misses the mark of God's standards. First John 5:17 states that "all unrighteousness is sin." Sin misses or falls short of righteousness. Therefore, sin is simply breaking God's laws.

Examples of Sin

The Word of God is filled with many laws. There are commands of adherence and commands of abstinence. The Ten Commandments are unquestionably laws of God. For example, the first commandment boldly states, "Thou shalt have no other gods before me" (Ex. 20:3). Any objects of dependence other than God or any concept of God that is not true to that which God reveals about Himself violates this first commandment. The third commandment states, "Thou shalt not take the name of the Lord thy God in vain: for the Lord will not hold him guiltless that taketh his name in vain" (Ex. 20:7). To use God's name carelessly, flippantly, or as an expletive is included in taking God's name in vain.[7] The fifth commandment admonishes, "Honor thy father and thy mother" (Ex. 20:12). To honor means to respect and obey with the right heart attitude. Disrespect and disobedience violate this standard. The ninth commandment says, "Thou shalt not bear false witness" (Ex. 20:16). Therefore, dishonesty or lying breaks this commandment. Other commandments prohibit

---

7. R. Laird Harris, Gleason L. Archer, Jr., and Bruce K. Waltke, eds. *Theological Wordbook of the Old Testament*, vol. 2 (Chicago: Moody Press, 1980), 908. "The primary meaning . . . is 'emptiness, vanity.' The evidence points to the fact that taking the Lord's name (i.e., his reputation) 'in vain' will surely cover profanity, as that term is understood today, or swearing falsely in the Lord's name. But it will also include using the Lord's name lightly, unthinkingly, or by rote."

murder, adultery, theft, and covetousness. Just these few com-mandments reveal that every human being breaks God's laws.

It takes only one murder to be a murderer, one theft to be a thief, and one lie to be a liar. Therefore, it takes breaking only one of God's laws to be a lawbreaker. "For whosoever shall keep the whole law, and yet offend in one point, he is guilty of all" (James 2:10). Therefore, every human is a criminal in God's sight. God's law exposes man's sin. The law does not remove sin; it reveals sin. Yet some people still think that if their good deeds outweigh their bad deeds, they will make it to heaven.

Disqualification of Sin

Jesus said, "Be ye therefore perfect, even as your Father which is in heaven is perfect" (Matt. 5:48). Whether speaking of justification or sanctification, the standard is always God Himself. God's holiness demands perfection. Thus, "all have sinned, and come short of the glory of God" (Rom. 3:23).

If three people were lined up at the Grand Canyon to see who could jump across, undoubtedly one would jump farther than the others. But obviously all would fall short of making it across. By way of analogy, the other side of the Grand Canyon represents God's standard of absolute perfection. Some people may look better compared to others; but compared to God, all fall far short of His standard of perfection.

Galatians 3:10 further explains, "For as many as are of the works of the law are under the curse: for it is written, Cursed is every one that continueth not in all things which are written in the book of the law to do them." In order to achieve heaven on one's own merit, one would have to be perfect, but no one is without sin. Therefore, salvation is not by works. Romans 3:20 declares, "Therefore by the deeds of the law there shall no flesh be justified in his sight." Ephesians 2:8-9 explains, "For by grace are ye saved through faith; and that not of yourselves: it is the gift of God: Not of works, lest any man should boast." Titus 3:5 affirms "not by works of righteousness which we have done."

Therefore, all are condemned under sin. Whether it is the sins of unrighteousness or the sin of self-righteousness, all are disqualified. Since God's standard is absolute perfection and all have sinned, no one meets the standard for heaven on his own merit or ability. Sin clearly disqualifies people from heaven. This is man's problem of sin.

The Penalty of Sin

In the phrase "Christ died for our sins," the word *died* addresses the second truth, which is the issue of judgment. Christ died for the sins of mankind because there is a penalty for man's sin. The following four warnings of judgment explain the penalty of sin.

Justice of Judgment

Romans 6:23 states, "For the wages of sin is death; but the gift of God is eternal life." Just as one earns wages at a job and would consider it unjust not to receive his proper wages, everyone earns death as the just wages for his sin. Romans 5:12 explains that "by one man [Adam] sin entered into the world, and death by sin; and so death passed upon all men, for that all have sinned." Physical death, which is the separation of the soul from the body, is not the only consequence of sin; there is also an eternal death. Even people who go to heaven die physically. Therefore, "the wages of sin" must be referring to more than just physical death. In fact, in Romans 6:23 "death" is not just the opposite of life, but of "eternal life." This indicates that death in this verse is an eternal death. Revelation 20:14 explains that at the Great White Throne Judgment, death will be "cast into the lake of fire. This is the second death." Therefore, the ultimate wages of sin is the second death, which is separation from God forever in the lake of fire.

Description of Judgment

The Bible describes hell as a literal place of eternal torment. John the Baptist warned of "fire unquenchable" (Luke 3:17). Jesus warned of "everlasting fire" (Matt. 18:8). In fact, Jesus preached more about hell than He did about heaven because He came to save people from the judgment of hell. The terminology Christ used of "everlasting fire" indicates that hell is both forever, since "everlasting" is the same word used by Christ in John 3:16 speaking of "everlasting life," and a place of literal torment in actual "fire." Hell is a second death of everlasting punishment in an actual lake of fire.[8]

As unthinkable as it may seem, hell is real. Hell is eternal separation from God in eternal fire. The same Bible that teaches eternal life in Christ teaches eternal death in hell.

Necessity of Judgment

God's judgment may seem harsh to man's thinking. Yet the Bible affirms that God is just. Deuteronomy 32:4 declares, "A God of truth and without iniquity, just and right is he." If God overlooked man's sin and let him into heaven anyway, justice would be violated. In fact, if God did not judge sin, it would violate His holiness and justice. Genesis 18:25 says, "Shall not the Judge of all the earth do right?" Justice demands that sin be judged.

---

8. Technically, *hades* is a temporal place of punishment prior to the Great White Throne Judgment, and *gehenna* is the eternal place of punishment following the justice meted out at the Great White Throne Judgment. The King James Version uses *hell* to translate both words. For an excellent discussion of the Greek terms relating to hell, see *The Doctrine of Eternal Punishment* by Mark Minnick (Woodridge, IL: Preach the Word Ministries, Inc., 1996).

Recipients of Judgment

Revelation 21:8 specifies "and all liars, shall have their part in the lake which burneth with fire and brimstone: which is the second death." Everyone fits into the category of liars. Therefore, everyone deserves his "part in the lake which burneth with fire and brimstone."

The first two truths of sin and judgment are bad news. First, God's holiness demands perfection; yet man has the problem of sin. Second, God's justice demands judgment; therefore, man deserves the penalty of sin. This is truly bad news. However, before one can benefit from the good news, he must understand and agree with the bad news. He must personally own his sin and realize his deserved destiny in hell. Sin not only disqualifies people from heaven, but sin also deserves judgment in hell. These facts ought to concern any thinking person.

The Payment for Sin

In the phrase "Christ died for our sins," the person of *Christ* emphasizes the third truth that highlights God's provision for man's problem. Although man deserves the penalty of sin, there is a satisfactory payment for sin. The following four blessings reveal this amazing payment.

Meaning of the Gospel

Christ is the heart of the gospel. The *gospel* is God's good news to sinful mankind. After comprehending sin and judgment, one realizes that the good news of salvation in Jesus Christ is glorious news.[9]

---

9. Paul says in I Corinthians 15:1, "I declare unto you the gospel which I preached unto you." Paul certainly did not huckster or peddle the gospel. Rather, Paul declared

Motive of the Gospel

Although God is holy and cannot tolerate sin, and although He is just and must judge sin, "God is love" (I John 4:8). However, God cannot and will not violate His holiness and justice. Yet God in His love did something that satisfied His holiness and justice. Romans 5:8 declares, "But God commendeth his love toward us, in that, while we were yet sinners, Christ died for us." The little word *for* indicates that Christ became man's substitute. God proved His love by providing a just way of escape through the sacrifice of His own Son on man's behalf. John 3:16 beautifully articulates the demonstration of God's love for all mankind: "For God so loved the world, that he gave his only begotten Son, that whosoever believeth in him should not perish, but have everlasting life."

Maker of the Gospel

Matthew 1:23 explains, "Behold, a virgin shall be with child, and shall bring forth a son, and they shall call his name Emmanuel, which being interpreted is, God with us." Christ came into the world as a man through the miracle of the virgin conception because only man can represent man, but He came as God because only God could do what He came to do. Jesus Christ is the Son of God, and yet He is "God with us." He is God come in the flesh (John 1:1, 14). Jesus, God robed in human flesh, is the reason for the good news because He sacrificed Himself for sinful man.

Message of the Gospel

"The gospel" (I Cor. 15:1) is the truth that "Christ died for our sins according to the Scriptures: And that he was buried, and

---

the gospel. He preached the gospel. The nuance of *declare* and *preach* imply a confrontation with truth focusing ultimately on the good news of salvation in Christ. The popular word *share* seems to weaken the biblical statement.

that he rose again the third day according to the Scriptures: And that he was seen" (I Cor. 15:3–5). This simple declaration of the gospel delineates two simple parts that focus on the death and resurrection of Jesus Christ.[10]

Christ Died, Proven by the Fact that He Was Buried

What was accomplished through Christ's death for man's sin? First, Christ suffered the judgment man deserves to suffer. The sinless Son of God took man's sin upon Himself. Isaiah 53:6 plainly says, "And the Lord hath laid on him the iniquity of us all." First Peter 2:24 affirms, "Who his own self bare our sins in his own body on the tree." All the sins man ever committed or will commit were, in actual fact, placed on Christ at the cross. This is amazing love. As the Lamb of God, Jesus could take away the sins of the world (John 1:29). Hebrews 1:3 pronounces "when he had by himself purged our sins." Christ singlehandedly suffered the judgment man deserves.

Second, Christ's payment is in full. After bearing the sins of the world, before He voluntarily gave up His spirit, Christ proclaimed with a loud voice, "It is finished" (John 19:30). Truly Jesus paid it all. Since Christ paid man's sin debt in full, there is nothing left for man to pay. Jesus saves, and He does all the saving. The payment of every individual's sin—past, present, and future— was sufficiently paid. No one, after paying the final payment on a mortgage, would continue to send in payments. Likewise, since Jesus paid the full price of man's sin, there is simply nothing left for man to pay.

---

10. Charles C. Ryrie, *So Great Salvation* (Wheaton: Victor Books, 1989), 39. Ryrie expounds, "Paul gives us the precise definition of the Gospel we preach today in I Corinthians 15:3-8. The Gospel is the good news about the death and resurrection of Christ. He died, and He lives—this is the content of the Gospel . . . He died for our sins and was buried (the proof of His death); He rose and was seen by many witnesses, the majority of whom were still alive when Paul wrote I Corinthians (the proof of His resurrection)."

Third, Christ's righteousness can be credited to man's account. Second Corinthians 5:21 says, "For he [God the Father] hath made him [God the Son] to be sin for us, who knew no sin; that we might be made the righteousness of God in him." This inspired statement articulates an exchange. Man's sin was credited to Christ so that Christ's righteousness might be credited to man. This exchange is the glorious truth of justification. To be justified is to be declared righteous.

Suppose someone were in debt far beyond his ability to ever pay. But suppose a multibillionaire pays off that person's debt, and not only pays off his debt, but credits a billion dollars into his account. That would be a wonderful transaction. However, the spiritual truth represented in this analogy is far greater. Man has a debt beyond his ability to pay. Even if a person were to be perfect in the future, he has already sinned in the past. Therefore, no one is able to meet God's standard of perfection on his own. But Christ paid every man's sin debt in full. Yet He does not leave man with a zero balance, for God demands perfection. Therefore, Christ makes provision for His perfect righteousness to be credited to man's account. If this transaction were to be applied to a man, then not only would his sin debt be paid, but God's standard of righteousness would be met. Instead of seeing man with his sin, God would see man with the righteousness of His Son. Therefore, God could righteously accept him into heaven without violating His holiness and justice. This is truly a glorious salvation. It is truly *good news*.

But what validates this good news?

Christ Rose Again, Proven by the Fact that He Was Seen

Paul, under inspiration, specifies some of the eyewitnesses of the risen Christ: "Peter," "the twelve," "five hundred brethren," "James," "all of the apostles," and then Paul himself (1 Cor. 15:5–8). In fact, he specifically states that Christ "was seen of above five hundred brethren at once" (I Cor. 15:6). More than five hundred eyewitnesses at one time would be overwhelming evidence in a court of law. The Scripture speaks emphatically that Christ bodily rose from the dead. In fact, the biblical record asserts and history affirms that the disciples of Christ, who had fled in fear when Christ was arrested and had hidden in fear when Christ's body was in the tomb, publicly proclaimed that they had seen the risen Savior. Many of them were martyred for their unabashed proclamation of the crucified and risen Christ as the only Savior. These disciples would not have been so bold had they not truly seen a risen Savior.

Jesus Christ died for man's sins and rose again to validate the claim. When He arose, He conquered death. Since death is the wages for sin, He also conquered sin. And since the second death is the ultimate penalty for man's sin, He conquered hell. Christ conquered sin, death, and hell. This is comprehensive good news.

The provision of salvation is perfect. However, not everyone avails himself of this salvific provision. Man is responsible to properly respond to this message of good news. The three truths of the problem of sin, the penalty of sin, and the payment for sin demand a decision.

The Decision of Faith/Repentance

After Paul declared the gospel, he said, "so we preach, and so ye believed" (I Cor. 15:11). The word *believed* sums up the right response to the good news of Jesus Christ. However, sometimes confusion surrounds the meaning of *believe*. Four biblical truths clarify the picture.

Offer of the Decision of Faith/Repentance: Universal

Who can make this vital decision? Romans 10:13 says, "For whosoever shall call upon the name of the Lord shall be saved." The specification "whosoever" includes everyone. However, many people "pray" supposedly to a higher being. What does it mean to call on the name of the Lord?

Meaning of the Decision of Faith/Repentance: Transferring One's Dependence/Changing One's Mind

Romans 10:14 asks, "How then shall they call on him in whom they have not believed?" The real issue in calling on the name of the Lord is not the outward act of prayer but believing in the heart. In Greek, to *believe* [*pisteuo*] is the verb form of the noun *faith* [*pistis*]. But what does it mean to believe? In Mark 1:15, Jesus said, "Repent ye, and believe the gospel." What does it mean to repent and believe the gospel?

Scripture articulates two aspects to one decision. Faith and repentance are not two decisions. Rather, they are like two sides of the same coin. Man's responsibility is *the* decision of faith and repentance, or simply "faith/repentance."[11]

Faith

Believe means "believe (in), trust."[12] In regard to salvation, the biblical usage emphasizes believing "in" or "on" Jesus (John 3:15,

---

11. That the two words represent one basic decision is seen in the scriptural usage of only one word in a given scenario. For example, Jesus told Nicodemus simply to *believe* (John 3:16), and Paul told the Philippian jailor simply to *believe* (Acts 16:31). On the other hand, in Paul's sermon on Mars' Hill, he simply used the word *repent* (Acts 17:30). More will be discussed in this regard in Chapter 8:"The Foundational Issue of Faith/Repentance."

12. Arndt and Gingrich, 661.

16, 36; 6:47; Acts 10:43; 16:31; Rom. 4:5).[13] The issue is not merely believing *about* Jesus but believing *in* Him. To believe in is to depend on.

The confusion in regard to believing arises from the common usage of the word *believe*. Often the word is used in the sense of merely believing *about*, which is understanding and agreeing without depending. For example, Luke 4:41 states, "And devils also came out of many, crying out, and saying, Thou art Christ the Son of God." Even the demons have a level of understanding and agreement, but they are obviously not on their way to heaven. Similarly, some understand *about* Jesus and may even agree with what they understand, but they are not depending *on* Jesus as their Savior. This acknowledgment of Jesus without depending on Jesus is often described as "easy-believism."

Easy-believism, or an acknowledgement-only decision, falls short of true faith for salvation for it does not involve the entire soul of man. The soul, or self, consists of the mind, the affections, and the will. All three aspects must be involved to have true faith. Just as a triangle must have three sides to be a triangle, faith must involve the mind, the affections, and the will to be true faith.[14] To understand (mind) and agree (affections) is necessary to depend on (will), but understanding and agreeing alone acknowledges Jesus without actually depending on Him. This is believing *about* Jesus without believing *in* Him.

Diagram 5.1 pictures this "common faith."

---

13. In the examples cited, the Greek incorporates *en* (John 3:15), *eis* (John 3:16, 36; 6:47; Acts 10:43), and *epi* (Acts 16:31; Rom. 4:5).

14. Even in the physical realm, this is manifested. For example, one may understand that a given chair can hold his weight. He may even agree that the chair would hold his weight if he sat on it. But it is not until he depends on the chair by sitting on it that he moves beyond believing *about* the chair to believing *in* the chair.

Diagram 5.1. Common Faith

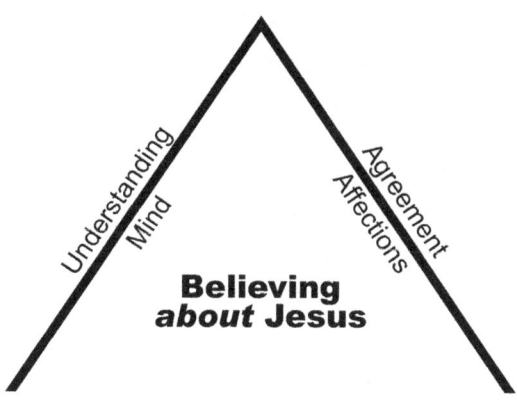

The clarification in regard to *believing* centers around the biblical emphasis of believing *in* Jesus (e.g., John 3:16). True faith for salvation moves beyond understanding the three truths (problem, penalty, payment) and agreeing with them to transferring one's dependence to Christ as one's Savior. Believing is taking one's confidence out of oneself and placing that confidence in Christ.

Diagram 5.2 pictures this "saving faith."

Diagram 5.2. Saving Faith

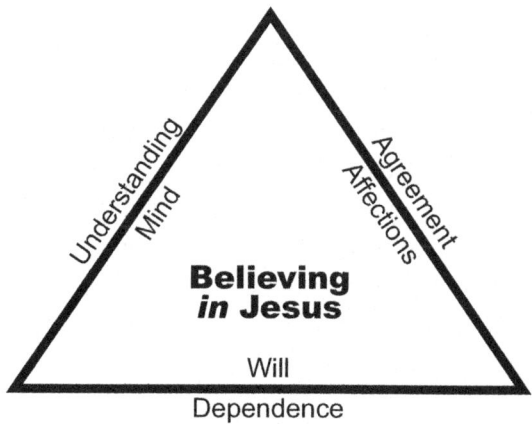

Dependence is the essence of faith. "To depend on" implies a transfer of trust. Therefore, it is impossible to have "always believed." Dependence presupposes understanding and agreement; however, it moves beyond the intellectual understanding and beyond the heart-felt agreement to the volitional transfer of dependence to Christ as one's Savior from sin and hell.

The story is told of a famous tightrope walker who had a tightrope stretched 1,100 feet across Niagara Falls. The tightrope was 160 feet above the raging waterfall. After he crossed, the crowd cheered wildly. He then approached the crowd with a wheelbarrow and asked, "How many of you *believe* that I could put a man in this wheelbarrow and take him across?" The crowd cheered, "I do! I do!" He pointed to a man cheering "I do!" and said, "You, sir, please get in." But the man bolted in the other direction.

What was wrong? That man believed that the tightrope walker could put a man—another man—in the wheelbarrow and take him across. But he was not willing to place his dependence totally on the tightrope walker to take him across. This dependence is the essence of believing. Salvation occurs when one places his dependence only on Jesus Christ to save him from sin and hell. As in the Grand Canyon illustration given earlier, Christ is the only way across the chasm between a sinful man and a holy God. Man must depend on Christ. This is believing *in* Jesus.

To believe in Jesus is to depend *only* on Jesus. A split trust reveals mistrust in Christ alone. Just as straddling one's weight on the halves of two adjacent chairs would reveal mistrust in either one of the chairs as an individual chair, so depending on Jesus plus something else reveals mistrust in Christ alone. Romans 3:28 says, "Therefore we conclude that a man is justified by faith without the deeds of the law." Faith in Jesus is "without the deeds of the law." Jesus saves, and He does all the saving. Therefore, He is the sole object of faith.

Repentance

Repent means "to change one's mind."[15] Simply put, to repent means to change one's thinking. Therefore, *repent* corresponds to *believe*, which means "to transfer one's dependence."

In believing, there must be understanding, agreement, and dependence. There is a similarity in repentance. To change one's thinking is not merely to understand in the mind or even agree in the heart, but to *change* one's thinking. In the definition "to change one's thinking," the word *thinking* corresponds to understanding (problem, penalty, payment), the word *one's* corresponds to agreement or the personalization of the facts understood, and the word *change* corresponds to dependence or the volitional transfer of trust. Therefore, *repent* corresponds with *believe*. Transferring one's dependence involves changing one's thinking.

Sin is the problem. It is grievous to a holy God. Judgment in hell is the consequence. God's justice demands it. But Christ is the answer. He is the only Savior. Repentance goes beyond understanding and agreeing with these truths to a change of way of thinking. This change of thinking is a turning to Christ as the Savior from sin and hell. This is the decision of faith/repentance.

Sin is the problem, but not sinning is not the solution—Christ is. When Christ moves into one's life by faith, He then can enable that person to victory over sin as he keeps depending on the indwelling Christ. But the key in the moment of salvation is to keep the focus on Christ, not reformation. Therefore, the way to really deal with repentance is to deal so thoroughly with sin as the problem and with judgment as the penalty and so thoroughly with Christ as the payment that people turn to Christ as the only answer.

To define repent as "to turn from sin(s)" without further clarifying what that means is unclear and potentially misleading. By itself the phrase "turning from sin(s)" may sound like a works-

---

15. Arndt and Gingrich, 511.

salvation. Certainly repentance should not be articulated in a way that feeds man's natural bent toward a meritorious salvation. "Turning from sin(s)" is legitimate when explained as an *inward* turn to Christ for salvation from sin and hell.

Repentance unto salvation is more clearly turning from the sin of unbelief, which is the sin of not depending on Christ. Repentance is turning to Christ from whatever is keeping a person from trusting Christ as Savior. In other words repentance is turning to Christ from whatever a person is trusting in, whether it involves a false security for a blissful life after death by trusting in a false god or self-righteous works, or a false security of short-sightedness that focuses simply on the material or sinful satisfaction of self-centered living without God. Although various passages indicate a judgment on sin(s), the sinner's responsibility for salvation is not to stop sinning (works), but to turn to Christ for salvation from sin and its penalty.

Some are concerned about an "easy-believism," or more clearly stated, an "acknowledgement-only" decision. The answer to this legitimate concern is not to add sanctification truth to salvation. The answer is to focus on that which the Holy Spirit convicts the world of: sin, righteousness, and judgment since "the natural man receiveth not the things of the Spirit of God . . . because they are spiritually discerned" (I Cor. 2:14). Therefore, the three truths of the gospel must be declared, for that is what the Spirit will use to convict an unsaved person. Dealing with sanctification truth is not what the Spirit uses to convict and convince *the world*. Furthermore, dealing specifically with sin, uncompromisingly with hell, and clearly with the finished work of Christ precludes giving true seekers the notion of a "ticket to heaven and license to sin."

Repentance is turning to Christ for deliverance from sin and hell. This is the decision of faith/repentance.[16]

---

16. In Chapter 8: "The Foundational Issue of Faith/Repentance," the concepts of faith and repentance will be addressed more thoroughly.

Promise of the Decision of Faith/Repentance: Forgiveness of Sins, Credited Righteousness, and Eternal Life

The Word of God connects some truly amazing promises to the condition of believing in Jesus. Acts 10:43 promises that "through his name whosoever believeth in him shall receive remission [forgiveness] of sins." Therefore, forgiveness of sins is a biblical motivation for believing in Jesus and a sure promise. Romans 4:7-8 states, "Blessed are they whose iniquities are forgiven, and whose sins are covered. Blessed is the man to whom the Lord will not impute sin." Through the transaction of faith past sins are forgiven and future sins will not be charged to one's account. Forgiveness of sins addresses man's negative account before a holy God.

Romans 10:4 promises "for Christ is the end of the law for righteousness to every one that believeth." Romans 4:5 states the same truth: "But to him that worketh not, but believeth on him that justifieth the ungodly, his faith is counted for righteousness." Credited righteousness is another exceeding great and precious promise to those who believe on Jesus. Credited righteousness addresses man's account positively before God.

But salvation is more than the cancellation of a sin debt and the positive credit of righteousness. Salvation is in a person. Of all the great promises of salvation in Scripture, the greatest emphasis, by sheer repetition, is eternal life. Jesus promises in John 6:47, "He that believeth on me hath everlasting life" (cf. John 3:15, 16, 36; 5:24). However, eternal life is not merely something forever; it is *Someone*. In 1 John 1:2, Jesus is referred to as "that eternal life." First John 5:20 states that Jesus Christ is "the true God, and eternal life." One who believes in Jesus receives the Eternal Life—the life of Christ. Can a person have eternal life just for a little while? That would be impossible, not only because one cannot have that which is eternal for a short period of time, but also because receiving eternal life is receiving a person (cf. John 1:12). The Christian life is receiving the life of Christ. This reception begins an inseparable union with Christ, since "he that is joined unto the Lord is one spirit" (I Cor. 6:17). Salvation is not based on what one continues to do or not do but on one's relationship with the eternal Son of God.

Necessity of the Decision of Faith/ Repentance: Mandatory

John 3:18 clarifies, "He that believeth on him is not condemned: but he that believeth not is condemned already, because he hath not believed in the name of the only begotten Son of God." Jesus said "Except ye repent, ye shall all likewise perish" (Luke 13:3). A decision must be made. To those who choose to transfer their dependence only to Jesus Christ to save them from sin and hell, God promises that He will forgive their sins, credit Christ's right-eousness to their account, and give them eternal life.

Conclusion

Table 5.1 summarizes the gospel as presented in this chapter.

Sin must be confronted. There is a tendency to deal with sin only in general terms. But if the Spirit is going to do His convincing work, sin must be dealt with specifically. It is "sins" (I Cor. 15:3) that the Spirit uses to convince of "sin" (John 16:8) so that people turn to Christ to deliver them from sin and its penalty.

The fact that there is a hell cannot be softened, but it should be declared with compassion. There is a tendency to general-ize hell as well. But again, if the Spirit is going to convince of judgment, the *rhemas* that teach this reality must be declared. However, it is not a matter of arrogantly telling a man where he is

Table 5.1. Gospel Presentation Chart

The Gospel I Corinthians 15:1–11	Holy Spirit Conviction John 16:8	Attributes of God	Reminders
Problem of Sin "Christ died for our **sins**."	Sin	Holiness	Be specific.
Penalty of Sin "Christ **died** for our sins."	Judgment	Justice	Do not soften this truth, but be compassionate.
Payment for Sin "**Christ** died for our sins."	Righteousness	Love	Glory in the gospel!
Decision of Faith/Repentance "and so ye **believed**."	Decision	Grace/ Mercy	Be crystal clear.

going. An older preacher said he did not like the way many evangelists preach on the subject of hell. He remembered the old-time evangelists who wept their way through their messages on hell. If an evangelist exhibits a lack of sensitivity to the awfulness of hell, he should get alone with God and ask Him to break his heart over the reality of hell.

Then when preaching the good news, there should be a glorying in the gospel. After the bad news, the good news ought to sound like good news. Again, perhaps there is a need to get alone with God and ask Him to open the eyes afresh to the glories of the gospel.

Finally, the decision of faith/repentance must be made crystal clear. Christ must be lifted up as the only answer to man's problem. The gospel must be articulated so clearly that any notion of self-dependence is exposed. The good news must be kept Christ-centered.

Adoniram Judson made one return to America. He had buried two wives, several children, and had suffered greatly. An itinerary was arranged for Judson to preach in churches. Crowds gathered to hear the legendary Adoniram Judson. On one occasion after preaching the gospel of Jesus Christ, he was told that his hearers were somewhat disappointed. They had hoped to hear some story of his adventures and trials. Upon hearing of their response, Judson replied, "Then I am glad they have it to say, that a man coming from the Antipodes had nothing better to tell than the wondrous story of Jesus' dying love."[17] What a glorious evangel!

17. Courtney Anderson, *To the Golden Shore The Life of Adoniram Judson* (Grand Rapids: Zondervan Publishing House, 1972), 462.

Chapter Six

THE GOSPEL TO SAINTS

"What shall we say then? Shall we continue in sin,
that grace may abound? God forbid. How shall we,
that are dead to sin, live any longer therein?"
Romans 6:1–2

In a conference on the Spirit-filled life, an evangelist preached on Galatians 2:20, which is Romans 6–8 in "nugget" form. After the service, a Christian lady stayed in her seat, somewhat overwhelmed. When the evangelist approached her, she said with tears in her eyes, "There's hope!"[1] Just as the gospel brings hope to the lost when the light of justification by faith dawns across the horizon of their hearts, so the gospel brings hope to defeated saints when the light of sanctification by faith shines across their hearts.

In Chapter 1 it was noted that Romans contains the most usages of *euangelion* (gospel) in the New Testament books. In Romans 1:16 Paul declares, "For I am not ashamed of the gospel of Christ." He then explains *the gospel* in a detailed

---

1. Taken from personal experience.

manner throughout the epistle.[2] Romans 1–5 explains justification by faith. But Paul anticipates a potential false conclusion that might be drawn from the fact that salvation is free by grace through faith, which he articulates in Romans 6:1, "What shall we say then? Shall we continue in sin, that grace may abound?" In other words, if salvation is truly free, why not get the free ticket to heaven and then live in sin? Amazingly, in response to this wrong conclusion, Paul does not re-articulate the gospel, making it "harder" to get saved. Rather, he states, "God forbid. How shall we, that are dead to sin, live any longer therein?" This pivotal point opens a new discussion on sanctification. Justification that is truly free by faith leads to sanctification that is also free by faith. New life by faith implies a forward look to new living by faith.[3] This Pauline emphasis sets the stage for the heart-thrilling drama of the gospel to the saints expounded in Romans 6-8. The foundation of this good news is given primarily in the first fourteen verses of Romans 6. As I Corinthians 15 is a classic passage on the gospel to sinners, Romans 6 is a classic passage on the gospel to saints.

Table 6.1 clarifies the differences between the gospel to sinners and the gospel to saints.

---

2. Romans 1–8 focuses on the plan of salvation, addressing both the gospel to sinners (1–5) as well as the gospel to saints (6–8). Romans 9–11, dealing with the problem of Israel's unbelief, focuses on the recipients of salvation, addressing both how God saves (by grace) and who God saves (through faith). Romans 12–16 focuses on the practical applications of salvation. For helpful insight on Romans 9–11, see John F. Parkinson, The Faith of God's Elect (Great Britain: Penfold Book & Bible House Ltd., 2002).

3. This thought is expounded well by Handley G. C. Moule in The Epistle to the Romans (London: Pickering & Inglish Ltd., n.d.), 156–62. Also Griffith Thomas says, "From ch. iii. 21 to ch. v. 21 the theme has been Justification by Faith in the Crucified Savior; now, from ch. vi. 1 to ch. viii. 39, it is Sanctification by Faith in the Risen Lord" (W. H. Griffith Thomas, St. Paul's Epistle to the Romans [Grand Rapids: Wm B. Eerdmans Publishing Company, 1980], 163).

Table 6.1. The Gospel to Sinners and Saints

The Gospel to Sinners	The Gospel to Saints
Justification by faith through the finished work of Christ	Sanctification by faith through the same finished work of Christ
Justification as the imputed righteousness of Christ	Sanctification as the imparted righteousness of Christ
Freedom from the penalty of sin	Freedom from the power of sin
Christ's death for man's sins, emphasizing substitution	The believer's death with Christ, emphasizing identification
The saving death of Christ	The saving life of Christ
Receiving the eternal life of Christ	Accessing the abundant life of Christ
Demands a response of faith for a new standing	Demands responses of faith for a new walking

As Satan seeks to confuse justification by faith with a "struggle theology" of works-justification, so he seeks to confuse sanctification by faith with a struggle theology of works-sanctification. Just as justification by faith confronts both unrighteous sinners and self-righteous sinners, so sanctification by faith confronts both worldly saints and self-righteous saints. And just as justification by faith is resisted by both the unrighteous, who do not want their sin to be exposed as a problem, and the self-righteous, who do not want their "filthy rags" to be exposed as insufficient, so sanctification by faith is resisted by both the worldly saints, who do not want their worldliness to be challenged, and the self-righteous saints, who do not want their condition of self-righteous rags to be challenged either. But just as the gospel to sinners is salvific good news to the unrighteous or self-righteous who will believe on Jesus for justification, so the gospel to saints is liberating good news to worldly or self-righteous saints who will depend on Jesus for sanctification.

The gospel to saints is that Jesus delivers from the power of sin all those who keep depending on Him. As sinners must respond rightly to the gospel to sinners, so saints must respond rightly to the gospel to saints. What is the essence of a right response to sanctification good news? Romans 6:3–14 articulates three combined responses involving the entire soul of man: mind, affections, and will. These collective responses are, by way of analogy, similar to the proper responses to justification good news.

Diagram 6.1 demonstrates this similarity.

Diagram 6.1. Combined Responses of the Soul

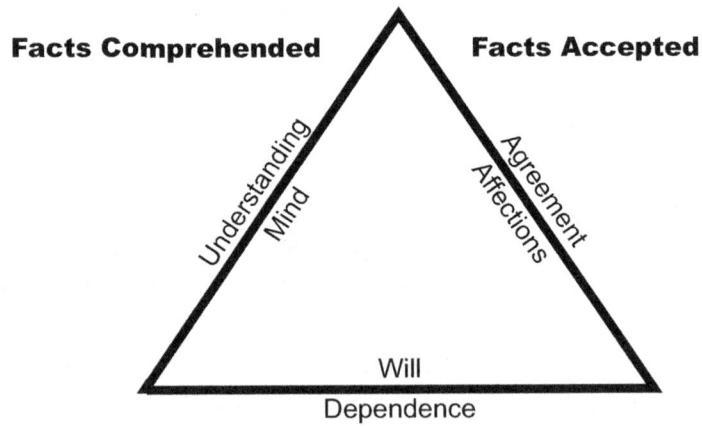

Facts Comprehended

Facts Accepted

Understanding

Mind

Agreement

Affections

Will

Dependence

Facts Trusted

Understand the Facts of Sanctification

Romans 6:3-10 delineates three sanctification facts observable by the wording in the text. The word *know* or *knowing* occurs three times, indicating that there are three facts that must be understood.[4]

Fact One: All Believers Are Saints

As the first fact for justification is that all unbelievers are sinners, the first fact for sanctification is that all believers are saints. To state this simple fact in greater detail: identification with the death of Christ necessitates identification with the life of Christ. The text unfolds this fact by starting with a truth statement, followed by a purpose statement,[5] and ending with a reason statement[6] (Rom. 6:3-5).

Truth Statement (3): "Know" (*agnoeo*)

Romans 6:3 asks, "Know ye not, that so many of us as were baptized into Jesus Christ were baptized into his death?" When a believer is placed into Christ at salvation, he is placed into Christ's death. For what purpose is the believer identified with Christ's death?

---

4. William F. Arndt and F. Wilbur Gingrich, *A Greek-English Lexicon of the New Testament and Other Early Christian Literature*, 2nd ed., revised F. Wilbur Gingrich and Fredrick W. Danker (Chicago: University of Chicago Press, 1979), 11. Verse 3 uses *agnoeo*, meaning "not to know, be ignorant." Here the sense is "Don't you know? You should know this." Stewart Custer, *A Treasury of New Testament Synonyms* (Greenville, SC: Bob Jones University Press, 1975), 112. Verse 6 uses *ginosko*, meaning "know by experience." Verse 9 uses *oida*, which denotes knowing "in the full absolute sense." But all three verses are emphasizing facts that the readers need to know.

5. Ibid., 376. The word *that* (*hina*) occurs strategically, meaning "in order that," denoting "purpose."

6. Ibid., 151-52. The word *for* (*gar*) expresses "cause" or "reason."

Purpose Statement (4): "that" (*hina*)

Romans 6:4 continues, "Therefore we are buried with him by baptism into death: that like as Christ was raised up from the dead by the glory of the Father, even so we also should walk in newness of life." The believer died with Christ for the purpose that he might live with Christ. The subjunctive "should walk" is the mood of probability, but as such indicates that the new walk is not automatic. Why is the believer now in a position to walk in newness of life?

Reason Statement (5): "For" (*gar*)

Romans 6:5 explains, "For if we have been planted together in the likeness of his death, we shall be also [united together] in the likeness of his resurrection." Union with Christ in His death demands union with Christ in His resurrection (life).[7] When the believer receives the eternal life of Christ, the Spirit of Christ joins the regenerated human spirit. Therefore, when the Holy One moves in, the believer becomes a "saint," which means "a holy one."[8] Thus, all believers are saints.

Fact Two: All Saints Are Free to Live Victoriously

As the second fact for justification is that all unbelievers are in bondage to sin and are headed to hell, the second fact for sanctification is that all saints are free to live victoriously (saintly) and are headed to heaven. To state this fact in another way: identification with the death of Christ liberates from sin as a master. Again the text unfolds this fact by starting with a truth statement, followed by a purpose statement, and ending with a reason statement.

---

7. W. Ian Thomas, *The Indwelling Life of Christ* (Sisters, OR: Multnomah Publishers, Inc., 2006), 54. Thomas states succinctly, "Christ gave Himself *for* us to give Himself *to* us" [emphasis original].

8. Arndt and Gingrich, 10.

Truth Statement (6a): "Knowing" (*ginosko*)

Romans 6:6*a* emphasizes, "Knowing this, that our old man is crucified with him." A believer's unregenerated spirit ["old man"] is crucified with Christ.[9] For what purpose is this death by crucifixion?

Purpose Statement (6b): "that" (*hina*)

Romans 6:6*b* continues, "that the body of sin[10] might be destroyed [rendered ineffective],[11] that henceforth we should not serve sin."[12] The crucifixion of the believer's unregenerated spirit frees him from forced service to the master of sin. The subjunctive "might be destroyed" is the mood of probability, but also indicates that which is not automatic. For what reason is this freedom from sin as a master?

Reason Statement (7–8): "For" (*gar*)

Romans 6:7 explains, "For he that is dead is freed from sin." Through the separation of death, sin is no longer the believer's master. Romans 6:8 further explains, "Now if we be dead with Christ, we believe that we shall also live with him." Separation from sin (the old master) is followed by union with Christ (the new master).

The first two sanctification facts address both the unregenerated condition and the regenerated condition. A person who is

---

9. That the "old man" refers to the spirit part of one's being is obvious from the simple fact that Paul is clearly not referring to a physical crucifixion of believers. Since physical death refers to the separation of the soul from the body, then the crucifixion of the old man must be referring to one's spirit.

10. The phrase "body of sin" may refer to the sin-cursed mortal body as in verse 12 "your mortal body." Moule comments that the mortal body is "a special field for the action of sin." (Handley G. C. Moule, *Studies in Romans* [Grand Rapids: Kregel Publications, 1977], 117.) Some, based on Colossians 3, take the phrase "body of sin" to mean the "grouping of sin" as in "body of truth." Therefore, no sin is unconquered. Either way sin has been rendered ineffective.

11. Arndt and Gingrich, 417.

12. The second *that is* taken from the infinitive and is not the word *hina*. However it continues to denote purpose.

unregenerated is alive physically because his soul is still united to his body, but he is dead spiritually because his spirit (within his soul) is separated from God. Human beings are "born dead" in the spirit part of their beings. That is, they are born separated from God because of the Fall of man in the Garden of Eden. Therefore, the unregenerated condition is biblically described as being "dead in trespasses and sins" (Eph. 2:1). The idea of "dead" is not death in the sense of a corpse, but rather death in the sense of separation. As physical death is the separation of the soul from the body, every human being is born dead or separated from God in his spirit. However, the unregenerated spirit that is dead to God (separated from God) is alive to sin (united to sin). "Dead in trespasses and sins" describes this unregenerated condition. Every person, regenerated or unregenerated, this side of heaven is aware of "sin that dwelleth in me" (Rom. 7:20) or indwelling sin. However, prior to salvation the unregenerated spirit is in an actual union with indwelling sin. In fact, this union is like a marriage (Rom. 7:1-4). Prior to salvation, indwelling sin is a person's husband, who acts as a taskmaster. Everything an unregenerated person does is done in union with sin. Therefore, "the plowing of the wicked is sin" (Prov. 21:4). Even the noblest efforts of unregenerated people are done in union with sin. This union defiles the motivation, makes it self-effort, producing man's righteousness, which is as filthy rags (Isa. 64:6), and falls short of the glory of God (Rom. 3:23).

The only way out of this tragic union is for one of the partners to die (Rom. 7:1-4). The good news is that when a person believes in Jesus for salvation, God identifies that person in the death of Christ. At that moment, in the spirit part of one's being, an actual separation from indwelling sin occurs. God also unites that person with Christ in His resurrection, allowing for a new union: "that ye should be married to another, even to him who is raised from the dead" (Rom. 7:4). At that point "he that is joined unto the Lord is one spirit" (I Cor. 6:17).[13] This is a new and glorious union with the Lord Himself. Therefore, indwelling sin is no longer a believer's husband or master. Although sin may come back and seek to influence, it has no more authority.[14] To yield to sin would be similar to working for a former boss when one now has a new boss. Not only would this be ludicrous, it would be a crime against the new boss to work for the competition instead. In scriptural fact, yielding to sin is committing spiritual adultery. James 4:4–5 expresses this betrayal with the words, "Ye adulterers and adulteresses, know ye not that the friendship of the world is enmity with God? whosoever therefore will be a friend of the world is the enemy of God. Do ye think that the scripture saith in vain, The spirit that dwelleth in us lusteth to envy?"

Since the believer is regenerated, he is actually free from sin as a master, and, therefore, free to live unto God who is his new master. As the unregenerated condition means that one is dead to God (separated from God) and alive to sin (joined to sin), so the regenerated condition means that one is dead to sin (separated from sin) and alive to God (joined to God). Therefore, all saints are free to live victoriously.

Diagrams 6.2 and 6.3 contrast the two conditions.

---

13. This inseparable union is a great foundation of faith for eternal security.

14. Evan Hopkins states, "Your old master, sin . . . may assert its power, but it has no authority." Quoted in Steven Barabus, *So Great Salvation* (Eugene, OR: Wipf & Stock, reprint ed., 2005), 90.

Diagram 6.2. Unregenerated Condition

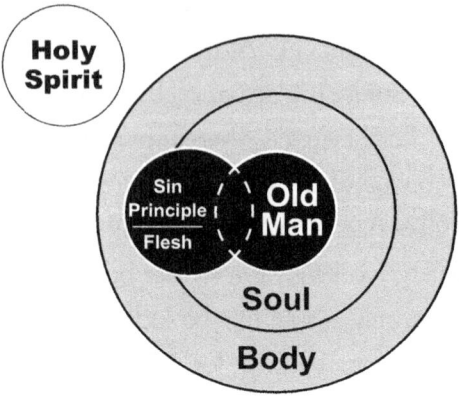

Diagram 6.3. Regenerated Condition

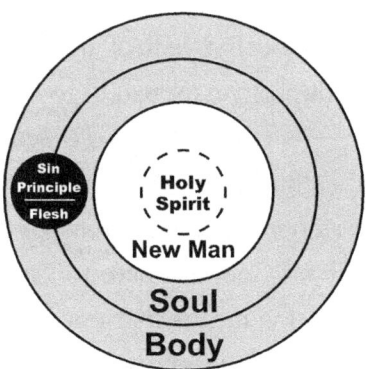

Fact Three: Christ Is the Victory!

As the third fact for justification is that Christ is the Savior, the third fact for sanctification is that Christ is the victory. To state this simple fact in greater detail: Identification with the death and resurrection of Christ finalizes the victory over death and sin. In this case, the text unfolds this fact by simply starting with a truth statement and ending with a reason statement.

Truth Statement (9): "Knowing" (oida)

Romans 6:9 emphasizes, "Knowing that Christ being raised from the dead dieth no more; death hath no more dominion over him." Christ's resurrection freed Him forever from death's dominion. Why is this resurrection so final?

Reason Statement (10): "For" (gar)

Romans 6:10 explains, "For in that he died, he died unto sin once: but in that he liveth, he liveth unto God." Christ's death to sin was once for all, and His life/living to God is forever. Every believer is in Christ. Therefore every believer died in Christ and is consequently free from sin's claim of death and was raised in Christ and is free to live to God.

The old man (unregenerated spirit) died with Christ and was raised with Christ a new man (regenerated spirit). Therefore, the old man is gone—forever.[15] It is impossible for the unregenerated spirit and regenerated spirit to coexist in the same body. The battle believers have with sin is not between the old man and the new man, but between the flesh (where indwelling sin still operates) and the Spirit. "For the flesh lusteth against the Spirit, and the Spirit against the flesh" (Gal. 5:17). Therefore, believers must "walk not after the flesh, but after the Spirit" (Rom. 8:4). Clearly the participants in the conflict are *flesh* and *Spirit*.[16] In passages like Galatians 5 and Romans 8, Paul uses the word *flesh*, not to mean merely the physical body, but the influence of indwelling sin

15. Colossians 3:9-10 renders the aorist more clearly than Ephesians 4:22 and 24 when it says "ye have put off the old man . . . And have put on the new man." The idea in Colossians 3 is that since a believer has put off the old man, he ought to put off the habits of the old man. Also, since the believer has put on the new man, he ought to put on the habits of the new man.

16. Some use the terminology "old nature" and "new nature." However, this can be confusing. If the old nature refers to the old man, then the old nature would be eliminated when the old man (unregenerated spirit) is replaced by the new man (regenerated spirit). If the old nature refers to the flesh where indwelling sin still operates, then the old nature still remains. If the old nature refers to indwelling sin, then the old nature still remains as an influence, but without authority.

within the body and soul of man. The human body of the believer is the temple of the Holy Spirit (I Cor. 6:19). What is warned against is the flesh as that part of man where the influence of indwelling sin is being yielded to rather than the Spirit.

For years many have used the illustration of two dogs to picture this battle between flesh and Spirit. Whatever dog is favored and fed the most is the one that wins. While it is true that every believer makes choices that influence who "wins," this illustration can be harmful. Are not the two dogs pictured in the mind's eye of equal size? Therefore, subconsciously this picture implies that part of the time one dog will win, and part of the time the other will. This thinking sets one up for inevitable defeat. The fallacy in the illustration lies in the fact that the participants in the conflict are not equals. Not even a small dog versus a large dog would give a correct picture. On the one hand, there is the *flesh* where the sin principle, or indwelling sin, still operates. But on the other hand, there is the *spirit*. Is this referring to the regenerated spirit or the Holy Spirit? The answer is both for "he that is joined unto the Lord is one spirit" (I Cor. 6:17).

This union of the regenerated spirit and the Holy Spirit is an amazing union. The regenerated spirit is a "new creature" (2 Cor. 5:17). This indicates that a creative act of God takes place at regeneration. This new creation is described as "his [God's] seed [*sperma*]" (I John 3:9). Therefore, something of the nature of God is implanted into the believer. This regenerated spirit is therefore "the new man, which after God is created in righteousness and true holiness" (Eph. 4:24).

This new spirit is then joined to Christ, the Eternal Life, through the Spirit. Literally, the believer who is severed from indwelling sin through death with Christ is raised that he might "be married to another, even to him who is raised from the dead." Therefore, it is the Spirit of the risen Christ who finished the work at the cross and was exalted to the right hand of the Father who joins the believer's regenerated spirit. It is the Spirit of the conquering, triumphant, enthroned Christ who moves into the believer, and when the believer is in fellowship with the Spirit, there is no contest with the flesh, for Christ is the victory—every time.

Diagram 6.4 compares the facts of justification with the facts of sanctification as they relate to the mind.

Diagram 6.4. Comparison of Justification Facts and Sanctification Facts: Mind

Justification Facts

Fact One: All unbelievers are sinners.

Fact Two: All unbelievers are in bondage to sin and headed to hell.

Fact Three: Christ is the Saviour!

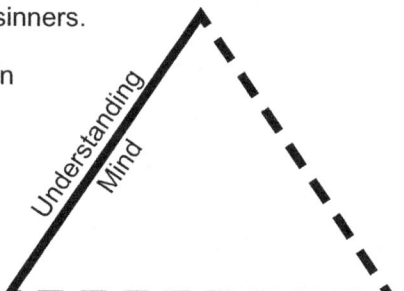

Sanctification Facts

Fact One: All believers are saints.

Fact Two: All saints are free to live victoriously and headed to heaven.

Fact Three: Christ is the Victory!

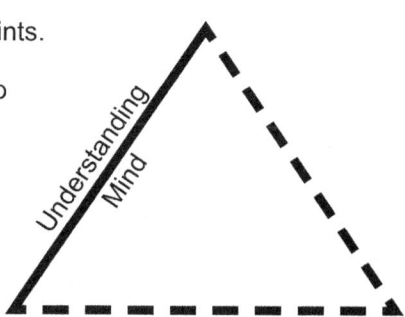

Personalize the Facts of Sanctification

Once sanctification facts are intellectually understood, the second combined response is to personalize what has been comprehended. Romans 6:11 admonishes, "Likewise reckon ye also yourselves to be dead indeed unto sin, but alive unto God through Jesus Christ our Lord." After presenting the facts, Paul under inspiration gives the first imperative in the text. However, this command is not directly to one's will, but to one's mind ("reckon") and to one's affections where one desires what he understands ("yourselves"). The word *reckon* is an accounting term. The same word is translated *conclude* (Rom. 3:28). The text urges every individual to come to the right conclusion by agreeing with God's conclusion. The command to "reckon" is a command to turn right knowledge into right thinking. Believers must conclude or think according to what actually is (the facts).

If a person actually has ten million dollars in his bank account, then he must "reckon," or account for, that fact by writing the accurate amount on the proper line in his checkbook or ledger. To write far less would be inaccurate as well as a hindrance to living according to one's worth. Likewise, the believer must "reckon," or account, spiritually according to the facts. He is separated from sin and joined to the all-sufficient, inexhaustible Christ. To think otherwise is inaccurate as well as a hindrance to living according to one's worth in Christ. The reason many believers do not live victoriously is that they do not think according to the facts. Rather, they think according to their defeated or ineffective experience. They think that the Spirit-filled life is for others, but somehow not for them. But "through Christ Jesus" the believer is "dead indeed to sin" and "alive unto God." Therefore, "reckon ye also yourselves to be dead indeed unto sin, but alive unto God through Christ Jesus our Lord." In Christ, the believer is separated from sin (the sinful life) and united to God (the holy life). Therefore, every believer must himself heartily agree with the facts. This hearty agreement is simply personalizing the facts of sanctification.

Fact One: I Am a Saint!

It is not a matter of merely understanding that all believers are saints, but personalizing that fact individually: "*I* am a saint." The reason some have difficulty claiming this is because they do not live very saintly. But every believer must think according to what actually is, not according to what may or may not seem to be. Yet many do not think according to the facts, even though they may understand them. Although believers were sinners positionally and are sinners practically through wrong choices, they are actually saints positionally, and, when that fact is embraced, may live saintly practically.

Fact Two: I Am Free to Live Victoriously!

It is not merely understanding that all saints are free to live victoriously (saintly), but personalizing that fact as an individual: "*I* am free to live victoriously." Every believer is separated from indwelling sin and united to the indwelling Christ and therefore is free to live victoriously by means of the victorious life of Christ. While it is true that every believer this side of heaven is able to sin because of still residing in human flesh, where indwelling sin still seeks to operate, it is also true that every believer is able *not* to sin because of the new inner union with the indwelling Christ. If one focuses on his ability to sin, he will experience sin. But if one focuses on his ability not to sin through his union with Christ, he will experience the victorious life of Christ. This focus is thinking rightly. To think otherwise is to insult Christ as a present deliverer.

Some focus on their bad habits and resign themselves to defeat, but this is not thinking correctly. It is placing one's experience on a higher level than God's Word. It is embracing a lie. The provision of sanctification means that bad, acquired habits may be replaced with good, acquired habits. No one was born with bad habits. Bad habits are acquired through many choices of yielding to the flesh both prior to salvation and as a carnal Christian who sadly keeps yielding to the flesh.[17] But the good news is that as a saint, the believer is free to live saintly by the power of the indwelling Christ. One is not a saint because he lives saintly; one may live saintly because he is a saint. As one walks in the Spirit, he is enabled to not fulfill the lusts of the flesh (Gal. 5:16). Step by step in this walk of surrender to the Spirit's leading and dependence upon the Spirit's enablement, the believer replaces bad, acquired habits with good, acquired habits.

---

17. Although some do not admit to the possibility of a "carnal Christian," Scripture seems to indicate otherwise for several reasons. First, 1 Corinthians 3 addresses the "brethren" as "carnal" (3:1-4). The word *carnal* from *sarkinos* (1 Cor. 3:1) and *sarkikos* (1 Cor. 3:3) means "fleshly," and, in context, emphasizes the ethical realm of the flesh, not merely physical flesh. Second, Galatians 5:16-18 and Romans 8:1-4 urge believers to walk "in" or "after" the Spirit, not the flesh. Honesty must admit that believers do at times yield to their flesh, thus the scriptural admonitions to yield to the Spirit. Christians who yield to their flesh are in those moments fleshly or *carnal* Christians. This is not a settled "state," but a condition of believers in the moments when they yield to their flesh.

Fact Three: Christ Is My Victory!

It is not merely understanding that Christ is the victory, but personalizing that fact: "Christ is *my* victory!" Christ is the victorious life; and since He lives in the saint, He is the saint's victorious life.

To access practical victory through Christ, one must embrace his positional victory in Christ. Right understanding is prerequisite to right thinking, and right thinking is prerequisite to right living. Positional reality is foundational to practical reality.

When an IMAX[18] features the perspective of riding in the cockpit of a fighter plane, the viewers experience the sensation of actually being in that plane. If the pilot begins to roll the plane, the sensation may actually cause the viewers to become sick to their stomachs. However, the viewers of the IMAX are not actually rolling in a plane. It is only an illusion. Their actual position is stationary. If the viewers focus on the illusion, they experience motion sickness (which is not an illusion). But this real experience is contrary to their actual position. However, if they stop looking at the illusion and focus on their stationary position, they experience their stationary reality. Likewise, when believers focus on the illusion of "Undoubtedly I will be defeated by the world and the flesh," they experience defeat (which is not an illusion). But this experience is contrary to their actual position in Christ. However, if they stop focusing on the illusion and focus on their victorious position in Christ, they experience the reality of victory in Christ.

Diagram 6.5 compares the facts of justification with the facts of sanctification as they relate to the affections.

---

18. IMAX® is a registered trademark of IMAX Corporation.

Diagram 6.5. Comparison of Justification Facts and Sanctification Facts: Affections

Justification Facts

Fact One: All unbelievers are sinners.

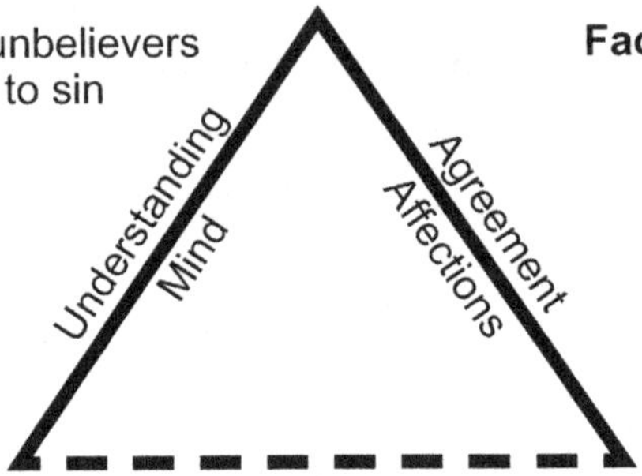

Fact One: I am a sinner.

Fact Two: All unbelievers are in bondage to sin and headed to hell.

Fact Two: I am in bondage to sin and headed to hell.

Fact Three: Christ is the Saviour!

Fact Three: I need Christ as my Saviour!

Understanding Mind Agreement Affections

Sanctification Facts

Fact One: All believers are saints.

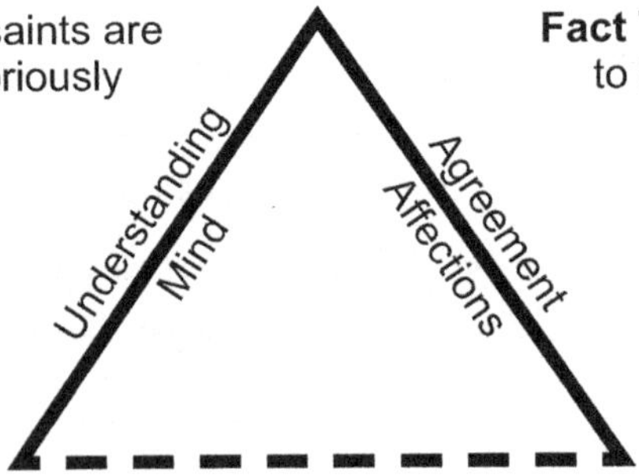

Fact One: I am a saint.

Fact Two: All saints are free to live victoriously and headed to heaven.

Fact Two: I am free to live victoriously and headed to heaven.

Fact Three: Christ is the Victory!

Fact Three: Christ is my Victory!

Understanding Mind Agreement Affections

The mind influences the affections, but the affections move the will.[19] Some believers do not have the facts straight. Yet some understand the simple facts that they are in Christ and Christ is in them. However, they do not think according to reality. For many the battle is lost by simply not reckoning rightly. For in order to exercise one's will correctly, one must think according to reality. Turning right knowledge into right thinking is personalizing the facts. Although this second response to sanctification facts is vital, there is yet a final response that is necessary for sanctification to proceed unhindered.

Depend on the Facts of Sanctification

The gospel to the saints demands three combined responses. After understanding the facts of sanctification and personalizing those facts, one must depend on sanctification facts. Understanding and agreeing without depending would be easy-believism on sanctification, just as understanding and agreeing without depending is easy-believism on justification. After Paul emphasizes sanctification facts and urges the personalization of those facts, he gives under inspiration three imperatives directly to the will. These commands address both the negative and positive side of real surrender and faith.

The Negative Side

The first two commands to the will are present-tense imperatives with a negative. This grammatical construction may indicate ceasing an action that is already in progress, or it may simply be a prohibition.

---

19. Evan Hopkins, *The Law of Liberty in the Spiritual Life* (Fort Washington, PA: Christian Literature Crusade, reprint ed., 1991). Hopkins expounds on this thought in his book which deals with the doctrine of sanctification. W. H. Griffith Thomas is quoted on the cover jacket of older copies of Hopkins's book as saying, "By far the best book available on the subject of holiness."

Stop Placing Oneself under Sin as an Authority

Romans 6:12 commands, "Let not sin therefore reign in your mortal body, that ye should obey it in the lusts thereof." Sin is allowed to reign or rule when the believer yields to indwelling sin.[20] But since sin is no longer the believer's master, the command is to stop letting sin rule. It is foolish for a saint to place himself under the authority of sin, since indwelling sin is not the believer's authority. Since sin is not the believer's master or boss, the believer does not have to obey sin.

In order to stop letting sin rule, the believer should confess his yielding to the flesh as sin and by faith accept the cleansing power of the blood of Jesus (I John 1: 7, 9).[21]

Stop Presenting One's Bodily Members to Sin To Be Used as Instruments of Unrighteousness

Romans 6:13 also commands, "Neither yield ye your members as instruments of unrighteousness unto sin." The word *yield* is translated as "present" in Romans 12:1. The command here is to stop presenting one's body parts to indwelling sin to be used as "instruments of unrighteousness."[22] For example, the practicality of the command is to stop yielding one's lips to indwelling sin to be used as an instrument of gossip, stop yielding one's eyes to indwelling sin to be used as an instrument of lust, stop yielding one's hands to indwelling sin to be used as an instrument of theft, and so forth.

After the Emancipation Proclamation, some slaves did not yet know of their new freedom. Since they did not understand the right facts, they felt obligated to obey their former masters.

---

20. "Sin 'reigns' when the will *goes with* solicitations to evil" [emphasis original] (Moule).

21. The concept of confession and a clean heart is explained in more detail in the next chapter.

22. Moule states, "Do not put them as weapons into the hand of sin to use for unrighteousness" (Moule).

Therefore, they kept yielding their bodies to the demands of their former masters. Similarly, after salvation some believers do not yet know of their new freedom from sin as a master. Since they do not understand the right facts, they feel obligated to obey their former master. Therefore, they keep yielding their bodies to the demands of indwelling sin. But based on sanctification facts, believers may stop yielding to sin and, therefore, stop presenting their body parts to be used by sin as instruments of unrighteousness.

The Positive Side

The next command addresses the same two applications on the positive side.

Start Placing Oneself under God as the Authority

Romans 6:13 commands, "but yield yourselves unto God, as those that are alive from the dead." Since God is, in fact, the believer's authority, the command is to start letting God rule. The believer is to surrender to God's leadership ("yield yourselves unto God") and depend on God's enablement ("as those that are alive from the dead"). Since the believer is alive in Christ (dead to/separated from sin and alive to/joined to the Lord), he must place himself under God as the new authority. This yielding is both directional and daily. The word *yield* in verse 13 is aorist, indicating the fact of an action and implying a directional turning point ("stop-start"). However, the same word *yield* is used in verse 16 in the present tense, indicating continuous action and implying a daily process. The combination of verb tenses shows that the gospel to the saints is not a once-for-all second blessing, but a repeated access of one's first blessing. This access is available when someone receives the indwelling life of Christ.

Start Presenting One's Bodily Members to God To Be Used as Instruments of Righteousness

Romans 6:13 continues, "but yield . . . your members as instruments of righteousness unto God." The command here is to start presenting one's body parts to God to actually be used as instruments of righteousness.[23] For example, the practicality of the command is to start yielding one's lips to God to be used as an instrument of encouragement, starting yielding one's eyes to God to be used as an instrument of purity, start yielding one's hands to God to be used as an instrument of wholesome labor, and so forth. In fact, a few verses later, Paul explains, "for as ye have yielded your members servants to uncleanness and to iniquity unto iniquity; even so now yield your members servants to righteousness unto holiness" (Rom. 6:19). The same muscles and body parts that were used as "servants to uncleanness" must now be yielded to God to be used as "servants to righteousness."

Both applications of the positive command indicate that from center ("yourselves") to circumference ("your members"), all must be yielded "unto God." Rather than just using the word *faith* or *believe*, the text describes faith with inspired precision. All is to be yielded to God. This is God-dependence, both for leadership and enablement. Depending on God's leadership and enablement is the life of faith. It is trusting to obey. The life of faith is not "just obey," for that indicates the flesh-dependence of works-sanctification. Nor is the life of faith "just trust," for that indicates easy-believism on sanctification (understanding and agreement only), which is passivity. Faith for sanctification without the step of obedience is not faith. Rather, the life of faith is "trust to obey," for when all three aspects of man's soul are involved, sanctification proceeds in power.

Diagram 6.6 compares the facts of justification with the facts of sanctification as they relate to the will.

---

23. Moule states, "Put them into the hand of God as weapons to use for righteousness" (Ibid.).

THE GOSPEL TO SAINTS ~ 153

Diagram 6.6. Comparison of Justification Facts and Sanctification Facts: Will

Justification Facts

Fact One: All unbelievers are sinners.

Fact One: I am a sinner.

Fact Two: All unbelievers are in bondage to sin and headed to hell.

Fact Two: I am in bondage to sin and headed to hell.

Fact Three: Christ is the Saviour!

Fact Three: I need Christ as my Saviour!

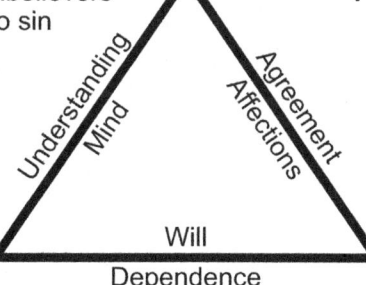

I depend on Christ [fact three] to save me from sin [fact one] and hell [fact two].

Sanctification Facts

Fact One: All believers are saints.

Fact One: I am a saint.

Fact Two: All saints are free to live victoriously and headed to heaven.

Fact Two: I am free to live victoriously and headed to heaven.

Fact Three: Christ is the Victory!

Fact Three: Christ is my Victory!

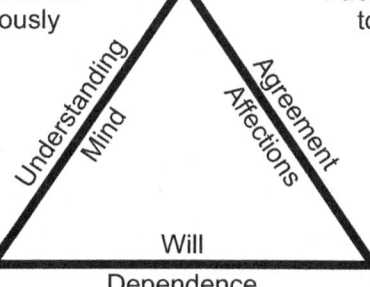

I depend on Christ to live His victorious life through me.

Conclusion

Romans 6:14 promises, "for sin shall not have dominion over you: for ye are not under the law, but under grace." When the facts of sanctification are understood, personalized, and depended upon, "sin shall not have dominion [rule] over you." This is glorious good news—the gospel to saints.

After laying the bedrock foundation of the gospel to the saints in Romans 6:1-14, Paul shows the interrelationship of positional truth and practical truth in Romans 6:15-23. In Romans 7:1-4 Paul provides an illustration of the truth just presented in Romans 6. In verses 5-6 he then recaps the purpose of salvation noting that prior to salvation "we were in the flesh [imperfect]. . . . But now we are delivered [aorist] . . . that we should serve in newness of spirit, and not in the oldness of the letter."

The phrase "that we should serve in newness of spirit" emphasizes that the positional deliverance opens the potential for practical deliverance. The article being absent before the Spirit emphasizes the operation or power of the Spirit as the key to real service and implies Spirit-dependence for Spirit-enablement. In contrast to this is the phrase "and not in the oldness of the letter." Self-dependent works of the law will not bring deliverance from the power of sin just as the works of the law do not bring deliverance from the penalty of sin. "Just as . . . [Paul] showed that law could not justify, so here he proves the additional truth, that it cannot sanctify."[24]

Paul then shows in detail in verses 7-24 that the law cannot deliver from sin positionally or practically. Verses 7-24 have a total silence regarding the Holy Spirit and reveal that even a regenerated man who attempts to "serve . . . in the oldness of the

---

24. Thomas, 190.

letter" will fail.[25] The failure of flesh-dependent efforts describes a condition, not a state. Believers do not have to go through a "stage" of carnality to get to spirituality. The issue is not two stages, but two conditions. Believers may vacillate between the condition of carnality (when they yield to the flesh or attempt obedience in the strength of the flesh) and the condition of spirituality (when they yield to the Spirit and depend on His power). Even a mature believer will find himself in the dilemma of Romans 7 when he depends on the flesh rather than the Spirit. "The point of the passage is that it describes a man who is trying to be good and holy by his own efforts and is beaten back every time by the power of indwelling sin. This is the experience of any man who tries the experiment, whether he be regenerate or unregenerate. The experiences here described are certainly not those of the Christian life as it ought to be. . . . And yet they may be true of many professed Christians as they now are."[26]

In Romans 7:25 Paul then relieves the dilemma of the failure of anything apart from the Spirit by emphasizing deliverance "through Jesus Christ our Lord." This deliverance is accessed through the apex of faith—"I thank God." Then in Romans 8 Paul shows the victory of walking after the Spirit and not the flesh. Yet the foundation for this victory is found in Romans 6:1-14.

When the believer stops yielding to sin and starts yielding to God, he is not "under the law, but under grace." Faith accesses

25. That Paul is referring to the regenerated man in Romans 7:14ff. is seen for several reasons. First, Paul uses "we" in verse 14 as he did in verse 6 when he spoke of those who have been delivered. Second, in verse 14 Paul switches to the present tense, and all the verbs beginning with "I am carnal" (Rom. 7:14) to the first half of verse 24 are in the present tense except for one (Rom. 7:18a). The present tense combined with an emphasis on "I" throughout the passage, and an absence of the Holy Spirit reveals the present failure of Paul when he does not depend on the power of the Spirit. Third, because Paul is regenerated he can say, "For I delight in the law of God after the inward man" (Rom. 7:22). Only a regenerated person can delight in God's law in the *inward* man. The word translated "inward" is *eso* and is used by Paul in Ephesians 3:16 translated "inner" in the phrase "to be strengthened with might by his Spirit in the inner man." Also *esothen* is used in 2 Corinthians 4:16 in the phrase "the inward man is renewed."

26. Thomas, 191.

grace. God-dependence accesses Spirit-enablement. God-dependence for steps of obedience accesses Spirit-enablement to actually take the steps. As power steering waits for the driver to set the direction before it activates, so God in His divine wisdom waits for the believer to set the direction before His life is manifested. The enablement is for "obedience unto righteousness" (Rom. 6:16) and "righteousness unto holiness" (Rom. 6:19) so that "ye have your fruit unto holiness [sanctification]" (Rom. 6:22). This is sanctification unhindered. This is sanctification by faith—the gospel to saints.

When faith choices are made (trust to obey), the principle of counteraction operates as the law of the Spirit counteracts and overcomes the law of sin. "For the law of the Spirit of life in Christ Jesus hath made me free from the law of sin and death" (Rom. 8:2). Through faith choices (Rom. 7:25), the positional truth of a believer's sanctification (Rom. 8:2) becomes practical as "righteousness" is "fulfilled" in those "who walk not after the flesh, but after the Spirit" (Rom. 8:4). This reality does not mean that "the law of sin" disappears, but that a greater law—"the law of the Spirit"—overcomes the lesser law. Just as corrective lenses do not cause near-sightedness to cease but rather counteract and overcome the near-sightedness as long as the lenses are worn (depended upon), so "the law of the Spirit" does not cause "the law of sin" (indwelling sin) to cease but rather counteracts and overcomes "the law of sin" as long as "the law of the Spirit" is depended upon. This is the gospel to saints.

"But if the Spirit of him that raised up Jesus from the dead dwell in you, he that raised up Christ from the dead shall also quicken your mortal bodies by his Spirit that dwelleth in you. Therefore, brethren, we are debtors, not to the flesh, to live after the flesh. For if ye live after the flesh, ye shall die: but if ye through the Spirit do mortify the deeds of the body, ye shall live" (Rom. 8:11-13). On the basis of "the Spirit" of the risen

Christ dwelling "in" the believer (v. 11) [understanding sancti-fication facts] and agreement with the reality that the debt is "not to the flesh, to live after [yield to] the flesh," but to the Spirit, to live after [yield to] the Spirit (v. 12) [personalizing sanc-tification facts], when the believer "through the Spirit" puts to death "the deeds of the body" (v. 13) [depending on sanctification facts], he "shall live." This is living in the Spirit or, more accurately, the Spirit living in and through the believer overcoming sin. This is the principle of counteraction. This is the gospel to the saints.

God-dependence for Spirit-enablement accesses the victori-ous life of Christ in the believer to be manifested through the be-liever. When union with Christ is accessed by faith, indwelling sin within the flesh is no match. The Spirit of Christ always wins. The provision of Christ's life is perfect. Sadly, the believer's application of the access by faith is imperfect. But when trusted, Christ is al-ways victorious. By responding rightly to sanctification facts, the believer may switch from being regularly defeated and surprised by victory to being regularly victorious and surprised by defeat. This is the gospel to saints.

The Christian life is not merely a set of correct doctrines or the form of right actions. The Christian life is a Life—His name is Jesus. Jesus is *the Christian Life*. Therefore, no one can live the Christian life but Christ. But at the new birth, Christ moves into the believer so that the believer may live, yet not the believer but Christ in the believer—the Christian Life. The believer's best for Christ falls short of the glory of God, but Christ's best in the be-liever meets the standard of God. Faith accesses the saving Life of Christ. It is the believer's privilege to depend on the indwelling Christ to live His victorious life through the believer, one step of faith at a time, and say, "Thank you, Lord."

This is the glorious evangel—the gospel to the saints!

Chapter Seven

SALVATION, ASSURANCE, AND REVIVAL

"I am come that they might have life,
and that they might have it more abundantly."
John 10:10
"And this is the record, that God hath given to us eternal life,
and this life is in his Son. He that hath the Son hath life, and
he that hath not the Son of God hath not life. These things
have I written unto you that believe on the name of the Son
of God; that ye may know that ye have eternal life."
1 John 5:11–13

Occasionally, a doctor will misdiagnose a patient. When this occurs, the prescribed help administered does not help and, at times, may even hinder. Obviously, a patient must be diagnosed accurately in order to receive the correct remedy. In like manner, preachers may misdiagnose someone's spiritual condition. When this occurs, the spiritual help administered does not help and, at times, may even hinder. It is vital, therefore, to diagnose accurately in the spiritual realm in order to give the correct spiritual remedy.

A diagnostician is "a specialist in diagnostics."[1] Evangelists specialize in the gospel in its full ramifications to both sinners and saints. For that reason, evangelists must be spiritual diagnosticians that specialize in gospel diagnostics. The combined texts of John 10:10 and 1 John 5:11-13 delineate three gospel-related issues: salvation (having eternal life), assurance (knowing one has eternal life), and revival (living that life abundantly). Since the issues of salvation, assurance, and revival affect eternal destinies and effective lives, evangelists must discern the difference between these issues in order to diagnose accurately and then offer the correct spiritual remedy.

Table 7.1 provides an overview.

Table 7.1. Gospel Diagnostic Chart: Overview

Issue	Clarification
Salvation	Being saved/having eternal life
Assurance	Knowing one is saved/has eternal life
Revival	Living one's salvation/life more abundantly

In order for an evangelist to be an accurate gospel diagnostician, he must know how to discern a person's spiritual need through the Word of God, and he must know the specific gospel remedies that correspond to specific spiritual needs—gospel remedies that clarify man's responsibility to access God's promised

---

1. *Webster's New World Dictionary*, 2nd college ed. (U.S.A.: William Collins and World Publishing Co. Inc., 1978), 388.

cures. By asking the right Bible-based questions, an evangelist may determine (provided the person is being honest) whether or not someone has fulfilled or needs to fulfill certain biblical responsibilities in order to experience God's promised cures.

Salvation

How can someone be saved? The gospel to sinners (detailed in Chapter 5) delineates three truths a person must understand and agree with and one decision that must be made. This choice, along with God's promise, is stated simply by Jesus in John 6:47: "He that believeth on me hath everlasting life." The condition is believing on Jesus; the promise is having eternal life. Therefore, regarding the issue of salvation, man's responsibility is the choice of faith, and God's promise is the promise of eternal life.

Man's Responsibility: The Choice of Faith
"He that believeth on me"

As noted in Chapter 5, believing on Jesus involves the whole soul of man: mind, affections, and will. Summarizing what it means to believe in Jesus will aid in knowing how to diagnose one's spiritual need. Each aspect of the soul may be represented by the sides of a triangle, and guides in the diagnostics.

Understanding (Mind)
The first side of the triangle represents the mind: understanding the facts of sin, righteousness, and judgment.

Diagram 7.1 pictures this understanding.

Diagram 7.1. Gospel Diagnostics: Understanding

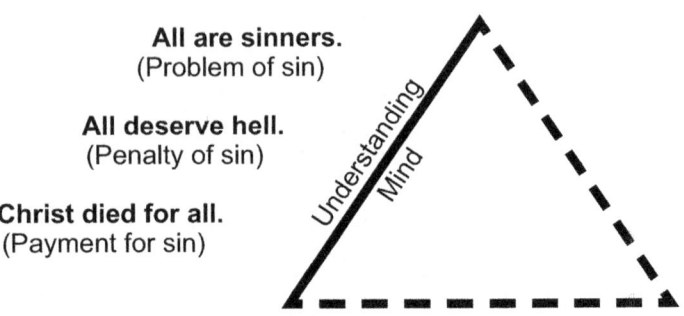

All are sinners.
(Problem of sin)

All deserve hell.
(Penalty of sin)

Christ died for all.
(Payment for sin)

To be brought to faith in Christ, unbelievers must first under-stand that all have sinned and deserve hell and that since Christ paid the penalty for all, He alone is the Savior. If someone does not understand the right facts, he cannot be saved until he does. Therefore, the first step in gospel diagnostics is to discern what a person understands regarding sin, righteousness, and judg-ment. The gospel diagnostician must always begin by discover-ing whether a person understands the three major truths of the gospel message to sinners. Questions help reveal what a person does or does not understand.

For example, consider the following diagnostic case. An evan-gelist met a lady visiting a church service. He asked her whether she knew that her sins were forgiven and that she possessed eternal life. She responded that she did. Then he asked what she was depending on to know this. She replied, "I believe in Jesus." He then asked, "Anything else?" She exclaimed, "Oh, yes! You must be baptized too." From a diagnostic standpoint, it is clear that this lady had a split trust. Therefore, it is legitimate to con-clude that she was not yet saved because she did not under-stand the fact of salvation by grace through faith in Christ alone.

The evangelist then showed the lady verses along the lines of John 6:47. When she saw the repeated emphasis on Jesus as the sole object of faith, she exclaimed with surprise, "I've never believed in Jesus!" After further explanation, she bowed her head and called on Christ alone to save her.[2]

Agreement (Affections)

The second side of the triangle of the soul of man represents the affections that must personalize the facts understood. Diagram 7.2 pictures this personalization.

Diagram 7.2. Gospel Diagnostics: Agreement

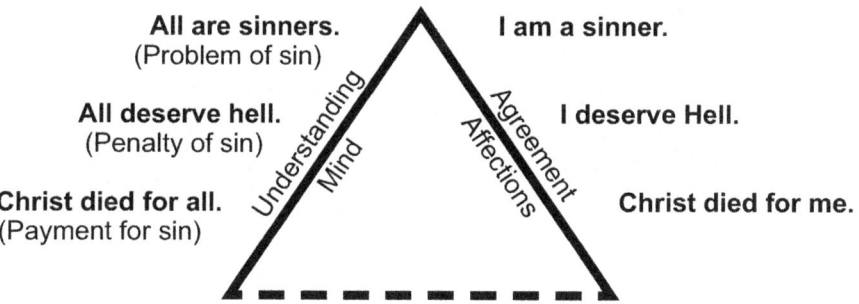

True faith for salvation must not only understand the right facts but also have a personal agreement with those facts. If someone does not agree with the facts (problem, penalty, payment) even though he understands them, he cannot be saved until he does. Therefore, the second step in gospel diagnostics is to discern whether or not someone agrees with the facts.

For example, consider the following diagnostic case. In a local church revival meeting an evangelist met an older gentleman who

_____
2. Taken from personal experience.

had just begun to attend that particular church. The gentleman turned ninety years old during the week of meetings, but he was in good health with a keen mind. The pastor informed the evangelist that the man was not yet saved and that they were praying for his salvation. In speaking with the gentleman, the evangelist discovered that the man clearly understood the facts of salvation as presented in the Bible. However, he did not agree that Jesus Christ is God.

From a diagnostic standpoint, it is clear that this man had not personalized who Christ is. Since Christ's person and work is the heart of the good news, it is fair to conclude that this man was not saved, even though he understood the biblical facts of salvation. His obstacle was a lack of agreement with a key fact. The deity of Christ is vital to Christ being able to be the Savior of the world.

Through a focused intercession and further gospel witness, the Holy Spirit did His convincing work. On Friday night after the service, the man said he was willing to trust Christ. When he prayed to express faith in Christ, his first words were "God, I thank you for convincing me that Jesus is God!"[3]

Dependence (Will)

The third side of the triangle represents the will that must be exercised in truly believing on Jesus. Diagram 7.3 pictures this volitional choice.

To understand the right facts and even agree with them is believing *about* Jesus. However, someone is not believing *in* Jesus until he depends *on* Jesus as his Savior. Although a right understanding and agreement are necessary, to understand and agree without depending on Christ is easy-believism—not true salvation. Prayer is often the expression of faith for salvation, but sometimes people go through the motions of prayer without actually trusting Christ to save them. Some say words without

---

3. Ibid.

Diagram 7.3. Gospel Diagnostics: Dependence

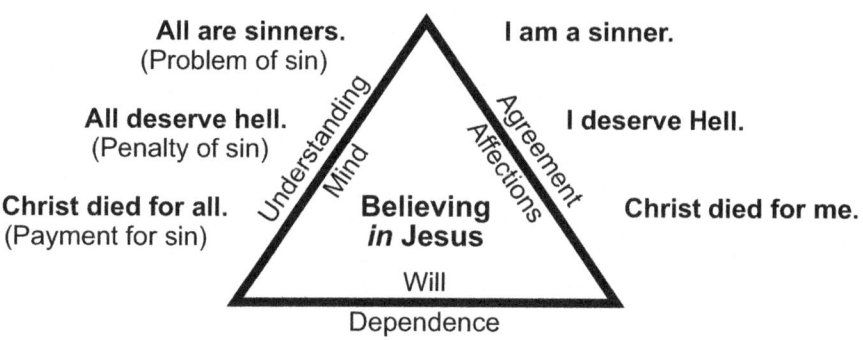

I depend on Christ to save me from sin and hell.

depending on Christ to actually do what He promised to do in saving them from sin and hell. If someone does not make the volitional transfer of dependence to Christ as Savior, he is not saved until he does. Therefore, the third step in gospel diagnostics is to discern whether or not someone has transferred his dependence to Christ to actually save him from sin and hell.

Since this point of the will is so vital, consider the following two diagnostic cases. First, an evangelist was witnessing to a couple at a park. The young lady seemed to have a clear testimony of salvation. However, the young man said that he understood and agreed but had never fully placed his trust in Christ to save him.

From a diagnostic standpoint, it is clear that this man believed *about* Jesus but had not yet believed *in* Jesus. He understood the right facts. He even gladly agreed with them. But, by his own admission, he had never experienced the transaction of faith. When challenged to do so, he bowed his head and, with tears, called on the name of the Lord.[4]

---

4. Ibid.

Second, an evangelist spoke with a man who had indicated by his raised hand during an invitation that he was not saved, but who had not responded beyond that. As the conversation began, the man said he had been "saved" when he was sixteen but that he was unsure of his spiritual condition. The evangelist asked, "When you were sixteen, did you have a basic understanding that you were a sinner?" He replied, "Yes." The evangelist asked, "Did you have a basic understanding that you were headed to hell?" Again, he replied, "Yes." The evangelist queried further. "Did you have a basic understanding that Jesus died for your sins, rose again, and offers you salvation?" Without hesitating, he replied, "Yes." (This addresses the first side of the triangle.) The evangelist then asked, "Did you agree with what you understood?" He answered, "Yes." (This addresses the second side of the triangle.) Finally, the evangelist questioned, "The best you knew, did you depend on Christ to actually save you from sin and hell?" (This addresses the third side of the triangle.) This time the man replied, "No." Upon further clarification, he said that although he had prayed as a young man, he had not actually trusted Christ to save him. He, more or less, hoped God would save him, but he had no sense of actually trusting Christ to save him, based on the promises.

From a diagnostic standpoint, based on this man's testimony, it appears that the volitional transfer of trust was lacking. Therefore, it is fair to conclude that he was not yet born again. He could be misstating reality; but based on his own testimony, he lacked faith in Christ as Savior.

When the evangelist emphasized taking God at His Word and challenged the man simply to trust Christ based on the promises, the man prayed, asking Christ to save him. He seemed joyous at the thought that God did what He promised, forgiving his sins and giving him eternal life.[5]

In summary, if a person does not understand the right facts, he is not saved. If he understands but does not agree with the

5. Ibid.

facts, he is not saved. Or if he understands and agrees but has never depended on Christ as Savior, he is not saved. Once the gospel diagnostician has discerned one's spiritual condition regarding salvation, he can prescribe the biblical remedy according to the need.

God's Promise: Having Eternal Life
"Hath everlasting life"

The moment one begins to believe in Jesus as Savior, he has (or begins having) eternal life. Since eternal life is forever, it is quite impossible to have eternal life for only a little while. Although one may doubt his salvation, if he, in fact, believed in Jesus as Savior, he has eternal life according to the multiplied promises of the gospel. Also, since Jesus is "that eternal life" (I John 1:2; cf. 5:20), when one receives eternal life, he receives Christ. The Spirit of Christ indwells the new believer. The regenerated spirit of the new believer is united to the Eternal Life. Since "he that is joined unto the Lord is one spirit" (I Cor. 6:17), God never cuts Himself off. The believer eternally possesses eternal life. This is true eternal security.

Assurance

How can someone know he is saved? The answer is found in the sure promises of the gospel. The focus of the classic assurance text in I John 5:11-13 emphasizes the object of faith with the words "And this is the record [testimony]." The key to assurance is focusing on God's promises in the gospel. The Apostle John, under inspiration, reviews the promises from his Gospel account: "And this is the record, that God hath given to us eternal life, and this life is in his Son. He that hath the Son hath [the] life; and he that hath not the Son of God hath not [the] life.[6] These things have I written unto you that believe on the name of the Son of God; that ye may know that ye have eternal life." The Apostle John reviewed the gospel promises for the purpose of cultivating assurance. The condition is focusing on the promises, and the promise is knowing that one has eternal life. Therefore, regarding the issue of assurance, man's responsibility is the focus of faith, and God's promise is the promise of knowing one has eternal life.

Before addressing the issue of assurance, two common misconceptions must be exposed. First, some think that it is impossible to have eternal life and not know it. However, when the Apostle John states "These things have I written unto you that believe on the name of the Son of God," he is indicating that he is writing to those who not only believe *about* Jesus but who believe *on* Jesus. Therefore, they have eternal life according to the promise of John 6:47. Yet he further states that he is writing "that [they] may know that [they] have eternal life." Since they have already believed on Jesus, they already have eternal life. But John is writing that they may *know* that they *have* eternal life. The point of his writing is that they might have the assurance of actually having eternal life.

A second common misconception is that if someone senses conviction that he needs to get saved, the conviction must be from the Holy Spirit and therefore he must need to get saved. However, this thinking does not take into account all the possibilities. It is true that if a lost person senses conviction that he needs to get saved, then the Holy Spirit must be the one convicting him of his need (John 16:8). But if a saved person (one who has understood, agreed, and depended on Christ as Savior) senses "conviction" that he needs to get saved, then it is a counterfeit conviction. It is to Satan's advantage to get a saved person to doubt his salvation. For when a born-again Christian has a season

---

6. The definite article inserted in the brackets is actually in the Greek text. Again, this reveals that Jesus is the Eternal Life.

of doubt, he is rendered useless in God's cause. He loses his joy since he is not sure that he is saved. He forfeits victory over sin since in doubting his salvation, he is in unbelief rather than faith and faith is the victory (I John 5:4). Also, he is ineffective in gospel witness, since he is not even sure that he is saved himself. Satan is a deceiver and a destroyer (John 8:44). He deceives the unsaved by giving them a false assurance, and he deceives the saved by giving them counterfeit conviction. Satan attempts to deceive the unsaved by telling them that they are saved, and he attempts to deceive the saved by telling them that they are not saved. Therefore, not all "conviction" is from the Holy Spirit.

Man's Responsibility: The Focus of Faith
"And this is the record"

The key to faith is not the subject of faith, but the object of faith. The object of faith is God, based on His Word. Man must believe on Jesus as Savior, based on the gospel promises. "Faith cometh by hearing, and hearing by the word [*rhema*/promises] of God" (Rom. 10:17). Therefore the key to assurance of salvation is to focus on "the record" of "the word of God." Assurance is by faith in the finished work of Christ founded on the sure Word of God.

Lack of assurance arises when someone switches focus from the object of faith to the subject (himself). Generally, this focus is either on one's Christian performance or one's salvation prayer. Regarding Christian performance, many wonder why they still continue to sin. They conclude that they are not saved and that if they could just get "really saved" (as if there is a difference), then they would experience victory. However, *victory is not automatic when one gets saved; it is by faith*. This will be discussed in more detail under the issue of revival. Regarding the salvation prayer, many people say things such as, "I'm not sure I really meant it," or "I'm not sure I said all the right words," or "I'm not sure I really sorrowed over my sin." However, focusing on the subject of faith is self-dependence. While it is true that the diagnostic questions "Did you understand? agree? depend?" involve the subject, the focus is on the object: "Did you understand, agree, depend—*on the right facts?*" The problem comes when someone subtly shifts focus from the object to the subject of faith. This wrong focus may produce a lack of assurance of salvation.

In either case of focusing on one's Christian performance for assurance or focusing on one's salvation prayer, the biblical remedy is to focus on the sure Word of God.

Consider the following diagnostic cases. An evangelist was asked to deal with a young man in his early twenties who regularly came forward at invitation times doubting his salvation. The evangelist showed the young man John 6:47: "He that believeth on me hath everlasting life." Looking the man in the eye, the evangelist asked if there had ever been a time when he had understood that he was a sinner headed to hell and that Christ was his only hope [understanding]. Had he therefore [agreement] placed his dependence on Christ alone to save him [dependence]. The man emphatically replied, "Yes!" The evangelist then asked, "Well, what do you have?" A blank stare was the man's only response. So the evangelist pointed to the words "hath everlasting life" and said, "You can depend on it. You can count on it. You can *know* it! Why?" Again, there was a blank stare. So pointing back to the words "hath everlasting life," the evangelist said, "Because it says so!" A smile slowly broke over the man's troubled face like a rainbow after the storm. With an "Ah!" of enlightenment, the man exclaimed, "Because it says so!" By focusing on the sure Word, he received assurance.[7]

The following case provides even more insight as a diagnostic study. An evangelist preached on a Sunday morning from John 3:1–18 on the new birth. Among the several that indicated a need to be born again was the wife of the music director in the church.

_____
7. Taken from personal experience. This scenario has been repeated many times.

She and her husband had attended a good Bible college. She was taken out for personal counsel, and before the service closed, she returned. The pastor announced that she had struggled with whether or not she was saved and so had trusted Christ as her Savior. While many rejoiced, the evangelist was uneasy. He had preached a simple gospel message that was not of the nature to cause saved people to doubt their salvation. Also, he knew enough of the young lady's background to know that she may have heard the kind of preaching that could cause a saved person to doubt his salvation.[8] Knowing that those who begin to doubt their salvation usually get disturbed whenever a gospel message is preached, the evangelist suspected that this young wife was most likely saved but in need of assurance.

Therefore, he asked the husband if he might ask his wife a few questions. The three met together a few nights later after a service. The evangelist asked the young lady whether she had ever prayed to trust Christ before. She answered that she had prayed many times, which is what the evangelist had suspected. Upon asking when was the first time she had prayed to trust Christ, she replied that it was when she was a child in elementary school.

So the evangelist began to ask gospel diagnostic questions: "When you prayed the first time, did you have a basic understanding that you were a sinner?" She emphatically replied, "Yes!" "Did you have a basic understanding that you deserved hell?" Again, she emphatically answered, "Yes!" "Did you have a basic understanding that since Christ died for your sins and rose again, that He is the Savior?" This was followed by another emphatic "Yes!"

---

8. Preaching that makes saved people doubt their salvation has come to be known as "get-lost preaching." While it is true that unsaved people must understand their lost condition before they can get saved, "get-lost preaching" can make truly saved people think that they are lost. In the sincere attempt to see lost people get saved, the gospel has sometimes been confused so as to also uproot the saints. Of all people, evangelists must keep the gospel crystal clear.

From a diagnostic standpoint, the young wife had, as a child, understood salvation facts. So the evangelist continued, "The best you knew, did you agree with the facts you understood?" Again, she responded emphatically, "Yes!"

From a diagnostic standpoint, this young lady had also, as a child, agreed with the salvation facts she had understood. Therefore, the evangelist then queried, "Did you, the best you knew how, depend on Jesus Christ to save you from sin and hell?" Once again, she replied in earnest, "Yes!"

From a diagnostic standpoint based on this lady's testimony, she had believed on Jesus in simple childlike faith and therefore had eternal life. Pointing to the Bible, the evangelist said, "That's all there is to it!" Then he asked her, "What caused you to doubt?" She answered, "I'm not sure I really meant it." This is focusing on one's salvation prayer, as noted previously. Also, she said, "And I'm not effective at leading people to Christ." This is focusing on one's Christian performance. She explained that she had some lost loved ones and wanted to see them saved. Since she was ineffective in reaching her loved ones, she concluded that perhaps she was not saved. She felt that if she could just get saved, then she would be effective in reaching them. Interestingly, that very burden for the lost was actually an evidence of salvation.

This young lady lacked assurance because she focused on her performance and her prayer, both of which focus on the subject of faith rather than the object. The evangelist continued, "Suppose you were drowning at sea. As you struggle up for what you think will be your last breath, you see a rescue boat nearby. So you cry out, 'Help!' What did you do? You transferred your dependence from your own self-struggle to someone who could help you." The evangelist continued, "You don't have to ask, 'Did I say "Help" right?'" At this point in the illustration, the young wife began to laugh. The evangelist continued, "You don't have to ask, 'I wonder if I really meant it?'" Then she began to cry. The evangelist continued further. "You don't have to ask, 'I wonder if there was enough emotion in my voice?'" By this time, the young lady was laughing and crying—laughing because she realized the foolishness of her error and crying because this lack of assurance had been such a traumatic issue in her life.

The evangelist explained that the key to assurance is the focus of faith and that she simply needed to focus on promises such as John 6:47—"He that believeth on me hath everlasting life"—because it says so. The young lady's joy returned, and she imbibed revival truth during the remainder of the meeting.[9] Revival truth demands faith, and someone cannot move forward in the life of faith until faith regarding the matter of assurance is settled. Therefore assurance of salvation is vital.

Salvation has never been based on how well someone performs. Salvation is always based on the sure Word of God. When someone believes on Jesus, he has eternal life—because the Bible promises it. Just as justification is by faith and sanctification is by faith, so likewise assurance is by faith.

God's Promise: Knowing One Has Eternal Life
"That ye may know [assurance] that ye have [actuality] eternal life"

When someone has understood salvation facts, agreed with them, and depended on Christ as Savior, that person has eternal life because the Bible, the sure Word, promises it. Assurance, therefore, arises when one focuses on "the record" of the sure Word. The promise of this Word-centered focus is "that ye may know that ye have eternal life."

The only infallible test of assurance is the infallible Word of God. Assurance comes from the "sure Word" (2 Pet. 1:19). All other tests of assurance are fallible. Other tests are helpful if they are

---

9. Taken from personal experience.

secondary to the primary test of the *sure Word*. However, if other tests are made primary, they can hinder rather than help because they are not infallible tests. Subjective tests, although valid, must be secondary to the objective test of the Word of God.

What about "evidence"? Although it is vitally important for a believer to demonstrate evidence of his salvation, the evidence "tests" are fallible. In fact, unsaved moralists can pass some evidence tests.

For example, some preachers say that if a person is truly saved, he will have a love for the Bible and will therefore read his Bible and go to church regularly. However, some unsaved moralists read the Bible, say prayers, and go to church every day. Therefore, the way to determine that an unsaved moralist is not saved is not an evidence test. Rather, the way to determine that an unsaved moralist is not saved is that he does not understand salvation facts. He believes in a works-salvation and is not depending on Jesus as Savior.

Yet some persist in making evidence tests *primary*. They maintain that if a person is truly saved, he will not habitually sin. Although they admit that a Christian may stumble, they maintain that he will not live in habitual sin. However, how can one infallibly define *habitual*? How much habitual sin cancels evidence? What if a Christian sins only once per day? Is this habitual? When faced with this obvious dilemma, some respond with discrepancies such as, "Well, what I mean is that if someone is a murderer or an adulterer, he can't be saved. As for me, well, I've just been bitter for twenty years!" The categorization of grosser sins and glossed-over sins can, at times, be humorous.[10]

---

10. Kevin Schaal, *From Law to Grace Keeping Mutually Dependent Concepts Distinct*. A paper presented at the Lansdale Leadership Conference, February 26, 2002. Schaal carefully explains, "We send a mixed signal concerning the law when we make any pet habit or lack thereof the litmus test for the veracity of a person's salvation. . . . We send mixed signals concerning the law and grace when we communicate that backsliding or sin is an impossibility for a true believer, or that a true believer might backslide but will never remain in that state. This is contrary to clear New Testament passages (Acts 5:1-11, I Corinthians 5:5, I Corinthians 11:30, and more). Certainly a changed life is an outward indication of a changed heart, but it is also possible for a believer to live in the flesh for a time—even till death. Certainly this type of person will face chastisement

Every Christian ought to have, and can have, evidence of his salvation by faith in the indwelling Christ. But *evidence is not automatic; it is by faith.* As salvation is not automatic but by faith, even so evidence of salvation through spiritual growth is not automatic but by faith. "Without faith it is impossible to please him" (Heb. 11:6). Growing in grace demands walking by faith (Rom. 5:2).

Real evidence comes through continual dependence on Christ. This continual dependence is abiding in Christ. Jesus said, "I am the vine, ye are the branches: He that abideth in me, and I in him, the same bringeth forth much fruit; for without me ye can do nothing" (John 15:5). If "without me ye can do nothing," then "with Me ye can do everything (you ought to do)." Jesus is defining *abiding* as continual dependence on Him. To be in Christ is to be saved. To abide in Christ is to be Spirit-filled because God-dependence (faith) accesses Spirit-enablement (grace). Without God-dependence for Spirit-enablement, true evidence is impossible, but by abiding in Christ, true evidence will be manifest as Christ abides in the believer, enabling the abiding one with His divine life." Evidence is actually evidence of the Spirit-filled life.

Every believer still faces the battle between the flesh and the Spirit (Gal. 5:17). A difficulty lies in the fact that unsaved flesh and saved flesh look the same. When a believer yields to the flesh, the works of the flesh are manifest (Gal. 5:19–21). When a believer yields to the Spirit, the fruit of the Spirit is manifest (Gal. 5:22–23). Therefore, the same person, even though he is regenerated, can "evidence" the works of the flesh or the fruit of the

---

as a son (even to point of death) and true conviction of the Spirit (Hebrews 12). But it is also true that he can quench the work of the Spirit in his heart."

11. Some mistakenly think that abiding is automatic to all believers. However, in John 15, Jesus acknowledges that the eleven disciples are "clean through the word" (John 15:3). That Christ is referring to salvation is clear by noting that just hours earlier, before Judas left the upper room, He said, "ye are clean, but not all" (John 13:10). After acknowledging that the disciples were already true believers in John 15:3, Jesus commanded in the next verse, "Abide in me, and I in you." Logically, if abiding was an automatic given for everyone who is saved, then Jesus would not need to command His disciples to *abide* in Him.

Spirit, depending on whether or not he makes choices of surrender and faith or choices of unsurrender and unbelief. This is why
Paul under inspiration urges the Galatian saints to make the right
choices of faith.

Change is God's plan for every believer—transformation into
the image of Christ (2 Cor. 3:18). However since change is primarily
manifested as one walks by faith and thus grows in grace, change
is not an absolute form of assurance. Yet it is a blessed secondary support. The key is to be careful to keep evidence tests secondary, since they are fallible.

Absolute assurance (objective assurance) in I John is through
the absolute Word (I John 5). But experiential assurance (subjective assurance) in I John is through the evidences of the Spirit-filled
life of abiding in Christ (I John 2–4). It is of no small significance
that *meno*, the word often translated "abide," occurs in I John 2–4
well over twenty times. This fact emphasizes that the evidences of
I John come through abiding in Christ, which, of course, means
that one is saved; for one cannot abide in Christ unless he is, first
of all, in Christ. Lack of evidence means one of two things, not
one of one. Lack of evidence could mean one is not saved since
one cannot abide in Christ unless he is in Christ. Or it could
mean one is saved but not abiding and is in need of revival. If this
latter condition is not diagnosed accurately, then one's real need
of revival may not be addressed.

If one who has been saved but is faltering in growth is not
diagnosed accurately and is led to get "saved again," it produces
confusion. For example, after a youth rally one teen exclaimed,
"Forty Christians got saved!" Now, do the ones who got "saved
again" get baptized again? And what happens when they find that
they keep sinning? Do they get "saved again"? Actually, when
those who have understood, agreed with, and depended upon
Jesus as Savior but are defeated in their Christian walk get "saved

again" (which is impossible), they are taking a step backward into unbelief because they are doubting that God did what He promised. Each time they get "saved again" in hopes of automatic transformation, they spiral downward into the abyss of unbelief.

Getting "saved again" confuses the real need of revival. If a saved person goes through the motions of getting saved again, then the real need of revival is not addressed. In fact, revival is actually undermined because the problem was not that a person was unregenerated but rather that he was walking "after the flesh" (Rom. 8:4) and therefore unsurrendered. Some who go through the motions of getting saved again view getting "saved again" or getting "really saved" as a quick fix for a defeated life when the real answer is walking the revival road.

If a person is misdiagnosed, then he does not receive the real help he needs. A man testified that when an evangelist preached to his church's youth group, half of the teens "got saved" again. He said it took one year for his son to recover and that other teens have never recovered and are completely defeated.[12] The problem was that some of the young people who got "saved again" actually needed revival.

Assurance is vital before one can ever move on to living the abundant life. Unwavering assurance arises from an unwavering focus on the sure promises of God. The evidences of the abiding life (I John 2–4) are blessed as a secondary assurance and as such are a great comfort. But since no one is perfect in the walk of faith, this subjective assurance is fallible. "If we receive the witness of men, the witness of God is greater . . . And this is the record" (I John 5:9–11). Objective assurance is found in the solid foundation of God's objective Word. Man's responsibility, therefore, is the focus of faith on the objective Word. God's promise is "that ye may know that ye have eternal life."

---

12. Taken from a personal conversation.

Revival

How can one live his salvation? Jesus said, "I am come that they might have life, and that they might have it more abundantly" (John 10:10). How can one live *abundantly*? The gospel to saints (detailed in Chapter 6) delineates three facts for sanctification that must be understood, personalized, and depended upon. This continuing message of the gospel is summarized in Colossians 2:6: "As ye have therefore received Christ Jesus the Lord, so walk ye in him." Christ is received by faith (John 1:12; 6:47); therefore, to "walk . . . in him" is to walk by faith. Regarding the issue of revival, man's responsibility is the walk of faith, and God's promise is living the abundant life.

Man's Responsibility: The Walk of Faith
"So walk ye in him"

The pathway of the revival road to access the abundant life of Christ involves both walking in the light as the means to deal with sin and walking in the Spirit as the means to keep from sin.

Walking in the Light: Confession and Faith (I John 1: 7, 9)

Although the truth of walking in the light can be greatly expanded, stated simply, the pathway of walking in the light demands two steps. The first step is confession. "If we confess our sins" (I John 1:9*a*) means "to say the same thing" as God says about one's sin.[13] That is to own the sin without making any excuses. Shifting blame is walking in darkness as one seeks to cover his tracks; whereas, walking in the light is real and sometimes painful honesty about one's sin before God and man (where

---

13. Fritz Rienecker and Cleon L. Rogers, *A Linguistic Key to the Greek New Testament* (Grand Rapids: Zondervan Bible Publishers, 1980), 786.

appropriate).[14] The second step is faith based on the promise "he is faithful and just to forgive us our sins, and to cleanse us from all unrighteousness." When thorough confession has been made, one must depend on the reality that God has truly forgiven and truly cleansed—because it says so.

Walking in the light is not sinless perfection; it is immediate confession. Immediate confession accesses immediate forgiveness. Therefore, the highway of holiness is the highway of lowliness as one learns to respond to the Holy Spirit's convicting light by quickly taking the steps of confession and faith.

Walking in the Spirit: Surrender and Faith (Gal. 5:16)

Galatians 5:16 says, "Walk in the Spirit, and ye shall not fulfill the lust of the flesh." The pathway of walking in the Spirit also demands two steps. The two steps are surrender and faith. These two steps are implied in Colossians 2:6. Since the Scripture clarifies, "As ye have therefore received Christ Jesus the Lord, so walk ye in him," the way to "walk . . . in him" or "walk in the Spirit" is the same way one "received Christ." One receives Christ by surrendering to the conviction of the Holy Spirit about sin, righteousness, and judgment, thus casting his dependence on Christ as Savior. Therefore, one walks in the Spirit by surrendering to the leadership of the Holy Spirit about the next step and depending on His enablement to take the step. Then "ye shall not fulfill the lust of the flesh" through the abundant life of Christ accessed by faith.

God's Promise: A Clean Heart and a Filled Life

When someone walks in the light, God promises to forgive, to cleanse, and to restore to fellowship (1 John 1:7, 9). This is

14. Roy Hession, *The Calvary Road* (Fort Washington, PA: Christian Literature Crusade Publications, reprint ed., 2006). Hession, from the revival in Rwanda, expands on the concept of walking in the light in a truly enlightening way in this classic, which has sold millions.

the clean heart. When someone walks in the Spirit, God promises victory over sin (Gal. 5:16). This is the filled life. Walking in the light is how to deal with sin. Walking in the Spirit is how to keep from sin. When one stumbles from the pathway of walking in the Spirit, he must immediately walk in the light. Then through the cleansing power of the blood of Jesus, he can return to walking in the Spirit. This is, in simple form, the revival road.

A man testified that he had trusted Christ but did not know how to grow spiritually. Since his life was largely one of defeat, he was often told that he was not saved. But going through the motions of getting saved again never brought him to a place of victory. Finally he despaired and dropped out of church for about ten years. This wrong choice led to a life of enslavement to sin. However, in the goodness of God he came into contact with a ministry that taught him how to access the victorious life of Christ. Through faith choices he began to grow spiritually. By God's grace he is a revived and thus a changed man.[15] If he had been diagnosed accurately to begin with and given the correct remedy, perhaps ten years of his life would not have been lost.

Conclusion

The evangelist must be a gospel diagnostician in order to discern the gospel prescription needed.

Table 7.2 overviews gospel prescriptions.

In seeking to diagnose someone's spiritual need, the evangelist must always begin with the gospel to sinners and discern whether or not someone has understood salvation facts, agreed with them, and depended upon Christ as Savior. The starting point is always one's understanding (doctrine). Once the issue of salvation is clearly settled, then the evangelist can proceed

---

15. Taken from a personal conversation.

Table 7.2. Gospel Prescription Chart

Issue	Spiritual Need	Gospel Remedy
Salvation	How can one be saved?	The Gospel to Sinners
Assurance	How can one know he is saved?	The Promises of the Gospel
Revival	How can one live his salvation?	The Gospel to Saints

Issue	Man's Responsibility	God's Promise
Salvation	The Choice of Faith (John 6:47)	Having eternal life
Assurance	The Focus of Faith (I John 5:11-13; Rom. 10:17)	Knowing one has eternal life
Revival	The Walk of Faith (Col. 2:6; I John 1:7, 9; Gal. 5:16)	Living the abundant life of a clean heart and filled life

to deal with assurance (if the problem is doubt) or revival (if the problem is defeat).

For example, if a person claims to be saved but looks and acts like the world, the gospel diagnostician must begin with the gospel and discern whether or not this person is saved. If he is not saved, then he must be led to Christ (gospel to sinners). If he clearly testifies to a saving faith but looks and acts like the world, then he is defeated and his obvious need is revival. Thus, he must be confronted with the need to walk in the light for cleansing and in the Spirit for victory (gospel to saints).[16]

If a person looks "good" but does not know whether or not he is saved, the gospel diagnostician must again begin with the gospel and discern whether or not he is saved. If he is not saved, then he must be led to Christ (gospel to sinners). If he clearly testifies to saving faith but doubts his salvation, his obvious need is assurance. Therefore, he must be pointed to the sure promises of the gospel where absolute assurance is found.

Having examined the distinctions between salvation, assurance, and revival, it may be helpful to apply gospel diagnostics to a few case studies. The goal of examining these true stories is to discern whether the real need was salvation, assurance, or revival. The order will be varied.

The first case study regards an unsaved older teen who had grown up in a non-Christian home with an alcoholic father. Although the teen had typical baggage from the world, when confronted with the gospel, he trusted Christ as his Savior. Then his alcoholic dad, after hearing the gospel, also trusted Christ to save him. The father quit drinking, started attending a Bible-preaching church, and began to grow spiritually. But after some time he took a drink—and "crashed" spiritually, going back to his alcoholism. The son, then in Bible college, phoned his dad and said, "Dad, you're a Christian. Christians don't drink." At first, his dad was angry. But later he called his son, admitting that he was a Christian and that he should not be drinking. So he got right with God, returned to the church, and began to grow spiritually again.[17]

---

16. If he rejects revival truth, especially over time, one may legitimately wonder if he is being honest about truly believing in Christ. Yet it is possible to be "saved; yet so as by fire" (I Cor. 3:15). Certainly there are times when only the righteous Judge knows the true condition of one's heart.

17. Account taken from a conversation.

Was this salvation, assurance, or revival? From a diagnostic standpoint, since the father had heard the gospel and trusted Christ, his real need was revival. If the son had said, "Dad, Christians don't drink. Since you're drinking, you're not a Christian," his father would have been misdiagnosed and would not have received the real help he needed. Getting "saved again" would have missed his real need to come clean about yielding to his flesh.

A second case study occurred when an evangelist preached at a teen camp. One night he announced that he was going to preach a salvation message. The next day a camp counselor, who was a preacher boy in Bible college, told the evangelist, "When you announced that you were going to preach a salvation message, I thought to myself, 'Am I going to doubt my salvation again?'" (This reveals he was used to hearing "gospel" messages that caused him to doubt his salvation). Then he proceeded to testify, "But about half-way through your message, I realized, 'I'm saved!'"[18]

Was this salvation, assurance, or revival? From a diagnostic standpoint, since the simple gospel caused this preacher boy to focus on gospel promises and since that focus revealed to him that he had received eternal life when he believed on Christ as his Savior, and since he then responded with joy, "I'm saved," this is a classic case of assurance.

A third case study took place when an evangelist preached in a certain church. He began the week preaching primarily to the saints for the first several days. After the Tuesday evening service, a deacon's wife called the pastor at 11:00 p.m. She asked if she and her husband could come over for some counsel. When they arrived, she explained that years before when her husband had gotten saved, she was thrilled something good was occurring in his life. She said he truly understood and got saved. But she went on to say that she did not understand but went through the motions of getting saved because she was excited for her

---

18. Taken from personal experience.

husband. With earnestness, she explained that through the years she had known all along that she was not saved. But now she was not able to continue without getting saved. So the pastor very simply declared the gospel and led her to Christ. She has rejoiced in her salvation ever since.[19]

Was this salvation, assurance, or revival? From a diagnostic standpoint, since this lady admitted that she did not understand the gospel at the time she prayed for salvation and had been troubled over the years, her real need was salvation.

When the "gospel" unsettles the saints with doubt, it is an unclear or imprecise gospel. The crystal clear gospel both comforts the saints and convicts the lost. Since the issues of salvation, assurance, and revival affect eternal destinies and effective lives, evangelists must discern the difference between these issues in order to diagnose accurately and then offer the correct spiritual remedy.

---

19. Ibid.

Chapter Eight

THE FOUNDATIONAL ISSUE
OF FAITH/REPENTANCE

*"And saying, The time is fulfilled, and the kingdom
of God is at hand: repent ye, and believe the gospel."*
Mark 1:15
*"As ye have therefore received Christ Jesus the Lord,
so walk ye in him: Rooted and built up in him,
and stablished in the faith, as ye have been taught,
abounding therein with thanksgiving."*
Colossians 2:6–7

Down through the centuries, theological extremes have produced theological extremes. The needed confrontation of one
extreme often produces a reaction that takes on the opposite
extreme. Certainly the gospel has not been exempt from this
pendulum effect. What does one need to know in order to
be saved? What constitutes in simple form the transaction of
salvation?[1] Where and how does the process of spiritual growth
fit into this picture?

---

1. Although some of this emphasis was explained in Chapter 5 dealing with "The
Gospel to Sinners," the review here is necessary in order to more thoroughly address
faith and repentance.

Jesus said, "Repent ye, and believe the gospel." Colossians 2:6–7 further instructs, "As ye have therefore received Christ Jesus the Lord, so walk ye in him: Rooted and built up in him, and stablished in the faith." The "walk" of spiritual growth is similar to how one "received Christ." How does someone "receive" Christ? John 1:12 answers this question explicitly by saying, "But as many as received him, to them gave he power to become the sons of God, even to them that believe on his name." Here "received him" is defined as "believe on his name." The issue is believing on Christ. Therefore, Colossians 2:6–7 teaches that the way one received Christ—by faith—is the way one grows spiritually—by faith. Since faith accesses grace (Eph. 2:8; Rom. 5:2), the walk of faith causes one to grow in grace (2 Pet. 3:18). The "walk . . . in him" is a walk of faith causing one to be "stablished in the faith." Therefore, faith (or faith/repentance) is the key issue for both salvation and spiritual growth.

The foundational issue of gospel extremes is one's understanding of faith/repentance. What is the proper understanding of faith and repentance? The Scripture unfolds four theological issues that provide the proper biblical balance of faith/repentance.

The Theological Essence of Faith and Repentance Is Similar

By focusing on each side of the theological coin of faith/repentance in the matter of salvation, the similarity of essence regarding faith and repentance is observed.

Faith

The verb *believe* simply means "to believe (in), trust."[2] The lexical wording *believe (in)* indicates more than a mental assent. It does not merely say "believe about." The wording *believe (in)* demands the idea of *trust* or *dependence.* "To depend on" articulates the key idea of the verb form. "To depend on" also implies one must choose to depend on. This choice of dependence is based on one's understanding and agreement with what is understood. Therefore, believing is volitional, or an act of the will, not just intellectual and affective. Systematic theology books and commentaries point out that there are three angles to believing: intellect (understanding), affections (agreeing), and volition (depending).[3]

What must one understand in order to be saved? Jesus said in John 16:8 that the Holy Spirit "will reprove the world of sin, and of righteousness, and of judgment." These same three truths are presented in the gospel declaration of I Corinthians 15:3: "Christ [righteousness] died [judgment] for our sins [sin]." Therefore, one must be convinced by the Holy Spirit of his sin, of his deserved judgment in hell, and of his need for the credited righteousness of Jesus Christ in order to be saved. Understanding these three truths is necessary for salvation. This involves the intellect. Heartfelt agreement with these truths is necessary for salvation. This involves the affections. However, to stop short with just understanding and agreement is not salvation.

2. William F. Arndt and F. Wilbur Gingrich, *A Greek-English Lexicon of the New Testament and Other Early Christian Literature,* 2nd ed. revised F. Wilbur Gingrich and Fredrick W. Danker (Chicago: University of Chicago Press, 1979), 661.

3. Charles Hodge, *Commentary on the Epistle to the Romans* (Grand Rapids: William B. Erdmans Publishing Company, 1967), 29. Louis Berkhof, *Systematic Theology* (Grand Rapids: William B. Erdmans Publishing Company, 1941), 503–5. As noted in Chapter 5, these three angles of the mind, the affections, and the will constitute the soul of man.

It would be an *acknowledgment-only* decision. Yet the demons acknowledge Christ. Luke 4:41 explains, "And devils also came out of many, crying out, and saying, Thou art Christ the Son of God." In that sense they believe about Christ. They even know that Jesus died and rose again. But obviously the demons are not on their way to heaven.

Many acknowledge Jesus Christ. They understand and agree with the basic truths of sin, righteousness, and judgment. But an acknowledgement-only "decision" without the volitional transfer of trust is not salvation. It is simply *easy-believism*.[4] It is the "one, two, three, repeat after me; slam, dunk, chalk 'em up on the charts" routine which gives people a false assurance of heaven. A lack of real emphasis on sin and judgment, dealing with it only in general terms, often produces this kind of shallow decision. True believing in Christ for salvation goes beyond the intellect and affections [acknowledgment] to the volition [dependence]. One must make the choice of transferring his dependence to Christ for salvation from sin and hell in order to be saved. This is as simple in a physical sense as a drowning person who, seeing a rescue boat going by, cries out, "Help!" and, therefore, is transferring his dependence from his own self-effort to someone else. In salvation, one transfers his dependence from his own self-effort to Christ.

The dependence must be only on Christ. To counter easy-believism, some have overreacted by embracing what has come to be known as "Lordship Salvation." The issue here is not whether or not Jesus is Lord. All sides of the debate within orthodoxy maintain the lordship of Christ. The issue revolves around what constitutes the "condition" of salvation. What exactly is man's responsibility in order to be saved?

---

4. The terminology *easy-believism* represents a decision that fails to actually transfer trust to Christ for salvation. However, the terminology is perhaps not the best choice of words. Since faith is not a work (Eph. 2:8–9; Rom. 4:5), in that sense it is "easy" to believe.

In countering easy-believism, the Lordship-Salvation position mistakenly goes beyond the volitional transfer of trust to Christ alone to an infringement on the finished work of Christ. For example, to say as some Lordship-Salvation proponents say that believing involves one's commitment to Christ to turn from or to be willing to turn from one's sinful life is making the person a part of the object of faith.[5] Believing is not one's commitment to Christ; it is one's dependence on Christ. The commitment to live right is a wrong dependence. The word *commitment* keeps the person making the commitment in control and, therefore still depending upon himself (his commitment). By contrast, the word *dependence* reveals the helplessness of the person depending because he is transferring his dependence to another. Galatians 3:24 clarifies this: "The law was our schoolmaster to bring us unto Christ, that we might be justified by faith." The law shows man he cannot meet God's standard of perfection and so brings him to Christ who met the standard for him. The law is a schoolmaster, not to bring man to reformation (self-dependence) but to Christ (God-dependence). Sin is the problem, but not sinning is not the solution—Christ is. The Lordship-Salvation position errs in adding ever-so-subtly to the object of dependence.

Some object, maintaining that believing involves surrender. This is certainly true if by *surrender* one means a yielding to the conviction of the Holy Spirit about sin, righteousness, and judgment so that one depends on Christ as Savior. Surrender must be viewed as dependence on Christ to do that which is impossible for

---

5. Millard J. Erickson, *Christian Theology* (Grand Rapids: Baker Books, 2002), 959. Erickson states, "The beginning of the Christian life requires a recognition of one's own sinfulness and a determination to abandon the self-centered way of life" and "Saving faith requires correct belief regarding the nature of God and what he has done. Correct belief is insufficient, however. There must also be active commitment of oneself to God." Erickson may be attempting to emphasize the volitional aspect of believing *in* Jesus, but words like *determination* and *active commitment* are not the same in meaning as *dependence*, and may unwittingly confuse the real meaning of faith.

man to do. True surrender in salvation is the obedience of faith. The obedience of faith for salvation is a cessation from works-dependence as one casts his dependence on the finished work of Jesus Christ. Romans 10:16 says, "But they have not all obeyed the gospel. For Isaiah saith, Lord, who hath believed our report?" In this context *obeyed* is explained as "believed." The obedience of faith for salvation is believing on Christ. However, although faith is obedience, faith is clearly not a work. Scripture states that faith is the antithesis of works. Ephesians 2:8–9 says, "For by grace are ye saved through faith . . . not of works." Faith is something man "does," but it is not a work. The Scripture is explicit on this point. Faith is obedience, but it is not a work. In this sense, faith/repentance is surrender and obedience. But faith in Christ is not a work, and if it is made a work, it is no longer faith. Romans 4:5 clarifies by saying, "But to him that worketh not, but believeth on him that justifieth the ungodly." To add one's commitment to live righteously to the transaction of salvation is to confuse "the simplicity that is in Christ" (2 Corinthians 11:3). Christ is the only one who saves, and He does all of the saving.

Repentance

The essence of believing or faith is to transfer one's dependence to Christ for salvation from sin and hell. What then is the essence of repentance? The verb *repent*, referring to salvation, is primarily from the Greek word *metanoeo*, which means "to change one's mind."[6] Since the Holy Spirit convinces the world regarding sin, righteousness, and judgment, the change of mind must be regarding these same three truths. To "repent" is to change one's mind about sin, about the need for Christ's righteousness, and about judgment in hell without it.

---

6. Arndt and Gingrich, 511.

Repent (*metanoeo*) comes from a compound word. The first word in the compound is *meta*, which, in this sense, means "after."[7] The second word in the compound is *noeo*, which means "perceive"[8] from the noun *nous*, which means "mind" or "way of thinking."[9] Therefore, *metanoeo* does mean "to change one's mind." As *metamorphosis* is a change of form, so *metanoia* (noun form of *metanoeo*) is a change of mind (way of thinking).

The issue is not just to understand in the mind (intellect) regarding sin, righteousness, and judgment, or even agree in the heart (affections), but to *change* one's mind (volition), trusting Christ (payment) to save from sin (problem) and hell (penalty). The issue of one's *mind* in repentance is one's *way of thinking*. One's way of thinking reveals what one perceives as absolute. It is one's grid of thinking which in that sense reflects what he is depending on. Therefore, *to change one's mind* is to exchange one's way of thinking, whether that be in regard to a false god (the religious idolater), works salvation (the self-righteous moralist), atheism, agnosticism, hedonism (the unrighteous sinner), or a combination.

As will be noted in the next major point, the emphasis of faith and repentance differs, but the essence is similar. *Believe* corresponds to *repent*, which means to change your thinking. There is a parallel with the understanding (mind), agreement (affections), and dependence (will) of believing in Jesus. *Thinking* corresponds to the understanding, *your* corresponds to the agreement, and *change* corresponds to the transfer of dependence. Therefore, faith and repentance are two sides of the same theological coin.[10]

---

7. Ibid., 510.

8. Ibid., 540.

9. Ibid., 544.

10. Henry C. Thiessen, *Lectures in Systematic Theology* (Grand Rapids: Wm. B. Eerdman's Publishing Company, 1981), 270. Thiessen explains, "True repentance never exists apart from faith. That is, one cannot turn from sin without at the same time turning to God. Conversely we may say that true faith never exists without repentance. The two are inseparably bound together." Berkhof states, "Moreoever, true repentance never exists except in conjunction with faith, while, on the other hand, wherever there

When one recognizes that his sin is taking him to hell and that Christ is his only hope (sin, judgment, righteousness), and then forsakes his wrong way of thinking by casting his dependence on Christ, he is repenting. The change of mind is about sin, righteousness, and judgment. Sin is the problem. Judgment is the consequence. Christ is the only Savior. Repentance abandons all wrong ways of thinking and trusts Christ alone for salvation from sin and hell.

To make repentance more than this exchange of ways of thinking is to make it something additional to the other side of the theological coin of faith. It makes two conditions for salvation, not one. Yet this violates Scripture. Acts 19:4 states, "Then said Paul, John verily baptized with the baptism of repentance, saying unto the people, that they should believe on him which should come after him, that is, on Christ Jesus." According to Paul, John the Baptist explained *repentance* as the choice to "believe on him . . . that is, on Christ Jesus." Thus, there is one condition for salvation, not two. When Peter explained the events at the house of Cornelius to the Jewish believers in Jerusalem, he said, "Forasmuch then as God gave them the like gift as he did unto us, who believed on the Lord Jesus Christ; what was I, that I could withstand God? When they heard these things, they held their peace, and glorified God, saying, Then hath God also to the Gentiles granted repentance unto life" (Acts 11:17–18). In this narrative "believed on the Lord Jesus Christ" corresponds to "repentance unto life." Again, the essence of faith and repentance must be similar.

Furthermore, while certain scriptural passages make clear the necessity of repentance for salvation (e.g., Luke 13:3; Acts 17:30),

---

is true faith, there is also real repentance. The two are but different aspects of the same turning—a turning away from sin in the direction of God" (Berkhof, 487). Augustus H. Strong, *Systematic Theology* (Valley Forge, PA: Judson Press, 1979), 836. Strong says, "Since repentance and faith are but different sides or aspects of the same act of turning, faith is as inseparable from repentance as repentance is from faith."

the Gospel of John speaks only of believing. And yet the Gospel of John was written "that ye might believe that Jesus is the Christ, the Son of God; and that believing ye might have life through his name" (John 20:31). Therefore, repentance must be in vital oneness with faith. Otherwise, one could not get saved through reading the Gospel of John, since John does not use the word *metanoeo* or *metanoia*. More specifically, one could not get saved through John 3:16. If this is the case, then Jesus did not thoroughly explain the gospel to Nicodemus.

The point is that when believing on Jesus is properly explained, then the concept of repentance is also being explained, even though the word may not be used. Conversely, when repentance is properly explained, then the concept of believing on Jesus is being explained as well, even though the terminology may not be used. For example, when Paul explains justification by faith in Romans, he does not use the verb *metanoeo* at all and uses *metanoia* only once (Rom. 2:5). It is not that Paul does not believe in repentance, for he does use the terminology in Acts. Rather, when Paul explains faith in Romans 1–5, he is explaining the concept of repentance.

The biblical study of the compounds of *metanoeo* and *metanoia* supports the definitions in the lexicon. This is not a case like "pineapple," which could be misleading when studying the two words of the compound. Rather, scriptural usage supports the definitions of "to change one's way of thinking" (verb) and "a change of way of thinking" (noun) regarding the problem of sin, the penalty of hell, and the payment of Christ.

To add something additional to the definition of *repent*, making repentance more than a turning to Christ for salvation from sin and hell, is to confuse the gospel. Jesus preached in Luke 13:3, "except ye repent, ye shall all likewise perish." Is this repentance more than a turning to Christ for salvation from sin and hell? It cannot be or salvation would be by works. But salvation is not by works (Eph. 2:8–9; Gal. 3:10–11; Titus 3:5). Therefore, *repent* must mean a turning to Christ for salvation from sin and judgment. Sin is the problem, but not sinning is not the solution—Christ is. Therefore, repentance is turning to Christ for deliverance from sin and its consequences.

The focus must always be on Christ, who is the sole object of dependence, whether the terminology employed is *faith* or *repentance*. In Acts 20:21 Paul described his ministry as "testifying both to the Jews, and also to the Greeks, repentance toward God, and faith toward our Lord Jesus Christ." His focus regarding both terminologies of *repentance* and *faith* was on the object of dependence. The focus of repentance as well as the focus of faith is on Christ as the answer to man's sin problem.

In contrast, some define *repentance* in a way that sounds like ceasing from sin or reformation. Phrases like "turning from sins" or "turning from sin" are used *without further clarification.* Some add the phrase "and turning to Christ," however, the emphasis of terminology is still primarily on turning from sins or sin, stated in a way that sounds like "to turn from committing sins" or "to stop sinning."[11]

---

11. Ralph Earle, *Word Meanings in the New Testament* (Grand Rapids: Baker Book House, 1989), 30. Earle states, "Deep repentance involves a real turnabout in life and prepares us to believe savingly in Jesus Christ." J. M. Lunde, "Repentance" in *New Dictionary of Biblical Theology,* eds. T. Edmond Alexander and Brian S. Rosner (Downers Grove: Inter-Varsity Press, 2000), 726–27. Lunde says, "All have turned away from God (Rom. 3:9–18), so there is a universal need for the corresponding turning away from sin (Rom. 2:5–10; 2 Cor. 12:21) and to God (1 Thess. 1:9; Acts 14:15; 15:19; 1 Pet. 2:25) . . . only those who have turned from their sinful ways will be forgiven." Both statements have confusing phrases like "turnabout in life" or "turned from their sinful ways" that sound like a works salvation. Leon Morris, *New Testament Theology* (Grand Rapids: Zondervan, 1990), 96. Morris says, "Repentance means that we abandon every evil way and opt to live radically new lives. Repentance means whole-hearted transformation. It is not the putting aside of a minor peccadillo or two. Jesus is calling for a reorientation of the whole life. This is further brought out in the call to believe the gospel. When God has spoken, those who hear must accept that divine word. This can be costly." It appears that Morris is confusing the *fruit* of repentance with the *turn* of repentance.

Is this not potentially confusing to an unsaved person whose human tendency is self-dependence (works) as a means of salvation? Does not "turning from sin(s)" without further clarification sound like reformation? But salvation is not by works.

Someone has mused, "If repent means turning from sins, why did Jesus die?" Christ died to save man from his sins because he cannot deal with his sins on his own. The terminology *turning from sin(s)* in some articulations of repentance sounds like "not sinning" or "doing good." Those who believe in salvation by grace through faith, and yet use these words do not mean what the terminology may convey to an unsaved person. Therefore, the meaning of repentance needs to be articulated more clearly.

For example, to say that in order to be saved one must "turn *and* trust," without further clarification, can be misleading. If the *trust* is one's moment of salvation (John 6:47), then what is the *turn*? The key is clarifying that the *turn* is the volitional *trust* in Christ for salvation from sin and hell. One's abandonment to Christ as Savior is the moment of faith/repentance. The *turn* to Christ is not reformation but rather the turn of trust for deliverance from the sin problem.

Repentance is entirely an *internal* issue. To whatever extent the Holy Spirit has convicted of sin(s), repentance is a dispositional change toward that sin(s), thus turning to Christ for deliverance from sin(s). In this sense there is a *turn*, but it is a turn of trust, not works.

The choice to turn to Christ as Savior is belief. The choice not to turn to Christ is unbelief. Practically speaking, the only sin that keeps a person out of heaven is unbelief (i.e., not depending on Christ). In John 16:9 Jesus said that the Holy Spirit convicts the world "of sin, because they believe not on me." Certainly *sins* reveal the root issue of the *sin* of unbelief. Yet the real issue is one's object of dependence, whether that is of the religious type or the irreligious. Every sin can be forgiven through faith in Jesus except the sin of not depending on Jesus as one's Savior.

In the sense of turning from sin as the problem leading to hell, repentance is the point of trust when one turns to Christ, who is life, from sin, which is death. But if one defines *repent* as "turning from sin(s)" without clarifying that the issue is "turning to Christ" for deliverance from sin because man cannot deal with sin on his own, it could be unclear and potentially misleading as it may imply to some that the turn would be actions (works). The articulation of the decision of faith/repentance must not in any way feed man's natural bent toward a meritorious salvation. However if one defines *repent* as "turning from sin(s)" with the clarification that the issue is "turning to Christ" because one now realizes his "lostness" due to sin, the definition has biblical validity.

The nature of one's wrong way of thinking will determine the details of the turn. For the religious idolater who is depending on a false god, faith/repentance for salvation is a ruing of the worthless idol, recognizing its deception, and an awakening to the worthiness of Christ. Therefore, the man flees to Christ as the one true God and Savior. First Thessalonians 1:9 reveals that the saints in Thessalonica had "turned to God from idols."

For the self-righteous moralist, faith/repentance for salvation is a ruing of self-righteousness as being "filthy rags" in God's sight and an awakening to the need for Christ's righteousness. Therefore, the man flees to Christ for true righteousness. Hebrews 6:1 clearly states "repentance from dead works, and of faith toward God."

For the unrighteous sinner, faith/repentance for salvation is a ruing of the life of sin or just not caring at all, realizing he is "undone," and an awakening to the mercy of God. Therefore, the man flees to Christ for mercy. In Luke 18:13 the publican cried out, "God be merciful to me a sinner." Clearly there is no sense of wanting God *and* sin(s).

Sometimes there is a mixture of the above. In all cases, there is an exchange of the wrong way of thinking for the right way of thinking. Therefore, repentance is a turning to Christ from whatever a person has been trusting in, whether false securities of the religious type (idolatry or works), or false securities of the irreligious type (atheism, agnosticism, materialism, hedonism, and so forth). Repentance is turning to that which the Holy Spirit has convicted of as the solution from that which the Holy Spirit has convicted of as the problem.

For example, in response to the question, "What must I do to inherit eternal life?" Jesus told the rich young ruler to sell his possessions, give to the poor, and follow Him. Is this a works-salvation? Not at all, rather Christ simply revealed this man's wrong object of dependence—his wealth. In fact, Christ explained this very point in Mark's account, by stating, "How hard it is for them that trust in riches to enter into the kingdom of God!" (Mark 10:24). The phrase "trust in riches" reveals that the issue is one's object of trust. In this case the trust involved placing a higher value on riches for satisfaction, rather than Christ (a short-sighted false security). Therefore, Christ challenged the rich young ruler to transfer his dependence from his wealth to Christ.

It is helpful in understanding repentance to recognize that the emphasis of Scripture is not turning from sin, but turning to Christ. Turning to Christ is primary, while turning from sin is a secondary corollary. This focus involves recognizing sin as the awful problem and hell as the sobering consequence but keeps the solution Christ-centered, unmixed with man's self-effort. This does not imply that sin does not need to be confronted, but all the more that sin must be confronted so that the law as a schoolmaster might point people to Christ. Sin must be presented as an unsolvable problem so that one recognizes the need for a miraculous salvation through Christ.

Acts 26:20 says, "Repent and turn to God." Here *epistrepho* ("turn") with "to God" is the explanation of *repent*. The phrase "turn to God" supports the understanding of repentance as being similar to faith. Also, *epistrepho*, the word for *turn*, is a key to understanding the scriptural *emphasis* of repentance.

Two times *epistrepho* is used explicitly with the concept of "from," in dealing with turning from the wrong object of dependence: "turn from these vanities [idols] unto the living God" (Acts 14:15), and "turned to God from idols" (1 Thess. 1:9). In addition *epistrepho* is used once with "from" in conveying the idea of turning from the satanic realm: "turn them from darkness to light, and from the power of Satan unto God" (Acts 26:18). These three "from" passages do not emphasize turning from sin but rather turning from the wrong trust to God.

Also, the verb *epistrepho* is repeatedly used in salvific contexts explicitly with only the concept of "to" in focusing on Christ as the Savior: "turn to the Lord" (Luke 1:16), "turned to the Lord" (Acts 9:35), "turned unto the Lord" (Acts 11:21), "turn . . . unto the living God" (Acts 14:15), "turned to God" (Acts 15:19), "turn . . . to light . . . unto God" (Acts 26:18), "turn to God" (Acts 26:20), "turn to the Lord" (2 Cor. 3:16), "turned to God" (1 Thess. 1:9), "returned unto the Shepherd and Bishop of your souls" (1 Pet. 2:25).

The explicit repeated emphasis of the scriptural usage of *epistrepho* is turning *to* the Lord, not *from* sin. This observation is an objective fact. Of these ten occurrences, eight use *epistrepho* with the preposition *epi* (Acts 9:35; 11:21; 14:15; 15:19; 26:18, 20; 1 Pet. 2:25) and two with the preposition *pros* (2 Cor. 3:16; 1 Thess. 1:9). The predominant usage of *epi*, which often means "upon," emphasizes that the turn of *epistrepho* in salvific contexts is a "turn of trust on the Lord."

The focus of repentance is a turning to Christ, which is essentially faith. In fact, Acts 11:21 uses *epistrepho* to define the word *believe*: "a great number believed, and turned unto the Lord." There is no *and* (*kai*) in the Greek. Therefore, the phrase "turned to the Lord" explains the word *believe*.

Salvation is by grace through faith and therefore not of works in any subtle way. This is not to say that repentance should not lead to a change of lifestyle, but rather that the essence of repentance itself is an exchange of ways of thinking as one turns to Christ for salvation from sin and hell. As noted in Chapter 6 regarding "The Gospel to Saints," justification, which is free by faith (Rom. 1–5), opens the way for sanctification, which is also free by faith (Rom. 6–8). This is why both John the Baptist and Paul call for those who have repented to follow through with a lifestyle that is appropriate to repentance or "meet for repentance" (Matt. 3:8; cf. Luke 3:8; Acts 26:20). "According to Scripture, repentance is wholly an inward act, and should not be confounded with the change of life that proceeds from it. Confession of sin and reparation of wrongs are *fruits* of repentance."[12] Repentance itself is not a change of behavior. It opens the way for a change in behavior by the power of the new life then received.

When the Holy Spirit convicts man of sin, he recognizes that sin, including his sins, is an offense to a holy God. When the Holy Spirit convicts man of judgment, he recognizes that hell is the just consequence for his sin(s). When the Holy Spirit convicts man of righteousness, he realizes his inability to meet God's standard of absolute perfection and his desperate need for the righteousness of Christ. At that point, man clearly sees that he cannot turn (cease) from his sin(s) or do anything of merit that is acceptable to a holy God, and, therefore, must turn to Christ to deliver him from sin and hell.

Jesus said, "They that are whole need not a physician; but they that are sick. I came not to call the righteous, but sinners to repentance" (Luke 5:31–32). Sick people do not turn from their sickness to a physician (i.e., they do not cease from their sickness to turn to a physician); they turn to a physician for deliverance from their sickness (because they loathe their sickness and desire healing). Similarly, sinners cannot turn from their sin(s) to Christ (i.e., they do not cease from their sinfulness to turn to Christ); they must turn to Christ, the Great Physician, for deliverance from their sin (because they loathe their sinfulness and desire healing).

---

12. Berkhof, 487.

Evangelists must keep the evangel clearly focused on Christ as the Savior who does all the saving. To emphasize man's responsibility in any way that diminishes a clear view of Christ as the only object of dependence confuses the good news. The only truly good news is that Christ welcomes all who flee to Him for salvation from sin and deliverance from the wrath to come. Furthermore, evangelists must make it clear that true repentance does not want Christ *and* sin(s). True repentance desires Christ to deliver from sin(s).

Therefore, repentance must have two major "guardrails" to be understood correctly. First, there must not be any mixture with works. Second, one cannot want Christ *and* his sin.

In summary, faith means a transfer of dependence, and repentance means a change of way of thinking. This exchange is a turning to Christ for salvation from sin and hell. The theological essence of faith and repentance is similar. However, further clarification is needed to have a proper understanding of faith/repentance.

The Theological Emphasis of Faith and Repentance Is Different

Since the essence of faith and repentance is similar, how does the emphasis differ? The essence of faith/repentance is to transfer one's dependence/change one's thinking. However, the emphasis of faith is the dependence now on Christ, and the emphasis of repentance is the transfer or exchange. In Mark 1:15, Jesus declares "repent ye, and believe the gospel." The usage of *repent* and *believe* shows the different emphases of the two words and does not indicate two conditions for salvation, or this statement would contradict multiple clear passages that show that man's responsibility is one condition (as noted earlier).

The fact that most occurrences of *believe* in regard to salvation are in the present tense (generally indicating continuous action) shows that one is now actually *depending* on Christ. Although *believe* is often in the present tense, the promises for salvation (e.g., forgiveness of sins and eternal life) are stated such that they are fulfilled the moment one first appropriates faith (e.g., "hath everlasting life," John 6:47). However, the idea is not to believe and then never believe again. The present tense indicating "is believing" allows for Christians to be referred to as "believers." Yet it is possible to doubt one's salvation. If not, verses such as I John 5:13 would be unneeded: "These things have I written unto you that believe on the name of the Son of God; that ye may know that ye have eternal life, and that ye may [continue to] believe on the name of the Son of God." Also, verses such as John 1:12 reveal that although *believe* is "is believing" (present tense), *receive* is in the aorist tense, indicating the fact of an action: "But as many as received him, to them gave he power to become the sons of God, even to them that believe on his name." *Received* refers to the moment of the transaction, and *believe* (or *is believing*) refers to the new dependence now on Christ.

While *believe* or *faith* emphasizes the new dependence now on Christ, *repentance* emphasizes the transfer or exchange. In passages that are most clearly salvific, the verb *metanoeo* occurs eleven times in the aorist tense (Matt. 11:20–21; 12:41; Luke 10:13; 11:32; Acts 2:38; 3:19; Rev. 9:20–21; 16:9, 11), ten times in the present tense (Matt. 3:2; 4:17; Mark 1:15; 6:12; Luke 13:3, 5; 15:7, 10; Acts 17:30; 26:20), and once in the future tense (Luke 16:30). The significant use of the aorist, indicating the fact of an action, seems to emphasize the moment of transfer. Interestingly, the Scriptures call Christians "believers" (Acts 5:14; I Tim. 4:12), not "repenters." Also, as already noted, the descriptive word *turn* (*epistrepho*) emphasizes the moment of the transfer of trust.

Although the theological essence of faith and repentance is similar, the theological emphasis differs. Having investigated these first two theological issues, how does sanctification relate to the biblical balance of faith/repentance?

The Concept of Faith/Repentance Is the Same for Salvation and the Spirit-filled Life

The Bible does not portray two kinds of faith/repentance: the one for salvation and the other for the Spirit-filled life of sanctification and service. Faith is faith. Repentance is repentance. The concept of faith/repentance is the same, although the purpose varies. Galatians 3:2-3 strongly asks, "Received ye the Spirit by the works of the law, or by the hearing of faith? Are ye so foolish? having begun in the Spirit, are ye now made perfect by the flesh?" Spiritual birth is by faith in Christ and not works (flesh-dependence). Spiritual growth is also by faith in Christ for the sanctifying work of the Spirit and not by flesh-dependence. Colossians 2:5b-7a states "your faith in Christ. As ye have therefore received Christ Jesus the Lord, so walk ye in him: Rooted and built up in him, and stablished in the faith." Just as one is saved by faith (salvation), he is to walk by faith (the Spirit-filled life). Both demand faith in Christ—in salvation to receive the Spirit and in the Spirit-filled life to access the Spirit's power. Therefore, the concept of faith/repentance is the same for both salvation and the Spirit-filled life of sanctification and service.

Although the concept of faith/repentance is the same for both salvation and spiritual growth, there is a difference of purpose. This difference must be understood to properly maintain the biblical balance on the issue of faith/repentance.

The Purpose of Faith/Repentance Is Different for Salvation and the Spirit-filled Life

The earthly goal of faith/repentance for salvation is to get to faith/repentance for the Spirit-filled life of sanctification and service. Salvation is the platform and necessary provision for the Spirit-filled life. The two are not totally separate, and yet they are distinguishable as one based upon the other. Faith/repentance for salvation is a once-for-all transaction whereby one transfers his dependence for a new position. Faith/repentance for sanctification and service is a repeated transfer of dependence for a new practice. The purpose of the former is for a new standing. The purpose of the latter is for a new walking. The former is for positional or credited (imputed) righteousness. The latter is for practical or enabled (imparted) righteousness. The former is for new life. The latter is for new living. The former is for Christ *in* you. The latter is for Christ *through* you. The former is for grace *to* you. The latter is for grace *through* you. Faith/repentance for salvation is for what you receive (i.e., forgiveness of sins, credited righteousness, eternal life). Faith/repentance for the Spirit-filled life is for what you do (i.e., obedience in the Christian walk and warfare). Therefore, care must be taken as to whether a passage is dealing with positional truth (salvation) or practical truth (sanctification).

Herein lies a key difference. The new position or standing of salvation involves no movement on the part of the one being saved unless the "receiving" is called movement. But the new practice or walking involves movement. The former is for what one receives (no movement). The latter is for what one does (movement). Walking involves movement. Faith/repentance for the Spirit-filled life of sanctification and service is tied to the *step* of the walk. The church of Ephesus was commanded to "repent, and do the first works" (Rev. 2:5). The walk of the Spirit-filled life demands the movement of steps in thought, word, or deed. The purpose of faith/repentance for the Spirit-filled life is a repeated transfer of dependence *to obey*. Simply put, it is God-dependence for Spirit-enabling to obey in thought, word, and deed.

For example, it is one thing for someone to say he believes God can bless soulwinning. That by itself is acknowledgment (easy-believism on soulwinning). However, it is another thing to depend on God to bless as one takes the step of declaring the gospel.

Faith for sanctification and service accesses the Spirit's power for the purpose of obedience in the Christian walk and warfare. When the dependence is tied to the step in thought, word, or deed, then the Spirit enables the one depending to actually take the step of obedience. This is not a matter of flesh-dependent activity, which produces hollow motions. This is a matter of God-dependent obedience, which accesses Spirit-enabled actions. Also this shows that the life of faith is not a life of passivity.

The distinction of purpose is vital to a proper understanding of the moment of salvation and the movement of walking in the Spirit. To confuse the two purposes is to cloud a free salvation with a works or bondage salvation. Horatius Bonar, in his book *Words to Winners of Souls,* says the following: "*We have not fully preached a free gospel.* We have been afraid of making it *too free,* lest men should be led into licentiousness; as if it were possible to preach too free a gospel, or as if its *freeness* could lead men into sin. It is only a free gospel that can bring peace, and it is only a free gospel that can make men holy."[13]

It is vital not to confuse the *do* of walking in the Spirit with the *receive* of salvation. In the effort to counter easy-believism, some have added sanctification truth (emphasizing the walk of the changed life) to salvation. However, unregenerate man cannot understand the Christian life, for "the natural man receiveth

---

13. Horatius Bonar, *Words to Winners of Souls* (Garland, Tex.: American Tract Society, 1981), 35 [emphasis Bonar's].

not the things of the Spirit of God . . . because they are spiritually discerned" (I Cor. 2:14). The only promise of the Spirit's
convincing work in the heart of an unsaved person is John 16:8:
"He will reprove the world of sin, and of righteousness, and of
judgment." Therefore, our gospel articulation must focus on
sin, righteousness, and judgment and not on the changed life
(walk) of sanctification. Dealing with sanctification truth is not
what the Holy Spirit uses to convince *the world*.

The Lordship-Salvation position violates this reality and gives
much emphasis to the walk of sanctification and service for the
moment of salvation. Sanctification and service passages are im-
properly used for the issue of salvation. But it is incorrect to
use Christian walk passages (e.g., Luke 9 and James 2) on the
issue of salvation. The debate is not that Jesus is Lord, but on
what constitutes the condition of salvation. Lordship-Salvation
confuses the condition for salvation with the condition for the
Spirit-filled life.

The Scriptures do teach a "Lordship Sanctification." The
Scriptures do teach *believers* to yield to the lordship of Christ
by surrendering to and thus depending on the Spirit of Christ
as Lord (leadership) and life (power). The Scriptures do strongly
teach that Christians must surrender to the leadership of the
Spirit and depend on the power of the Spirit to truly honor God.
This is simply the Spirit-filled life for holiness and service. But to
add an emphasis on lifestyle changes to the moment of salvation
is at best confusing and at worst false doctrine.

For example, someone wrote, "We are not saved on the merit
of those works, but we will not be saved without them."[14] How
does this statement differ from Acts 15:1? "And certain men which
came down from Judea taught the brethren, and said, Except ye
be circumcised after the manner of Moses, ye cannot be saved."
Paul and Barnabas strongly disputed this false teaching according to Acts 15:2. Galatians 2 discloses that later Paul "withstood"

---

14. Taken from a personal letter.

Peter "to the face" (2:11) publicly (2:14) for giving credence to this same type of thinking by not eating with the Gentile believers for fear of "them which were of the circumcision" (2:12). Peter did not teach the Galatian error, but he gave credence to it by his associations. Yet Paul publicly confronted him. To cloud the gospel with any type of works-dependence is a serious matter.

The right solution to the problem of acknowledgment-only (easy-believism) decisions is to deal specifically with sin as that which offends God's holiness, uncompromisingly with hell as just judgment, and clearly with the finished work of Christ as the only object of dependence for salvation. If sin and hell are dealt with thoroughly, then the sinner sees his need of a Savior, just as the sick man sees his need of a physician. This emphasis precludes giving anyone the notion of a "quick ticket to heaven and license to sin" without violating the true freeness of salvation. Then once one is saved, he must be taught the Spirit-filled life to grow spiritually.

Although salvation involves massive positional and inward change (e.g., a new spirit and the indwelling Spirit), practical outward change occurs as one accesses the Spirit of Christ by faith to live (walk) the Christian life. True change that pleases God comes as a believer walks by faith and thus walks in the Spirit. Any other change is self-change, which does not please God because it is not of faith. "But without faith it is impossible to please him" (Heb. 11:6). Flesh-dependence brings bondage. God-dependence accesses the life and liberty of the Spirit for the freedom of the true Christian walk.

Conclusion

The foundational issue of gospel extremes is one's understanding of faith/repentance. How important is it? It could cost the very souls of men and women. For example, someone once witnessed to a lady who operated a country/western radio station. After hearing the gospel, this lady indicated she wanted to be saved. Then the one witnessing said that she must stop operating the radio station in order to be saved.[15] This is the overreaction of the Lordship-Salvation position to the easy-believism problem. Tragically, she then backed out of her decision to get saved. Far better would it have been to see her trust Christ for salvation and then on that basis teach her how to grow spiritually through the power of the Spirit and deal with the lifestyle issue. It was not a matter of her bringing up the issue as something she would cling to over salvation. It was made an issue to her as a part of the object of dependence. Evangelists must learn to declare the gospel—plus nothing, minus nothing.

The biblical balance of faith/repentance reveals the importance of declaring the gospel to sinners (sin, judgment, credited righteousness based on the finished work of Christ, and the decision of faith/repentance) in order to see people saved and then declaring the gospel to saints (the truth of the Spirit-filled life) in order to see people grow spiritually. This precision of emphasis keeps the evangel crystal clear to both sinners and saints.

---

15. Taken from a personal conversation with the believer in this story.

Part Four

FOCUS ON

EVANGELISM

Chapter Nine

EVANGELISM APPLIED

"They . . . went everywhere preaching the word."
Acts 8:4

The gift of the evangelist is the Spirit-empowered declaration of truth for the cause of revival and evangelism. Although pastor-teachers, as well as all believers, are to fulfill the Great Commission, the evangelist is to be a leading voice of the evangel. The evangelist specializes in the evangel—both the gospel to sinners and the gospel to saints.

Jesus declared, "I will build my church" (Matt. 16:18). Christ began His church with "the foundation of the apostles and prophets, Jesus Christ himself being the chief corner stone" (Eph. 2:20). Once the foundation was laid, Christ continued and still continues building His church through "evangelists; and some, pastors and teachers; For the perfecting of the saints, for the work of the ministry, for the edifying of the body of Christ" (Eph. 4:11-12).

How does Christ continue building His church through *evangelists* in particular? The answer is through *evangelism* applied. The evangelist (*euangelistes*) is to evangelize (*euangelizo*) with the evangel (*euangelion*). But how is evangelism applied scripturally? The biblical precedent provides three observations regarding the application of evangelism.

A Specialized Objective

The Christ who said "I will build my church" gave leadership gifts ultimately for the edifying or building of the body of Christ. This building up of Christ's body involves both a qualitative or spiritual growth (e.g., "grow up into him in all things") and a quantitative or numerical growth (e.g., "maketh increase of the body"), both of which build the body "unto the measure of the stature of the fullness of Christ" (Eph. 4:11–16).

The specialized objective of the evangelist is to lead in building the body of Christ both quantitatively and qualitatively through the specialized focus on the evangel.

Evangelizing Sinners

Since the evangel begins with the gospel to sinners, then the evangelist must obviously preach the gospel to those without Christ. This aspect of the evangel addresses building Christ's church quantitatively. Although every believer is to witness to the unsaved around him, the evangelist is responsible for public or mass evangelism. In Chapter 1 it was noted that of the fifty occurrences of the verb *euangelizo* used of men preaching the gospel, forty-nine were used in contexts of public ministry. When the public nature of the evangelist's responsibility is seen in conjunction with building Christ's church, there are two obvious applications of mass evangelism.

Mass Evangelism for the Purpose of Establishing Churches

In unevangelized regions, the purpose of mass evangelism is to establish local churches. The Gospel accounts reveal that much preparation for establishing churches was accomplished during the time of Christ's earthly ministry. In fact, *euangelizo* is used a total of nine times in the Gospel narratives (primarily in Luke) of men evangelizing lost sinners. *Euangelizo* is connected to John the Baptist (Luke 3:18), the Lord Jesus (Matt. 11:5; Luke 4:18, 43; 7:22; 8:1; 16:16; 20:1), and the apostles (Luke 9:6; 16:16).

The book of Acts records the actual establishment of local churches. It is no accident that *euangelizo* is found in conjunction with *ekklesia* in the establishment of these churches. With the sending of the Spirit, the first local church to be established was the church in Jerusalem. Initially, Acts 2:47 and 5:11 refer to the new assembly as "the church." Acts 8:1 says "the church which was at Jerusalem," and Acts 11:22 says "the church which was in Jerusalem." Peter and the apostles, as already noted, are connected to the verb *euangelizo* and were used to establish this first church, with James eventually becoming the pastor. In fact, Acts 5:42 describes the ministry in the formation of the Jerusalem church with "and daily in the temple, and in every house, they ceased not to teach and preach [*euangelizo*] Jesus Christ."

Then through persecution the gospel spread so that "they that were scattered abroad went everywhere preaching [*euangelizo*] the word" (Acts 8:4). This involved Philip, who later is called "Philip the evangelist" (Acts 21:8), going to Samaria "preaching [*euangelizo*] the things concerning the kingdom of God, and the name of Jesus Christ" (Acts 8:12). Many believed, but Philip did not stay to actually establish the church since the Spirit led him to the desert to evangelize the Ethiopian eunuch.[1] Presumably a church in Samaria was established.[2] This assumption is validated

---

1. This is the only time *euangelizo* is used in a one-on-one situation.

2. As noted in Chapter 1, many are implicitly designated as evangelists through the use of *euangelizo* and were involved in establishing churches (e.g., the Apostle Paul). However, it is interesting that the only man explicitly designated as an "evangelist" in Scripture (Acts 21:8) does not in the scriptural record actually plant a church. Although Philip laid the groundwork and presumably a church later formed, Philip is not seen in Scripture as *only* a church planter. This seems odd if the claim is correct that evangelists are only missionary church planters. While it is true, as this chapter is demonstrating, that evangelists may be involved in establishing churches, to make this the only application of evangelism is an unscriptural limitation.

by the statement in Acts 9:31 after the conversion of Saul: "Then had the churches rest throughout all Judea and Galilee and Samaria, and were edified." Acts 9:31 is the first usage of the plural *churches* and indicates that the dispersion of believers from Jerusalem, "who went everywhere preaching [*euangelizo*] the word," led to the founding of several churches in the surrounding regions. The specific reference to Judea and Samaria reveals a fulfillment of Acts 1:8.

The next specific local church explicitly established in Scripture is the church in Antioch. The dispersion believers "traveled as far as . . . Antioch . . . and . . . spake unto the Grecians, preaching [*euangelizo*] the Lord Jesus (Acts 11:19–20). Through "the hand of the Lord . . . a great number believed" (Acts 11:21). Then through the ministry of Barnabas, the new believers were grounded (Acts 11:23–24). Finally, both Barnabas and Paul for "a whole year . . . assembled themselves with the church, and taught much people" (Acts 11:26). Acts 13:1 describes "the church that was at Antioch." The unnamed evangelists used with the verb *euangelizo* (Acts 11:20), along with Barnabas and Paul, who elsewhere are also connected to the verb, were used of God to establish this church in Antioch.

The first missionary journey of Paul and Barnabas was clearly in unevangelized regions. Therefore, the primary ministry of this first missionary journey was to establish churches. Although their ministry was broader than the explicit usages of *euangelizo*, the verb is used in the ministry at Antioch of Pisidia (Acts 13:32), Lystra, Derbe, and the cities of and region around Lycaonia (Acts 14:6–7, 15). Passing back through the then-evangelized areas, Paul and Barnabas "ordained them elders in every church" (Acts 14:23). This usage of *church* is the next geographic reference in the inspired history of Acts.

After Paul chose Silas for the second missionary journey, "he went through Syria and Cilicia, confirming the churches" (Acts 15:41). Who planted these churches? Syria and Cilicia were not a part of the first missionary journey. Also Paul is here "confirming," not establishing, these churches. However, it is possible that Paul founded these churches during his extended stay in Tarsus since they were in that region and he obviously knew of them and was welcomed by them when he came with Silas.[3]

The second missionary journey eventually included new regions that were unevangelized. The verb *euangelizo* is used to describe the purpose of the call of God to the region of Macedonia (Acts 16:10). Paul's obedience led to the establishing of churches throughout that region.

The repeated usage of *euangelizo* in conjunction with *ekklesia* in the establishment of churches reveals that mass evangelism for the purpose of establishing churches is a definite application of evangelism.

Mass Evangelism through Established Churches

In areas where churches have been established, mass evangelism is applied through the existing churches. The church at Jerusalem began in Acts 2. By the end of the chapter, the new believers are labeled as "the church" (Acts 2:47). But mass evangelism did not stop once the church was established. Through the continued preaching of Peter and John in a mass evangelism context at the Temple, "many . . . believed . . . about five thousand" (Acts 4:4).[4] Again, after referring to "the church" as an established church (Acts 5:11), "the apostles" continued ministering, resulting in "multitudes" believing and being "added to the Lord" (Acts 5:12-14).[5]

---

3. After Paul's conversion, he came to Jerusalem. Because of a threat on Paul's life, the brethren in Jerusalem "sent him forth to Tarsus" (Acts 9:30). Referring to this brief time in Jerusalem, Paul said, "Afterwards I came into the regions of Syria and Cilicia." In Acts 11:25, Barnabas departed "to Tarsus, for to seek Saul." The intervening years from Acts 9:30 to Acts 11:25 appear to be about nine or ten years. This would have been enough time to plant the churches referred to in Acts 15:41.

4. It should be remembered that Peter and John are specifically connected to the verb *euangelizo* in Acts 8:25 and therefore are evangelists by implication. This point was examined in Chapter 1 more extensively.

5. The apostles are directly connected to *euanglizo* in Luke 9:6; 16:16 and in Acts 5:42 in the context at hand.

After the church in Antioch was founded (Acts 11:19–21), Barnabas came, and through his ministry "much people was added unto the Lord" (Acts 11:24).[6]

On his second missionary journey, Paul revisited the churches that were established on his first journey. As a result of Paul's ministry to these established churches, not only "were the churches established in the faith," but they also "increased in number daily" (Acts 16:5).[7]

After establishing a nucleus of disciples in Ephesus (Acts 18:19–21), Paul returned, and a nucleus of twelve men expanded so that "all they which dwelt in Asia heard the word of the Lord Jesus" (Acts 19:7–10). This mass evangelism resulted in the statement "So mightily grew the word of God and prevailed" (Acts 19:20), causing "no small stir" (Acts 19:23).[8]

Both applications of mass evangelism for the purpose of establishing churches and also through established churches have been applied throughout church history.

Equipping Saints

Not only does the specialized objective of evangelism involve evangelizing sinners, it also includes equipping saints. In the previous chapters it has been noted repeatedly that the gospel has a dimension to saints in addition to sinners. This aspect of the evangel addresses building up Christ's church qualitatively. Ephesians 4:12 clearly teaches that evangelists are given "For the perfecting [equipping][9] of the saints, for the work of the ministry, for the edifying of the body of Christ." By God's grace, evangelists must equip "the saints" to do "the work of the ministry."

6. Barnabas is connected to *euangelizo* in Acts 13:32; 14:7, 15, 21; and 15:35.

7. Paul is directly connected to *euangelizo* in Acts 13:32; 14:7, 15, 21; 15:35; 16:10 and 17:18, as well as throughout his Epistles (see Chapter 1).

8. Rick Flanders details this amazing work of revival and mass evangelism in an article entitled "Twelve Men and a Preacher" (*Revival*, no. 1 [2007]: 12–15).

9. Fritz Rienecker and Cleon L. Rogers, *A Linguistic Key to the Greek New Testament* (Grand Rapids: Zondervan Bible Publishers, 1980), 531.

Although pastors also equip the saints in a multi-faceted way, evangelists equip the saints in a specialized way. The specialized purpose of evangelists focuses on the evangel. In regard to equipping the saints, this focus involves both strengthening the saints through the gospel to the saints and training the saints in declaring the gospel to sinners.

Strengthening the Saints

The missionary journeys of Paul beautifully illustrate evangelism applied to both sinners and saints. The first journey involved establishing churches (Acts 13–14). The second missionary journey involved both strengthening the existing churches (Acts 15:41–16:5) and establishing new churches (Acts 16:6–18:22). The third journey predominantly involved strengthening existing churches, although new territory was also reached (Acts 18:23–21:16).

Inspiration incorporates several words to describe Paul's ministry to the saints. On his return through the newly formed churches at the end of his first journey, Paul ministered by "confirming the souls of the disciples, and exhorting them to continue in the faith" (Acts 14:22). *Confirming* translates from *episterizo* meaning "to strengthen."[10] As may be obvious, *exhorting* translates from *parakaleo*, meaning "to urge, to encourage."[11] Interestingly, *continue* translates from *emmeno*, meaning to "stay" or "remain (in)."[12] The closely related word *meno*, often translated "abide," is a key concept regarding the Spirit-filled life of the believer abiding in Christ (God-dependence) and Christ abiding in the believer (Spirit-enablement).[13] The phrase "continue in the faith" certainly conveys the necessity of the life of faith.

---

10. Ibid., 297.

11. Ibid., 648.

12. William F. Arndt and F. Wilbur Gingrich, *A Greek-English Lexicon of the New Testament and Other Early Christian Literature*, 2nd ed. rev. F. Wilbur Gingrich and Fredrick W. Danker (Chicago: University of Chicago Press, 1979), 255.

13. In John 15:4–5, Christ defines *abide* by stating that "without me ye can do nothing," which implies that "with Me you can do everything you ought to do." The implication is that God-dependence accesses Spirit-enablement. A careful investigation of John 6:56 teaches the same truth when examined in light of John 6:47 and 54.

At the beginning of his second journey, Paul traveled through Syria and Cilicia, "confirming the churches" (Acts 15:41). Again, *confirming* translates from *episterizo*, meaning "to strengthen." Then as a result of Paul's ministry further west into Galatia, "so were the churches established in the faith" (Acts 16:5). *Established* translates from *stereoo*, meaning "to make firm, to strengthen."[14]

At the beginning of his third journey, Paul returned to Galatia and Phrygia, "strengthening all the disciples" (Acts 18:23). Here *strengthening* translates from *sterizo*, again meaning "to strengthen" (like *episterizo*).[15] Referring to his ministry in Macedonia, Paul gave "them much exhortation" (Acts 20:2). The word *exhortation* is simply the participle form of *parakaleo*.

The major emphasis of Paul's ministry to existing churches was *strengthening* them. True strength is found not in the flesh but in the Spirit, who imparts the life of Christ. Christ in the believer is the "engine" necessary to empower Christian living. The access to "Christ in you" (Col. 1:27) so that "I live, yet not I, but Christ liveth in me" is by "faith" (Gal. 2:20).

If one wonders what Paul taught to strengthen the new churches, one has but to study the Pauline Epistles directed to churches, particularly Romans, First and Second Corinthians, Galatians, Ephesians, Philippians, and Colossians, all of which have portions explaining the gospel to the saints. For example, Chapter 1 overviewed the extent of the gospel (*euangelion*) in the books of Romans, Galatians, and Ephesians. Also, in Acts 19, the first truth Paul stressed to the new Ephesian converts regarded a right understanding of the Holy Spirit. This emphasis is the heart of the good news of the indwelling Christ as the strength for all obedience.

With various terminologies being used over the centuries (some more theologically precise than others), many evangelists have preached the importance of the Spirit-filled life. For example,

14. Rienecker and Rogers, 301.
15. Ibid., 311.

speaking of D. L. Moody's emphasis to the saints and especially to Christian workers, one biographer described it as "spreading the good news of the Holy Spirit."[16] Moody gave a series of talks at his Northfield Conference that were later published in a book entitled *Secret Power*. These talks represent Moody's heartbeat.

The thesis of Moody's talks and book was simple. The church lacked the power to change lives because it leaned too much on elements beside prayer, the Word, and the Holy Spirit. The late-nineteenth-century church, he argued, is like an army being defeated because it refuses to use its weapons. The church did not need new buildings, new organs, new choirs, or new measures. "That is not what the Church of God needs today. It is the old power that the Apostles had." Moody insisted that the Holy Spirit will transform the ministers and enable them to use the "sword of the Spirit"—the Bible. "If a man is not filled with the Spirit, he will never know how to use the Book." Moody stressed that Spirit-filled men preach the Word, not themselves, and that such workers must be continually filled with power from on high, rather than rely on any single experience from the past. "The fact is, we are leaky vessels, and we have to keep right under the fountain all the time to keep full of Christ, and so have fresh supply." Moody likened the Spirit-filled worker to an irrigated field in California's Sacramento Valley. The irrigated field is green and it stands in stark contrast to the non-irrigated field where the soil is dry, the vegetation is brown and dry, and no fruit will come forth.

Moody stressed that all disciples—not just preachers and missionaries—need this grace, and it is freely offered to them. He continually stressed Jesus' promise of the

16. Lyle W. Dorsett, *A Passion for Souls: The Life of D. L. Moody* (Chicago: Moody Press, 1997), 351.

Spirit in John 14, 15, and 16 as a promise to the church from the first century onward. Only the Comforter, Counselor, and Teacher—the Spirit—will give us wisdom, discernment, and power to do work that has eternal consequences. Work relying on anything but Him will ultimately be fruitless.[17]

To strengthen the saints, evangelists must confront the sins of the converted life and the sin of flesh-dependent ministry (self), lift up Christ as the answer through the cleansing of His blood and the enabling of His Spirit, demand surrender (to the Spirit's leadership) and faith (in the Spirit's power) as the access to the provision of Christ, explain the reality of Christ's actual life accessed by faith for holiness and service, and emphasize God-dependent, Spirit-enabled service in the cause of the gospel.

Training the Saints

Strengthening the saints focuses on accessing the engine power of Christ in the believer for the purpose of victory over sin and power in service. *Training* the saints focuses on instructing the saints in declaring the gospel and thus fulfilling the Great Commission through the power of the Spirit. This training equips the saints to do "the work of the ministry" (Eph. 4:12). The leadership gift of the evangelist is, by divine enablement, keenly aware of the evangel—not so the evangelist would be the only one to evangelize, but so he can equip the saints to evangelize. One of the purposes of the gift is to provide divine understanding in the specialized focus of the evangel in order to teach others.

A glimpse of this is seen in Paul's ministry on his second missionary journey: "And so were the churches established in the faith, and increased in number daily" (Acts 16:5). The ministry to the churches resulted in ministry through the churches. The churches were strengthened and trained, resulting in effective ministry to the unsaved around them.

---

17. Ibid., 348–49.

An example of this dynamic in the twentieth century comes from the life and ministry of John R. Rice. Through his periodical entitled *The Sword of the Lord* and his "Sword" conferences, many were equipped and inspired to reach the lost around them. Whole churches moved forward in reaching the unsaved as a result of Rice's ministry.[18]

Practical Methodologies

The first observation noted regarding the application of evangelism was a specialized objective. The second observation concerns practical methodologies. Practical Spirit-led methodologies were used in the New Testament to preach to the lost and to equip the saints. Although many subcategories have been used historically, the general categories are seen in the New Testament.

Evangelism through Spoken Preaching

Of fifty-five usages of the verb *euangelizo* in the New Testament, twenty-six occur in narrative literature: Matthew (1), Luke (10), and Acts (15). Although more could be studied than the contexts where *euangelizo* occurs, these contexts reveal simple but practical methodologies for preaching the gospel. In fact, the venues used include the two obvious possibilities: outside and inside.

By biblical precedent, the open-air venue has provided an excellent means for mass evangelism. Strictly regarding *euangelizo* in the gospel narratives, John the Baptist evangelized in the wilderness (Luke 3:18; cf. 3:2–3 and Matt. 11:7), Jesus evangelized

---

18. For more information regarding Rice's ministry, see *Man Sent from God: A Biography of Dr. John R. Rice* by Robert Sumner (Murfreesboro: Sword of the Lord Publishers, 1959).

in the desert (Luke 4:43; cf. 4:42) and in villages and cities (Matt. 11:5; cf. 11:1–4; Luke 7:22; cf. 7:12ff; 8:1), and the disciples evangelized "through the towns" (Luke 9:6). Without the explicit use of *euangelizo*, Jesus preached to the multitude on land from a boat (Luke 5:1–3), from mountain settings as with "the Sermon on the Mount" (Matt. 5:1–8:1), from desert places as with the feeding of the five thousand (Luke 9:10ff), and so forth. The open-air venue provided large enough settings for mass evangelism.

Strictly regarding *euangelizo* in the history recorded in Acts, Philip evangelized in Samaria (Acts 8:4–5, 12), in the desert (Acts 8:35), and in cities (Acts 8:40). Peter and John evangelized "in many villages of the Samaritans" (Acts 8:25), and unnamed men evangelized in Antioch (Acts 11:20). Paul and Barnabas evangelized in cities and their outlying regions (Acts 14:6–7, 15, 21), and Paul evangelized in the "market" (Acts 17:17–18). These settings imply, at least in part, the open-air venue. Other outdoor settings are either stated or implied throughout Acts but without the explicit use of the word *euangelizo*.

Throughout history some evangelists have followed in the train of open-air preachers. Perhaps most notable is George Whitefield who, when facing the dilemma of having the doors of the Church of England closed to him, simply utilized the open-air venue.

> Whitefield's idea of preaching in the open air did not originate with himself. It had been put into his mind by his exchange of letters with a fearless, tireless, dynamic Welshman, Howell Harris. For three years this man had been exhorting immense throngs of his fellow-countrymen out of doors and had been used of God in the awakening of hundreds.[19]

> Whitefield was profoundly influenced by Harris's example. Field preaching opened up prospects which moved him to the depths of his being. Here was a means of reaching the vast untouched multitudes and here was a

19. Arnold Dallimore, *George Whitefield*, vol. 1 (Edinburgh: The Banner of Truth Trust, 1970), 233.

deliverance from all dependency on the availability of the churches or the Society Rooms. Here was a gloriously free and wondrously promising form of evangelism and in all the vigour of his nature he wanted to launch into it right away. "Howell Harris and I are correspondents, blessed be God," he wrote. "May I follow him as he does Jesus Christ."[20]

When Whitefield broke from the status quo against public opinion, God blessed abundantly. Soon he was preaching to thousands. In an area where coal miners came to hear Whitefield preach, he described what has become a classic scene:

> Having no righteousness of their own to renounce, they were glad to hear of a Jesus who was a friend of publicans, and came not to call the righteous, but sinners to repentance. The first discovery of their being affected was to see the white gutters made by their tears which plentifully fell down their black cheeks, as they came out of their coal pits. Hundreds and hundreds of them were soon brought under deep convictions, which, as the event proved, happily ended in a sound and thorough conversion. The change was visible to all, though numbers chose to impute it to anything, rather than the finger of God.[21]

Whitefield introduced John Wesley to *field preaching*. Both John and Charles then regularly applied the method with others to follow.

Although many other names might be mentioned, in the mid-twentieth century James A. Stewart from Scotland used the open-air forum. Trained early in street preaching, by age 16 or 17, Stewart experienced hundreds of people staying to listen to the

---

20. Ibid., 249.
21. Ibid., 263–64.

"boy preacher."[22] Knowing many times of real revival and awakening, especially in Eastern Europe, Stewart preached to as many as ten thousand in the open air.[23]

The other obvious venue is preaching inside in structures made by man. Regarding the use of *euangelizo* in the Gospel narratives, Jesus evangelized in the synagogue(s) (Luke 4:18; cf. 4:16–17; 4:43; cf. 4:44) and in the Temple at Jerusalem (Luke 20:1). In the record of Acts, the apostles evangelized in "the temple, and in every house" (Acts 5:42), and Paul and Barnabas evangelized in the synagogue(s) (Acts 13:32; cf. 13:14–15) and also in a house or some sort of structure, if the church in Antioch met in a building (Acts 15:35).

Obviously evangelists have preached in church buildings, civic auditoriums, camp-style tabernacles, and the like throughout church history. For example, one historian noted, "The circuit riders spoke wherever they could gain a hearing—in log cabins, court houses, school houses, taverns, or in the open air."[24] Evangelists with the fire of God in their hearts must preach and will find a way to do so.

Evangelism through Written Preaching

The four inspired Gospel accounts articulate the gospel in written form. Interestingly, the four writers of the Gospels soon came to be known as "The Evangelists" among early church writers. Written preaching exploded as a venue for preaching the gospel with the advent of the printing press. Since that time a number of evangelists have taken advantage of the printed page.

---

22. Detailed accounts are given in James A. Stewart's autobiography *I Must Tell* (Asheville: Revival Literature, 2007), 18–29, and in his biography by Ruth Stewart, *James Stewart: Missionary* (Asheville: Gospel Projects Inc., 1977), 12–25.

23. Ruth Stewart, 166.

24. Kenneth Scott Latourette, *A History of Christianity*, vol. 2 (Peabody, MA: Prince Press, 2005), 1040.

A Pervading Presence

A third observation of biblical precedent in the application of evangelism regards the repeated surges given to the early church through the power of Pentecost. The exalted Christ poured out His Spirit on the Day of Pentecost (Acts 2:16-17, 33). This Pentecostal blessing launched the age of Pentecost, for the Holy Spirit has not yet been sent back.

Peter under inspiration slightly changed the wording as he quoted Joel 2:28. This inspired change affects the timing of the outpouring of the Spirit. Although the timing indicated in Joel is yet future, Peter declares "in the last days, saith God" [different wording from Joel] "I will pour out of my Spirit upon all flesh" (Acts 2:17). The outpouring of the Spirit is promised for the time period known as "the last days." According to Peter's statement "this is that" (Acts 2:16), the last days began on the Day of Pentecost and continue through the entire church age. But what is the outpouring of the Spirit, and how did it impact the evangelism of the early church?

The Definition of the Outpouring of the Spirit

The clearest biblical definition of the outpouring of the Spirit appears in Ezekiel 39:29, where God says, "Neither will I hide my face any more from them: for I have poured out my spirit upon the house of Israel." The word *face* often is translated as "presence" (e.g., Isa. 64:1). In this divine statement, the phrase "I have poured out my Spirit" is explaining the first phrase "Neither will I hide my [presence] any more from them." In other words, the outpouring of God's Spirit is explained as the manifestation of God's presence.

In the New Testament the manifestation of God's presence is spiritual, not physical. But it is just as real as if it were a physical manifestation. Wherever God pours out His Spirit, whether it is with few or many, those in that vicinity are suddenly aware of the presence of God. This consciousness of God produces an atmosphere that has rent through the powers of darkness, pushing back their deceptions and allowing for the Word of God to have free course and the glory of its full weight on hearts. This type of atmosphere makes it as conducive as possible for the saints to be broken and revived and for sinners to be saved without violating the human will.

The spiritual manifestation of God's presence is also powerful but difficult to describe because it is an unseen presence. Generally, writers describe man's response to this convicting presence. When God pours out His Spirit, sometimes it is immediately powerful like waves crashing over the rocks, and sometimes it is increasingly powerful like the tide rising until the rocks are fully submerged. In the end, the results of both are the same.

The outpouring of God's Spirit quickens hearers to the weight of God's truth. There is a difference between a man preaching as a Spirit-filled man and a Spirit-filled man preaching in an atmosphere saturated with the presence of God. The former is a quickened preacher that, by God's grace, will impact some in the audience as rivers of living water flow. The latter is both a quickened preacher and quickened hearers that, by God's grace, produce a greater impact as both living waters flow and the deluge of rain floods.

The consciousness of God produces a conviction of sin as evidenced in Isaiah 6. When he saw the Lord, Isaiah cried out, "Woe is me! for I am undone" (6:5). The awareness of the presence of God produces an awareness of any sin that separates from God. With this type of exposure of sin, man either runs to God in brokenness or runs from God in rebellion. There is no middle ground.

For example, when God poured out His Spirit at the beginning of the Lewis Revival, Duncan Campbell relates, "The awful presence of God brought a wave of conviction of sin that caused even mature Christians to feel their sinfulness, bringing groans of distress and prayers of repentance from the unconverted. Strong men were bowed under the weight of sin and cries for mercy were mingled with shouts of joy from others who had passed into life."[25]

The Demonstration of the Outpouring of the Spirit

In Acts 2 "the multitude came together" (2:6) as God had poured out His Spirit, and the praying saints "were all filled with the Holy Ghost" (2:4) and began declaring "the wonderful works of God" (2:11). When Peter preached in this atmosphere, the audience "pricked in their heart" cried out, "What shall we do?" (2:37). As a result, 3,000 "gladly received his word" and then "were baptized" and "added" to the original 120. That the floodtide of blessing was real is seen in the fact that the 3,000 new believers "continued steadfastly" (2:42) and "the Lord added to the church daily such as should be saved" (2:47).

Did this level of blessing cease? Not at all, for in Acts 3 the lame man was healed, giving Peter another audience, and in Acts 4 "many of them which heard the word believed; and the number of the men was about five thousand" (4:4). After the beginnings of persecution, the saints prayed and "when they had prayed, the place was shaken where they were assembled together; and they were all filled with the Holy Ghost, and they spake the word of God with boldness" (4:31) and "with great power gave the apostles witness . . . and great grace was upon them all" (4:33).

In Acts 5 "believers were the more added to the Lord, multitudes both of men and women" (5:14). Although more

25. Andrew Woolsey, *Channel of Revival: A Biography of Duncan Campbell* (Edinburgh: The Faith Mission, reprint ed., 1982), 118.

persecution arose, they "ceased not to teach and preach Jesus Christ" even "daily in the temple and in every house" (5:42).

In Acts 6 "the word of God increased; and the number of disciples multiplied in Jerusalem greatly" (6:7). In Acts 7 Stephen preached in an atmosphere charged with the presence of God—made clear by the description that his hearers "were cut to the heart" (7:54). But they stoned him to death.

A question may arise as to why the response of the hearers in Acts 2 differed so greatly from that in Acts 7. Both accounts indicate the preacher was filled with the Spirit, and both accounts evidence the truth of God's Word having incredible weight on the hearers through the outpouring of the Spirit. The difference seems to lie in the hearers' hearts. The audience in Acts 2 primarily consisted of religious seekers who had come to Jerusalem (2:5). However, the hearers in Acts 7 primarily were religious leaders who had already hardened their hearts (6:9-12; 7:51-53).

In Acts 8 through Philip's ministry in Samaria, "the people with one accord gave heed" (8:6), and "there was great joy in that city" (8:8). In Acts 9 through Peter's ministry (including healing), "all that dwelt at Lydda and Saron . . . turned to the Lord" (9:35), and throughout Joppa "many believed" (9:42).

In Acts 10 at the house of Cornelius, "the Holy Ghost fell on all them which heard the word" (10:44) so that those present believed (cf. Acts 11:17). In Acts 11 through the evangelization at Antioch, "a great number believed" (11:21), and through the ministry of Barnabas "much people was added unto the Lord" (11:24). After more persecution in Jerusalem, "the word of God grew and multiplied" (12:24).

In Acts 13 on Paul's first missionary journey, at Pisidian Antioch "came almost the whole city together to hear the word of God" (13:44), "many . . . believed" (13:48), and "the word of the Lord was published throughout all the region" (13:49). In Acts 14 at Iconium "a great multitude both of the Jews and also of the Greeks believed" (14:1). At Derbe "they taught [made disciples of] many" (14:21).

In Acts 16 "the churches . . . increased in number daily" (16:5). In Acts 17 at Thessalonica "some of them [Jews] believed . . . and of the devout Greeks a great multitude, and of the chief women not a few" (17:4), and at Berea "many of them believed" (17:12). In Acts 18 at Corinth "many of the Corinthians believed" (18:8).

In Acts 19 through Paul's ministry at Ephesus, "all they which dwelt in Asia heard the word of the Lord Jesus" (19:10). "So mightily grew the word of God and prevailed" (19:20).

The final chapters of Acts relate Paul's productive ministry even while under arrest.

The level of ministry in Acts is more than just Spirit-filled men preaching to dull hearers. Repeatedly, the hearers were made to face the reality of God by an awareness of His presence. This manifestation of God's presence literally produced either revival or riot. As Jesus had taught in John 14–16, both great blessing and great persecution accompanied the powerful ministry of the Spirit.

It must also be noted that in the atmosphere of the outpouring of the Spirit, great miracles were manifested at times, gaining large hearings for the preached Word. However, miracles did not accompany every scenario, particularly in Acts 11 in the work at Antioch, in Acts 13 at Pisidian Antioch, in Acts 14 at Iconium, in Acts 17 at Thessalonica and Berea, and in Acts 18 at Corinth. Therefore, it is the outpouring of the Spirit, not the work of miracles, that is the key to greater impact.

During seasons of refreshing from the presence of the Lord, not only are churches revitalized, but multitudes of sinners are awakened. The church grows both qualitatively and quantitatively. History abounds with examples of this dynamic impetus to the body of Christ through the outpouring of God's Spirit in revival.[26]

---

26. Richard Owen Roberts, *An Annotated Bibliography of Revival Literature* (Wheaton: Richard Owen Roberts Publishers, 1987). This extensive bibliography records over 6,000 entries of revival-related sources.

May evangelists of every generation apply evangelism as the evangelists of the early church did, looking to God for divine aid so that it may be said in every generation as it was said of them: "And the hand of the Lord was with them: and a great number believed, and turned unto the Lord" (Acts 11:21).

Chapter Ten

THE PASSION OF THE EVANGELIST

"And it shall come to pass in the last days, saith God,
I will pour out of my Spirit upon all flesh . . ."
Acts 2:17
"But ye shall receive power, after that the Holy Ghost is
come upon you: and ye shall be witnesses unto me
both in Jerusalem, and in all Judea, and in Samaria,
and unto the uttermost part of the earth."
Acts 1:8

During the early days of the . . . Lewis Awakening,
there was a remarkable movement in the village of Arnol.
There had been no response during the first few meetings, and a time of prayer was convened in a house at the
close of an evening meeting. As one man was praying, all
present became aware that prayer had been heard and
that the Spirit of God was being poured out upon the
village. They left the house to discover that the villagers
also were leaving their cottages and making their way, as
though drawn by some unseen force, to one point in the
village. There they congregated and waited, and when Mr.
Duncan Campbell commenced to preach, the Word took

immediate effect. In a few days that small community had been swept by the Spirit of God, and many souls had been truly converted to God.[1]

Do not accounts of this nature stir the hearts of God-called evangelists? Is there not a passion that cries out, "Lord, do it again"? When evangelists are filled with the Spirit, do not certain Scripture passages pulsate in their veins: "Wilt thou not revive us again: that thy people may rejoice in thee?" (Ps. 85:6); "O Lord, I have heard thy speech, and was afraid: O Lord, revive thy work in the midst of the years, in the midst of the years make known; in wrath remember mercy" (Hab. 3:2); "Oh that thou wouldest rend the heavens, that thou wouldest come down, that the mountains might flow down at thy presence!" (Isa. 64:1).

The passion of the evangelist is the outpouring of the Spirit. What is the reason for this passion, and how is this heartbeat expressed? Two scriptural issues answer these two major questions.

The Reason for the Passion

The reason the passion of the evangelist is the outpouring of the Spirit lies in the similarity between the purpose of the evangelist and the results of the outpouring.

The Purpose of the Evangelist

The purpose of the evangelist is to specialize in the gospel of Jesus Christ—the gospel to sinners and the gospel to saints. When preaching to the unsaved, the evangelist is to declare the good news of salvation. When preaching to the saved, the evangelist

---

1. Arthur Wallis, *In the Day of Thy Power* (Columbia, MO: Cityhill Publishing, 1990), 79.

is to declare the good news of revival. The former focuses on the reception of eternal life. The latter focuses on restoration to the abundant life.

The burden of the evangelist is that sinners be confronted with the problem of sin, the penalty of hell, the sufficient payment in Christ, and the responsibility to believe in Jesus by turning to the Lord, away from all other false trusts. The burden of the evangelist is also that saints be equipped with the Spirit-filled life for holiness and service. In both cases the objective is that the Lord Jesus be pleased by means of the evangel directing people to Christ as the deliverer from both the penalty and power of sin.

These emphases have been touched on repeatedly in previous chapters. In summary, the purpose of the evangelist is to preach the evangel for the purpose of seeing sinners receive Christ and saints revived with the life of Christ.

The Results of the Outpouring

In the previous chapter it was noted that the outpouring of the Spirit is the spiritual, powerful manifestation of the presence of God, producing an atmosphere of God-consciousness, moving saints to be restored to spiritual life (revival) and sinners to receive eternal life. The phraseology *the outpouring of the Spirit* focuses on God's divine moving, whereas the word *revival* focuses on man's received blessing when he responds in brokenness to God's moving. The outpouring focuses more on the cause, and revival and evangelism more on the effect. This effect delineates the results of the outpouring. In short, the results are twofold: the saints are revived (i.e., restored to spiritual life), and sinners are saved (i.e., receive eternal life). The two results of the outpouring perfectly correspond to the purpose of the evangelist: revival and evangelism.

Acts 1–2 provide a New Testament example of this great truth. One hundred twenty believers were touched with the life of heaven, and three thousand souls were born into the kingdom of heaven. Both saints and sinners were mightily changed by the larger measure of the Spirit's outpouring.

Jonathan Goforth's book *By My Spirit*, which is his testimony of the outpouring of the Spirit in Manchuria, recounts:

> Moreover, as far as our observation has led us, we have concluded that there must first be deep conviction among the true followers of Christ before any expectation can be entertained of moving others. From our experience we are able to state that in every instance where this necessary first stage has been reached, the unconverted in the audience have broken down completely.[2]

Revival among the saints leads to an awakening among the lost. For example, Goforth described one moving of God with the following:

> The Christians were most responsive. They came under conviction, confessed their sins, acknowledged their faults one to another and made restitution for wrongs done. This had a startling effect upon the unsaved. Men and women by the score confessed their belief in Jesus Christ for the first time. Among these were several noted scholars and a number of prominent kiln owners.[3]

Andrew Murray, who was privileged to see the outpouring of the Spirit during his ministry in South Africa, states, "When God's Spirit is poured out upon the church, and men and women, who are now struggling on in feebleness, are clothed with the garments of

---

2. Jonathan Goforth, *By My Spirit* (Elkhart, IN: Bethel Publishing, 1983), 15.
3. Ibid., 102–3.

praise and the power of the Spirit, the world will soon share the blessing . . . A revival among believers is the great need of our day. A revived church is the only hope of a dying world."[4]

When the outpouring of the Spirit reaches the unawakened, they are suddenly awakened. Speaking of the First Great Awakening, Jonathan Edwards reports:

> The work of God is carried on with greater speed and swiftness, and there are often instances of sudden conversions at such a time. So it was in the apostles' days, when there was a time of the most extraordinary pouring out of the Spirit that ever was! How quick and sudden were conversions in those days . . . So it is in some degree whenever there is an extraordinary pouring out of the Spirit of God, more or less, in proportion to the greatness of that effusion.[5]

Herein is the similarity between the purpose of the evangelist and the results of the outpouring. The two-fold purpose of the evangelist and the two major results of the outpouring of the Spirit are the same: revival among the saints and salvation among the lost. Is it any wonder that the passion of the evangelist is the outpouring of the Spirit? Is there any better equipping for usefulness than a true reviving of the saints? Is there any greater harvesting of souls than the mass harvests of an outpouring? Although there ought to be thankfulness for personal revivals and for souls plucked one by one from the burning, is there not a need for mass revival and mass evangelism through mighty outpourings of God's Spirit? The work of a lifetime without the outpouring may be seen quickly with one powerful outpouring of the Spirit of the living God.

---

4. Andrew Murray, *Revival* (Minneapolis: Bethany House Publishers, 1990), 18.

5. Jonathan Edwards, *The Works of Jonathan Edwards*, vol. 1 (Edinburgh: The Banner of Truth Trust, 1974), 539.

The Responsibility of the Passion

What responsibility do evangelists have regarding the outpouring of the Spirit? Since evangelists are for the cause of revival and evangelism, they have a very definite responsibility in seeking the outpouring of the Spirit. Broadly speaking, evangelists must lead in revival praying and revival preaching. Giving oneself "continually to prayer and to the ministry of the word" (Acts 6:4) is the responsibility of every preacher. For evangelists the burden is praying for revival and preaching for revival.

Praying for Revival

While one's whole life should be walked by faith, the heart cry of the evangelist for the outpouring of the Spirit is expressed through God-dependent prayer. The issue is not prayer-dependence, as if putting in enough praying somehow merits favor with God. The issue is recognizing one's desperate need for the unleashed power of the Spirit of God and casting one's reliance upon God to pour out His Spirit based on His promises.

This kind of praying is prompted by the Spirit as He shows the failure of flesh-dependent efforts and the desperate need for His enduement and manifest presence. Furthermore, one must come to the foundation of faith, which is "the word [*rhema*] of God." It is the Spirit who guides one to this specific truth, gripping one with the reality of the promise (John 16:13–14). The convincing work of the Spirit provides the "evidence" of the promise of God needed to exercise faith. In Hebrews 11:1, the word *evidence* is the noun form of the verb "to convince" in John 16:8. Holy Spirit convincement is divine initiation. However, God makes man responsible to call on Him to then fulfill His promise. At this point the praying is not because one believes God *can* fulfill His promise but because one is convinced God *will* fulfill His promise.

For example, after giving the promise of "rivers in the desert" in Isaiah 43:19-21, God reveals His people's unbelief in verse 22: "But thou hast not called upon me . . . thou hast been weary of me." It is a tragedy to not ask God to fulfill His promises. This unbelief prevents God's people from accessing the fulfillment of the promises and reveals the sad reality of being "weary" of God. God confronts His people with their sins in verses 22-24. In verse 25 God reassures the believers of their eternal security in spite of their sins. Then He speaks of chastening them in verses 26-28. Finally, He offers the water of the Spirit again in the next verses, Isaiah 44:1-5. The key phrases are "I will pour water upon him that is thirsty," and "I will pour my spirit." The promise implies the condition that one must be *thirsty*. Man is responsible to seek God to fulfill His promises.

Scripturally and historically, it has been only a few that God brings to the foundation of faith for revival. It was the apostles who received the promise of Holy Spirit power in Acts 1:4-5, and then with a few others "continued with one accord in prayer and supplication" in verse 14. Not all those saved under John the Baptist's and Christ's ministries were there praying. Yet God poured out His Spirit in Acts 2.

It was Peggy and Christine Smith, two godly elderly sisters, whom the Spirit moved to claim Isaiah 44:3 in the late 1940s. They claimed that promise through effectual, fervent prayer. At their encouragement, their pastor and a few men joined in the intercession. After a total of about eighteen months, the Spirit was poured out on the island of Lewis from 1949-1953. This outpouring has come to be known as the "Lewis Revival."

God brought Jonathan Goforth to the conviction that the "greater works" of John 14:12 should be realized. He began an intensive study of the Holy Spirit in Scripture. His heart cry was the Holy Spirit in power. In 1906, as Goforth finished preaching, one Chinese evangelist said with breaking voice, "Brethren, He for Whom we have prayed so long was here in very deed tonight."[6]

---

6. Goforth, 19-21.

In 1907 the Korean Revival took place. Jonathan Goforth went to Korea during this time. He writes, "The Korean movement was of incalculable significance in my life because it showed me at firsthand the boundless possibilities of the revival method . . . Korea made me feel, as it did many others, that this was God's plan for setting the world aflame."[7] Upon returning to China, Goforth told the Korean story. Many were stirred to call upon God for an outpouring of His Spirit. After an unusually blessed conference among the missionaries, Goforth writes, "Before we finally separated to our different stations, scattered throughout the length and breadth of the country, we resolved that no matter where we were or what we were doing, we would pray every day at four o'clock in the afternoon until the Divine blessing fell upon the Church of China."[8] In 1908 God began pouring out His Spirit in Manchuria and a mighty moving of God took place.

After the distraction of the Revolutionary War and the effects of enormous immigration, America desperately needed revival by the 1780s. A few small fires burned in various places in the early 1790s. But in 1795 when the "Circular Letter" circulated through a number of churches, urging hungry souls to seek God for a mighty revival, "The Concert of Prayer" began. By the late 1790s a second great awakening had spread across the eastern states. J. Edwin Orr, the revival historian, documents "The Concert of Prayer" lasting through at least 1830. It should be no surprise that the awakening itself continued for over three decades.[9]

Evangelists must pray in faith for the outpouring of the Spirit. Therefore, evangelists must seek the Lord for the foundation of faith for an outpouring of the Spirit. When the Spirit provides *evidence* of God's will through the convincement of His promise, then evangelists must call upon the Lord in believing prayer to fulfill His promise, leading others to do the same.

---

7. Ibid., 23.

8. Ibid., 25.

9. J. Edwin Orr, *The Eager Feet* (Chicago: Moody Press, 1975), 1-200.

However, prayer by itself misses another vital responsibility in seeking the outpouring of God's Spirit.

Preaching for Revival

Revival preaching without revival praying is powerless. Revival praying without revival preaching lacks detonation, but revival praying with revival preaching is explosive. Revival preaching ignites the gunpowder of revival praying.

Revival preaching must confront the need. Evangelists must confront sin as the problem and exalt Christ as the solution. This truth was expanded in Chapter 3 when dealing with confrontational preaching. The dynamic of revival preaching is needed to both awaken the lost to their need of Christ as Savior and to arouse the saints to their need of the Holy Spirit as Sanctifier.

Evangelists must declare the truth regarding the need for the ministry of the Holy Spirit. John R. Rice points out:

All great soul-winning evangelists believe in a definite enduement of power of the Holy Spirit. So did Charles H. Spurgeon, so did John Wesley, so did Charles G. Finney, so did D. L. Moody, so did R. A. Torrey, so did J. Wilbur Chapman. Terminology may differ, but all . . . believe that Christians need and can have a definite enduement of power for soul-winning.[10]

As noted in the previous chapter, D. L. Moody emphasized the ministry of the Holy Spirit as an absolute necessity for effective ministry. He not only preached on the Holy Spirit, but his life was "in demonstration of the Spirit and of power" (I Cor. 2:4). As a result Moody "had a wide and profound influence through the length and breadth of Protestantism in the English-speaking

---

10. John R. Rice, *The Evangelist* (Murfreesboro, TN: Sword of the Lord Publishers, 1968), 193–94.

world, especially that of the Evangelical tradition, and through it upon much of mankind."[11]

The declaration of the truths of the Spirit involves an emphasis on the filling of the Spirit and the outpouring of the Spirit. "In times preceding revival it is common to find among believers of various persuasions a fresh emphasis on the person and work of the Holy Spirit."[12] In Chapter 4, entitled "A Supernatural Gift," and in Chapter 6, entitled "The Gospel to Saints," the filling of the Spirit was discussed. Every believer needs divine enabling to do God's will. Therefore, evangelists need to preach on the fullness of the Spirit because the Spirit's power is the vital truth in equipping the saints for service.

Evangelists also must preach on the outpouring of the Spirit. Once Jonathan Goforth came to this conviction, he regularly preached on this grand theme. After the outpouring of the Holy Spirit in Manchuria, Goforth left to preach in London and then in Toronto (which was his home). He addressed the General Assembly of his mission board.

> When at last he arose before that great audience of ministers and church leaders, Goforth spoke for twenty minutes with such power and intensity, a marked stillness reigned throughout his address. His plea was for them as leaders, teachers, and professors to humble themselves before the Lord and seek the Holy Spirit's outpouring as did the Korean missionaries. This he held out as the church's only hope if retrogression and disaster were to be avoided.[13]

Years later someone wrote of Goforth, saying:

---

11. Kenneth Scott Latourette, A History of Christianity, vol. 2 (Peabody, MA: Prince Press, reprint ed., 2005), 1255.

12. Wallis, 69.

13. Rosalind Goforth, Goforth of China (Minneapolis: Bethany House Publishers, 1937), 204–5.

He lived in the Holy Spirit's presence so that no power on earth could shake his confidence. In meetings he seemed like a man who was clearing the track for a powerful locomotive that was waiting only for a clear track and that would not come until the track was clear. He was as sure of the Spirit as of tomorrow's sun, and just as sure that only clouds of sin could obscure His glory.[14]

Every God-called evangelist must learn, live, and declare the glorious truths of the Spirit of the living God. When God guides individuals to His truth, they may expect His promises to be fulfilled.

The passion of the evangelist is the outpouring of the Spirit—for "times of refreshing . . . from the presence of the Lord." Outpourings may be seasonal, but seasons should be regular. Just as the Spirit-filled life should be the normal life of the believer, seasonal outpourings of the Spirit should be the normal life of the church. Whenever outpourings of the Spirit are not regular, the cause is man's unbelief, not God's promises. Just as unbelief prevents individuals from experiencing the victorious life of Christ, so unbelief hinders the church from knowing the mighty outpouring of God's manifest presence.

This deadly enemy of unbelief comes to the evangelist in two forms. One form of unbelief is flesh-dependence. This is the sincere evangelist who depends on the "arm of the flesh." But "the flesh profiteth nothing" (John 6:63). The other form of unbelief is the opposite end of the pendulum swing, and that is fatalism. This philosophy says that even if people pray, God may or may not send revival. It is all up to God's sovereign choice. But this ignores the fact that God's purposes are revealed through His promises (made personal by the convincing work of the Spirit) and that God's promises must and can be obtained through faith. Hebrews 11:33 states "who through faith . . . obtained promises."

14. Ibid., 334.

This is a matter of God's way. This makes man responsible to exercise faith in order to obtain God's promises. "Ye have not, because ye ask not" (James 4:2). When God's will is revealed through the Word and the Spirit—*ye have not, because ye ask not*. This is a matter of faith, not fatalism.

Repeated examples of the explosive power of praying for revival combined with preaching for revival may be found in J. Edwin Orr's account of the early twentieth-century revivals that affected at least fifty-seven nations.[15]

When evangelists lead in revival praying and revival preaching, they are "promoting" revival, not through fleshly formulas, but through expressions of God-dependence. This emphasis of seeking God for His reviving presence is the "revivalist" dimension of the evangelist. J. Edwin Orr maintains that the word *revivalist* came into use by 1820 describing those who promote religious revivals.[16] In this sense, every evangelist ought to be a revivalist. In fact, the early part of the second great awakening was referred to later as applying "sane *revivalism*."[17]

Conclusion

Whenever evangelists preach in an atmosphere charged by the presence of God, although there will often be persecution, the church will advance through real revival and effective evangelism.

For example, Ireland in the fourth century revealed all the signs of a pagan culture. In this setting, Patrick, known as "St. Patrick," exemplified the work of the evangelist with the dynamic of the outpouring of the Spirit. Although legends often embellish

---

15. J. Edwin Orr, *The Flaming Tongue* (Chicago: Moody Press, 1975), 1-200.

16. J. Edwin Orr, *The Event of the Century* (Wheaton: International Awakening Press, 1989), xii. Interestingly, the word *revivalist* came into use before Charles Finney was even converted.

17. Ibid., xiv [emphasis original].

his story, Patrick's autobiographical *Confession* provides more trustworthy information.

As a teenager in Scotland, he was kidnapped by Irish pirates and forced into slavery. By God's grace Patrick was gloriously converted. Then he escaped and returned to his homeland. After over a decade of spiritual growth, he returned to Ireland in response to the call of God—this time as a slave to Christ, not to the Irish. Throughout thirty years of ministry in Ireland, Patrick baptized thousands and started well over two hundred churches.[18] "During his lifetime ministry, the nation changed from paganism to 100,000 believers."[19] This is more than the work of a Spirit-filled man. Undoubtedly, God had poured out His Spirit.

Patrick's story differs little from accounts in the book of Acts. The key was the combination of a Spirit-filled man and hearers convicted by the outpouring of the Spirit. In fourth century Ireland, the nature of the need was primarily evangelism.

Another evangelist from Scotland, used both in the reviving of the church and the awakening of the lost, is William Chalmers Burns. Born in 1815, Burns was instilled with a longing for revival from his father during times of family worship.[20] Born again in 1831, young Burns immediately felt and surrendered to the call to preach.[21] As he grew spiritually, "Burns . . . wept for hours in deep soul-agony on behalf of a backslidden church and for lost souls going to hell."[22] The heart of Burns is revealed by the following anecdote:

---

18. Ken Curtis, et al. eds., *Glimpses*, no. 75 (1996): 1–2; Ed Reese, "Patrick: Apostle of the Irish" in *Reese Chronological Encyclopedia of Christian Biographies* (Chattanooga: AMG Publishers, 2007), 63. Reese claims Patrick started 365 churches.

19. Reese, 63. Reese emphasizes "both Catholics and Protestants claim him, but history shows the Celtic (branch of the Indo-European family of languages) Church did not become Catholic until A.D. 664. The celebration of St. Patrick's Day continues on March 17th, a tribute to one whose doctrine was much like a modern-day Baptist."

20. James A. Stewart, *William Chalmers Burns* (Asheville: Revival Literature, n.d.), 10–11.

21. Ibid., 14–16.

22. Ibid., 19.

When he was seventeen years of age, he was brought by his mother from the quiet surroundings of Kilsyth to the great bustling city of Glasgow. His mother was separated from her son while she was shopping, and when she retraced her steps to find him she discovered him in an alley with great tears streaming down his face. She could see he was suffering great agony. His surprised mother exclaimed, "Willie, my boy, what ails you? Are you ill?" "O Mither! Mither!" he cried. "The thud of these Christ-less feet on the way to hell breaks my heart!"[23]

Later during Burns' preaching ministry, his hearers experienced the dynamic of the Spirit of God falling upon them. His brother provides an eyewitness account of July 23, 1839, in Kilsyth, Scotland. The climax of the meeting is recorded as follows:

In urging sinners to an immediate closing with Christ in the offers of his grace, he had made use of the obvious and very common figure of a life-boat bringing hope and deliverance to the side of a foundering vessel; when in developing the idea and dwelling on it, the whole scene seemed to pass in living reality before his eyes—the doomed bark rolling helplessly amid the wild waves, and rapidly settling down; the crouching, trembling throng clinging to the gunwale, and the light buoyant skiff leaping up towards them amid the blinding spray, so near that they might almost touch it; and as he saw them still hesitating and wasting in fatal inaction the last moments of opportunity, he cried aloud as one might do from the summit of a neighbouring headland on the shore, "Are you in? are you in? Flee for refuge to lay hold of the hope set before you; now or never." There was in his whole style

---

23. Stewart, 18–19.

and manner at this moment, as frequently afterwards at similar times, a dramatic vividness and energy; which reminded one of what we read of in Whitefield;—a vividness and energy, however, which in my brother's case was not in any measure due to a graphic poetic fancy, but simply to an intense and awful realization of eternal truths. As to the scene itself which followed, I can think of no better description than the account of the day of Pentecost, in the second chapter of the Acts, of which both in its immediate features and in its after results, and in everything except the miraculous gift of tongues, it seems to me to have been an exact counterpart.[24]

The reference to this historical event being a *counterpart* to the Day of Pentecost is quite accurate. What took place involved both the filling of the Spirit in the preaching of Burns and the outpouring of the Spirit regarding the hearing of the audience. As mentioned in the previous chapter, this is the difference between a man preaching as a Spirit-filled man and a Spirit-filled man preaching in an atmosphere saturated with the presence of God. The former quickens the preacher, and some are blessed. The latter quickens the hearers as well, and many are blessed.

This dynamic is explained further by William Burns' brother:

It is from this time that we must date a remarkable change in my brother's manner of preaching . . . "For weeks before he was full of prayer; he seemed to care for nothing but to pray. In the day-time, alone or with others, it was his chief delight, and in the night watches he might be overheard praying aloud. Yet during this time the power that rested upon himself did not affect his preaching; it was sensible, clear, orthodox, unobjectionable; and in that indeed

24. Islay Burns, *Memoir of the Rev. William C. Burns* (reprint ed.; Stoke-on-Trent: Tentmaker Publishers, 2005), 97–98.

he never altered; for in the midst of whatever excitement, there was never any eccentricity or extravagance of doctrine, or even the extreme pressing of any one point; but a steadfast keeping within lines of received truth, as not expecting conversion by any special way of stating the gospel, but by the power of the Spirit accompanying it. For a season, however, before the Kilsyth communion, he seemed two different men in private and public—his own spiritual strength so far exceeding what appeared in the pulpit. But then the Lord, who had strengthened David to slay the lion and the bear in the recesses of the mountains, sent him forth to triumph over Goliath before the hosts of Israel. He had been asking, seeking, knocking, for the Holy Spirit; that Spirit came upon him with power; and the Lord added unto the church daily such as should be saved, multitudes both of men and women."[25]

What was the result of this season of refreshing from the presence of the Lord?

The movement thus begun in a manner so remarkable, went on steadily, and for weeks thereafter seemed only to grow in solidity and depth. Meetings for prayer and preaching of the gospel were held every successive night, generally in the church, and occasionally, when the weather favoured, in the market-place or in the church-yard. Crowds of inquirers flocked at every invitation to the vestry or the manse to seek spiritual counsel from the minister and his assistants. Prayer-meetings both of the old and young sprang up everywhere in the village and the surrounding hamlets."[26]

---

25. Ibid., 98–99.
26. Ibid., 99.

The impact of this moving of God through a surrendered vessel affected thousands, both sinners and saints alike. The church was transformed from her backslidden lethargy, and multitudes were translated from darkness to light.

It is no wonder that the passion of the evangelist is the outpouring of the Spirit. The manifest presence of God is the greatest dynamic needed to promote the cause of revival and evangelism. Each generation is responsible for its generation. The need is great. God's glory is at stake. The promises are sure. May every true evangelist experientially know revival praying, revival preaching, and most of all—the revival Presence!

Bibliography

Alexander, J. A. *Isaiah*. Grand Rapids: Kregel Publication, 1992.

Anderson, Courtney. *To the Golden Shore: The Life of Adoniram Judson*. Grand Rapids: Zondervan Publishing House, 1972.

Armstrong, John H. *Five Great Evangelists*. Great Britain: Christian Focus Publications, 1997.

Arndt, William F., and F. Wilbur Gingrich. *A Greek-English Lexicon of the New Testament and Other Early Christian Literature*, 2nd ed. rev. F. Wilbur Gingrich and Fredrick W. Danker. Chicago: University of Chicago Press, 1979.

Barabas, Steven. *So Great Salvation*. Eugene, OR: Wipf & Stock, 1952.

Bonar, Horatius. *Words to Winners of Souls*. Garland, TX: American Tract Society, 1981.

Burns, Islay. *Memoir of the Rev. William C. Burns*. Stoke-on-Trent: Tentmaker Publications, 1870.

Chapell, Bryan. *Christ-Centered Preaching*. Grand Rapids: Baker Books, 2000.

Custer, Stewart. *A Treasury of New Testament Synonyms*. Greenville, SC: Bob Jones University Press, 1975.

Dallimore, Arnold. *George Whitefield*. Vol. 1-2. Edinburgh: The Banner of Truth Trust, 1970.

Dorsett, Lyle W. *A Passion for Souls: The Life of D. L. Moody*. Chicago: Moody Press, 1997.

Edwards, Jonathan. *The Works of Jonathan Edwards*. Vol. 1. Edinburgh: The Banner of Truth Trust, 1974.

Friedrich, Gerhard. *"euaggelizomai, euaggelion, proeuaggelizomai euaggelistes."* In *Theological Dictionary of the New Testament.* Vol. 2. ed. Gerhard Kittell, 707–37. Grand Rapids: Wm. B. Eerdmans Publishing Co., 1964, 1993.

Gaebelein, Frank E., ed. *The Expositor's Bible Commentary.* Vol. 2. Grand Rapids: Zondervan Bible Publishers, 1978.

Goforth, Jonathan. *By My Spirit.* Elkhart, IN: Bethel Publishing, 1983.

Goforth, Rosalind. *Goforth of China.* Minneapolis: Bethany House Publishers, 1937.

Hession, Roy. *The Calvary Road.* Fort Washington, PA: Christian Literature Crusade Publications, 1950.

Hiebert, D. Edmond. *Second Timothy.* Chicago: Moody Press, 1958.

Hopkins, Evan. *The Law of Liberty in the Spiritual Life.* Fort Washington, PA: Christian Literature Crusade, 1952.

Jones, Bob, Sr. *Evangelism Today.* Greenville, SC: Bob Jones University Press, 1955.

Jones, Laura. *The Life and Sayings of Sam P. Jones.* Atlanta: Franklin-Turner Company, 1907.

Latourette, Kenneth Scott. *A History of Christianity.* Vol 2. Peabody, MA: Prince Press, 2005.

Minnick, Mark. *The Doctrine of Eternal Punishment.* Woodridge, IL: Preach the Word Ministries, Inc., 1996.

Morris, Leon. *New Testament Theology.* Grand Rapids: Zondervan Publishers, 1990.

Moule, Handley G. C. *The Epistle to the Romans.* London: Pickering & Inglish Ltd., n.d.

Murray, Andrew. *Revival.* Minneapolis: Bethany House Publishers, 1990.

Orr, J. Edwin. *The Eager Feet: Evangelical Awakenings, 1790–1830.* Chicago: Moody Press, 1975.

_____. *The Event of the Century: The 1857-1858 Awakening.* Wheaton: International Awakening Press, 1989.

_____. *The Flaming Tongue The Impact of the Early 20th Century Revivals*. Chicago: Moody Press, 1975.

Parkinson, John F. *The Faith of God's Elect*. Great Britain: Penfold Book & Bible House Ltd., 2002.

Pickering, Ernest. *Biblical Separation: The Struggle for a Pure Church*. Schaumburg, IL: Regular Baptist Press, 1979.

Reese, Ed. *Reese Chronological Encyclopedia of Christian Biographies*. Chattanooga, TN: AMG Publishers, 2007.

Rice, John R. *The Evangelist*. Murfreesboro, TN: Sword of the Lord Publishers, 1968.

Rienecker, Fritz, and Cleon L. Rogers. *A Linguistic Key to the Greek New Testament*. Grand Rapids: Zondervan Bible Publishers, 1980.

Roberts, Alexander, and James Donaldson, eds. *Ante-Nicene Fathers*. 10 vols. 1885; reprint, Peabody, MA: Henderickson Publishers, Inc., 2004.

Roberts, Richard Owen. *An Annotated Bibliography of Revival Literature*. Wheaton, IL: Richard Own Roberts Publishers, 1987.

Robertson, A. T. *Word Pictures in the New Testament*. Nashville, TN: Broadman Press, 1930.

Ryrie, Charles C. *So Great Salvation*. Wheaton, IL: Victor books, 1989.

_____. *The Holy Spirit*. Chicago: Moody Press, 1997.

Schaff, Philip, and Henry Wace, eds. *Nicene and Post Nicene Fathers*. 2nd ser., 14 vols. 1890; reprint, Peabody, MA: Hendrickson Publishers, Inc., 2004.

Stewart, James A. *Evangelism Without Apology*. Grand Rapids: Kregel Publication, 1960.

_____. *I Must Tell*. Asheville, NC: Revival Literature, 2007.

_____. *William Chalmers Burns*. Asheville, NC: Revival Literature, n.d.

Stewart, Ruth. *James Stewart: Missionary*. Asheville, NC: Gospel Projects, Inc., 1977.

Strong, Augustus H. *Systematic Theology*. Valley Forge, PA: Judson Press, 1979.

Sumner, Robert L. *Man Sent from God: A Biography of John R. Rice*. Murfreesboro, TN: Sword of the Lord Publishers, 1959.

Thayer, Joseph Henry. *A Greek-English Lexicon of the New Testament*. Grand Rapids: Baker Book House, 1984.

Thiesson, Henry C. *Lectures in Systematic Theology*. Grand Rapids: Wm. B. Eerdmans Publishing Company, 1981.

Thomas, Ian. *The Indwelling Life of Christ*. Sisters, OR: Multnomah Publishers, Inc., 2006.

Thomas, W. H. Griffith. *St. Paul's Epistle to the Romans*. Grand Rapids: Wm. B. EerdmansPublishing Company, 1980.

Tow, Timothy. *John Sung, My Teacher*. Singapore: Christian Life Publishers, 1985.

_____. *The Asian Awakening*. Singapore: Christian Life Publishers, 1988.

Trench, Richard C. *Synonyms of the New Testament*. Grand Rapids: Wm. B. Eerdmans Publishing Company, 1983.

Tyler, Bennet, and Andrew Bonar. *Asahel Nettleton: Life and Labours*. Edinburgh: The Banner of Truth Trust, 1996.

Vincent, Marvin R. *Word Studies in the Greek New Testament*. Grand Rapids: Wm. B. Eerdmans Publishing Company, 1980.

Wallis, Arthur. *In the Day of Thy Power*. Columbia, MO: Cityhill Publishing, 1990.

Walvoord, John F., and Roy B. Zuck. *The Bible Knowledge Commentary, New Testament Edition*. Wheaton: Victor Books, 1983.

Wigram, George V. and Green, Jay P. *The New Englishman's Greek Concordance and Lexicon*. Peabody, MA: Henderickson Publishers, Inc., 1982.

Woolsey, Andrew. *Channel of Revival: A Biography of Duncan Campbell*. Edinburgh: The Faith Mission, 1982.

Young, E. J. *The Book of Isaiah*. Vol. 3. Grand Rapids: Wm. B. Eerdmans
Publishing Company, 1972.

Made in the USA
Monee, IL
13 July 2021

72719815R10144